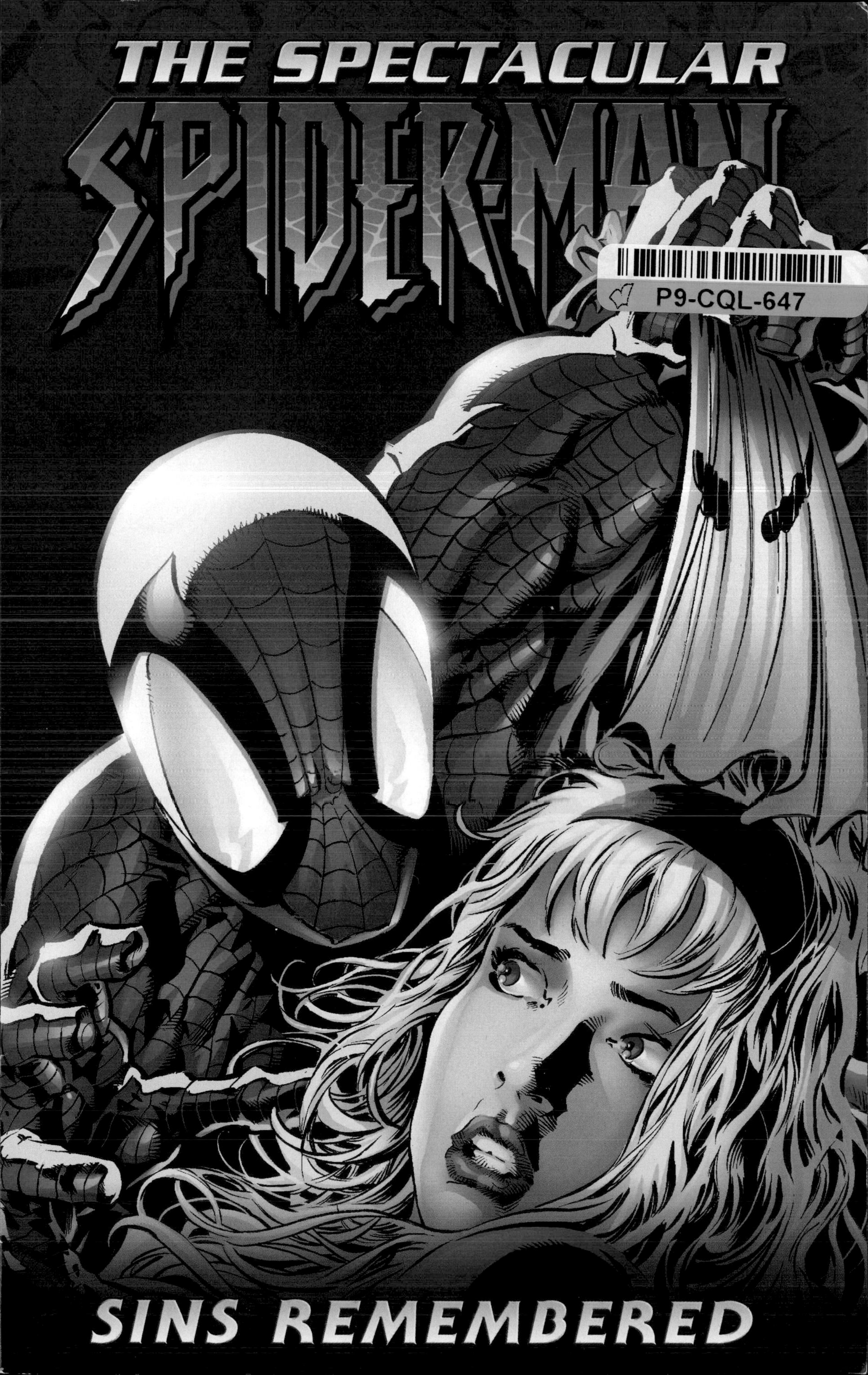
THE SPECTACULAR
SPIDER-MAN
SINS REMEMBERED

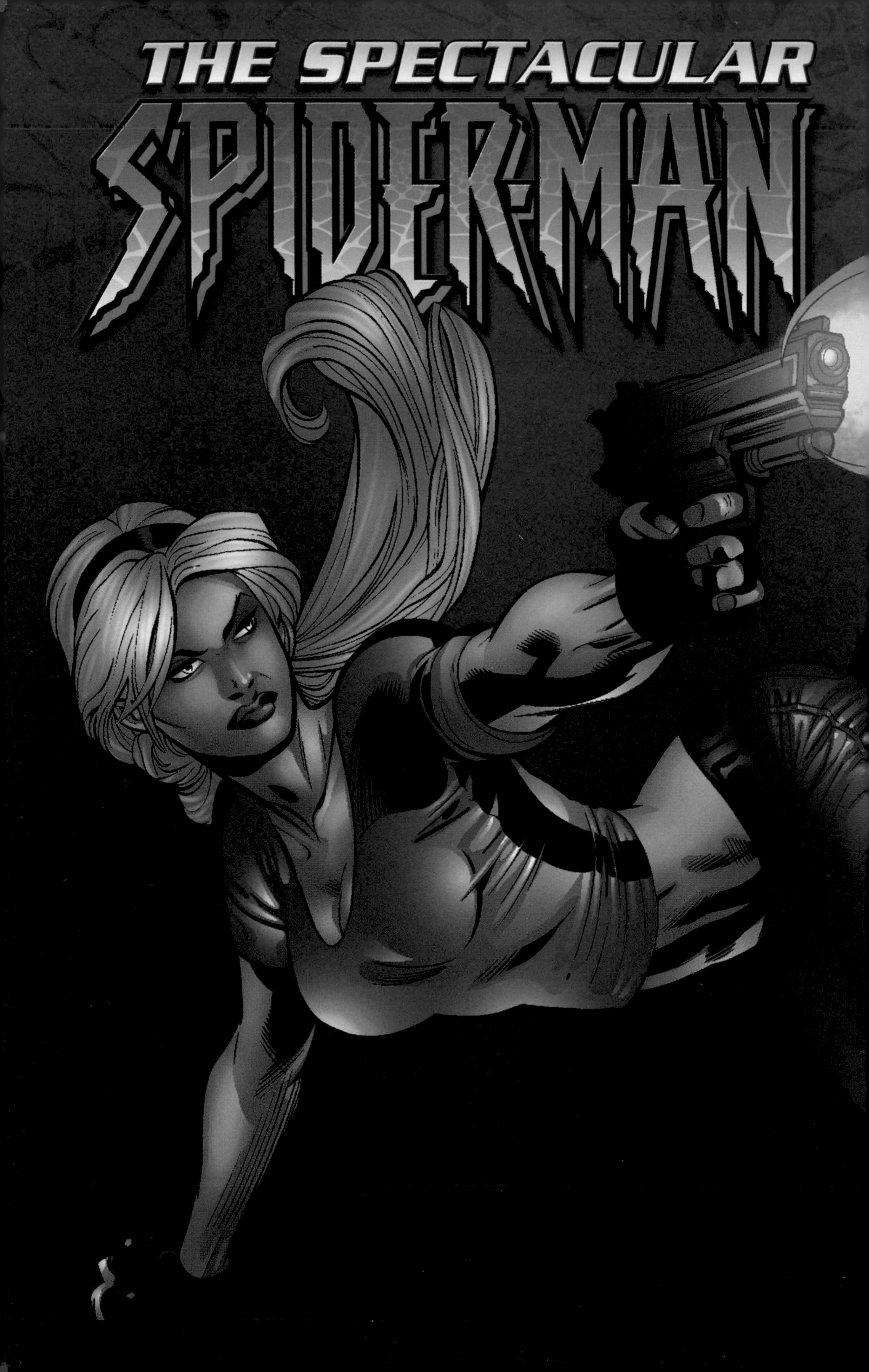
THE SPECTACULAR
SPIDER-MAN

SINS REMEMBERED

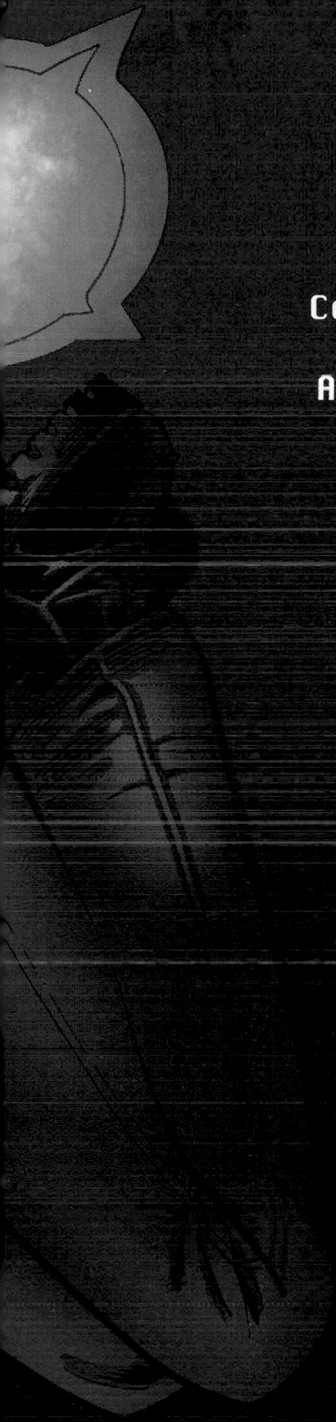

Writer: Sara "Samm" Barnes

Penciler: Scot Eaton

Inker: Cam Smith

Color Art: Studio F & Chris Sotomayor

Letterer: Virtual Calligraphy's Cory Petit

Covers: Greg Land, Matt Ryan & Justin Ponsor

Assistant Editors: Andy Schmidt, Nicole Wiley, Molly Lazer & Stephanie Moore

Editor: Tom Brevoort

Special thanks to
J. Michael Straczynski & Axel Alonso

Collection Editor: Jennifer Grünwald

Senior Editor, Special Projects: Jeff Youngquist

Director of Sales: David Gabriel

Production: Loretta Krol

Book Designer: Patrick McGrath

Creative Director: Tom Marvelli

Editor in Chief: Joe Quesada

Publisher: Dan Buckley

THE SPECTACULAR SPIDER-MAN

SINS REMEMBERED

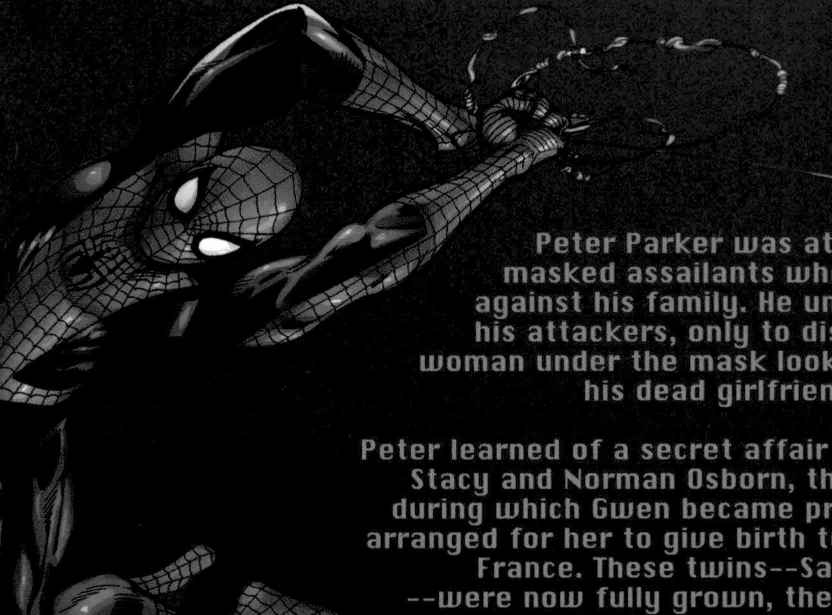

Peter Parker was attacked by twin masked assailants who made threats against his family. He unmasked one of his attackers, only to discover that the woman under the mask looked exactly like his dead girlfriend, Gwen Stacy!

Peter learned of a secret affair between Gwen Stacy and Norman Osborn, the Green Goblin, during which Gwen became pregnant. Osborn arranged for her to give birth to their twins in France. These twins--Sarah and Gabriel --were now fully grown, the Goblin formula in their blood resulting in superhuman strength, but also in the twins aging extremely rapidly.

Peter, as Spider-Man, beckoned Gabriel and Sarah to the top of the Brooklyn Bridge, where he told them the truth about their parentage. Sarah believed him, but Gabriel attacked, prompting the police down below to fire at the three. Spider-Man kicked Gabriel into the East River, while Sarah was shot.

Gabriel survived the fall and fled to one of Osborn's hidden lairs. There, a prerecorded message informed Gabriel that he was to inherit the Osborn legacy. Accepting his father's offer, Gabriel injected himself with Goblin serum, becoming the Gray Goblin.

Meanwhile, Sarah lay dying in the hospital. Peter gave her a blood transfusion, leaving him weakened when the Gray Goblin attacked. Sarah chose to save Spider-Man, shooting her brother's glider with a security guard's revolver. The glider exploded, sending Gabriel crashing into the harbor.

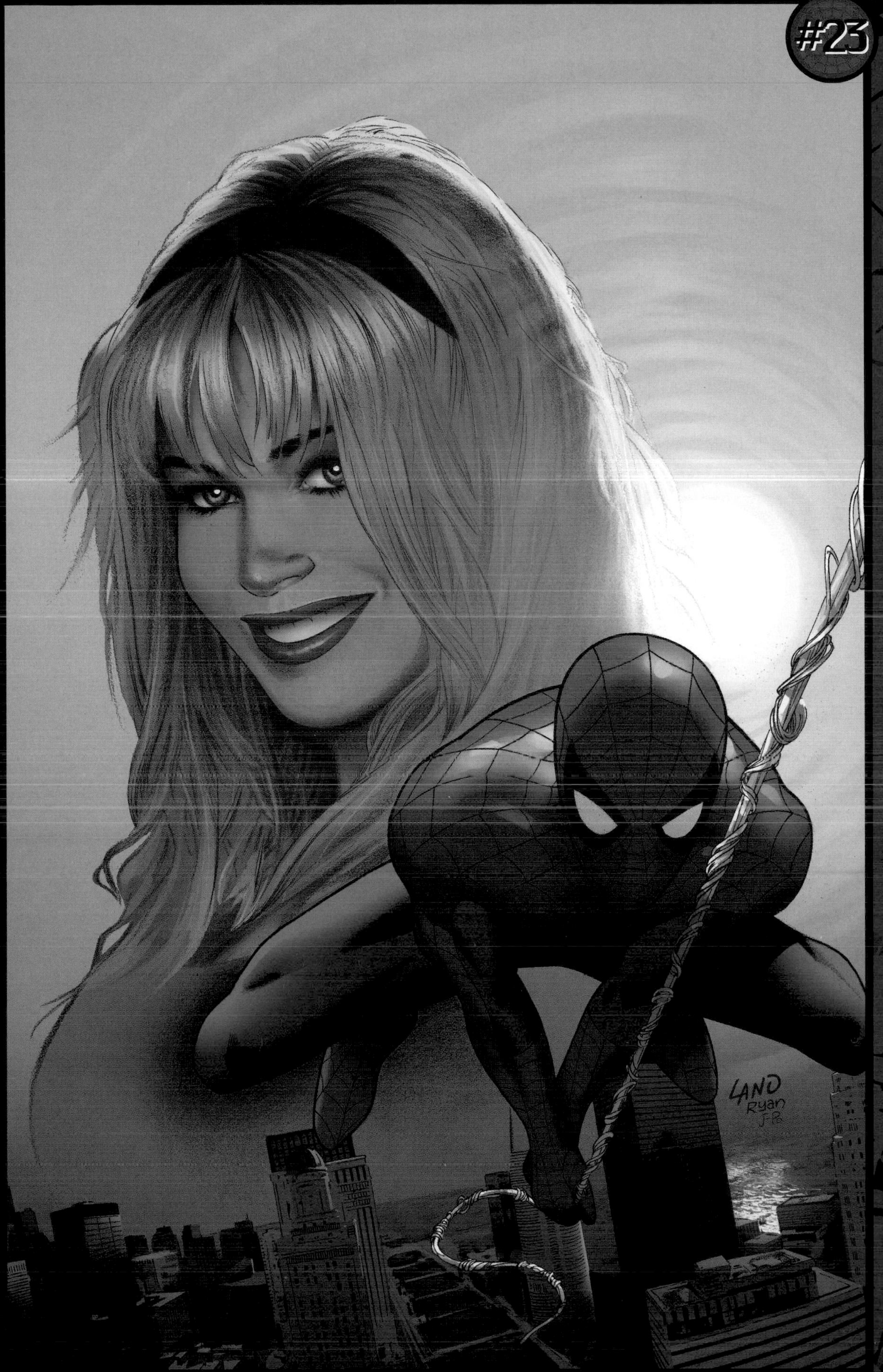
#23
LAND
Ryan
J-Po

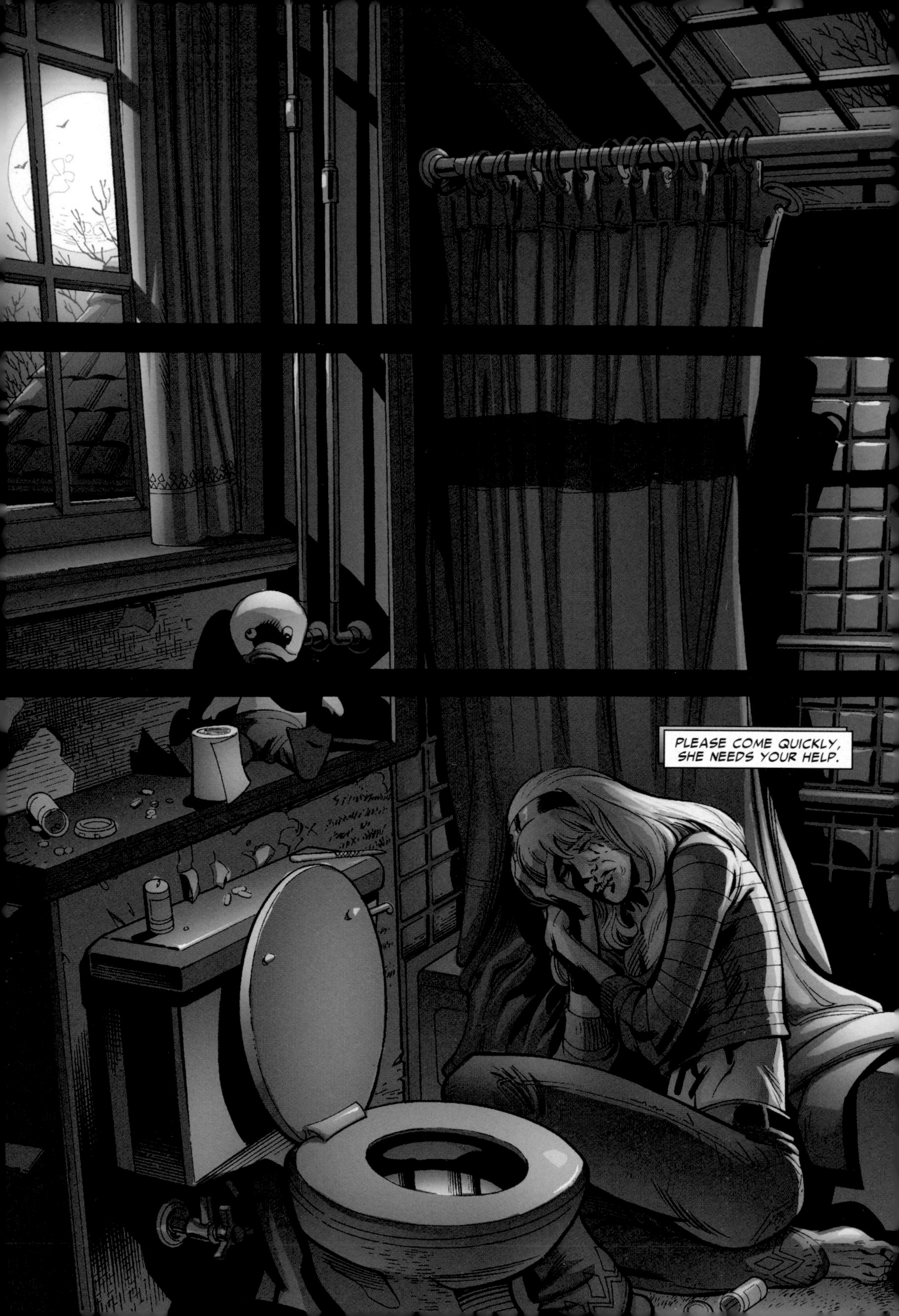
PLEASE COME QUICKLY, SHE NEEDS YOUR HELP.

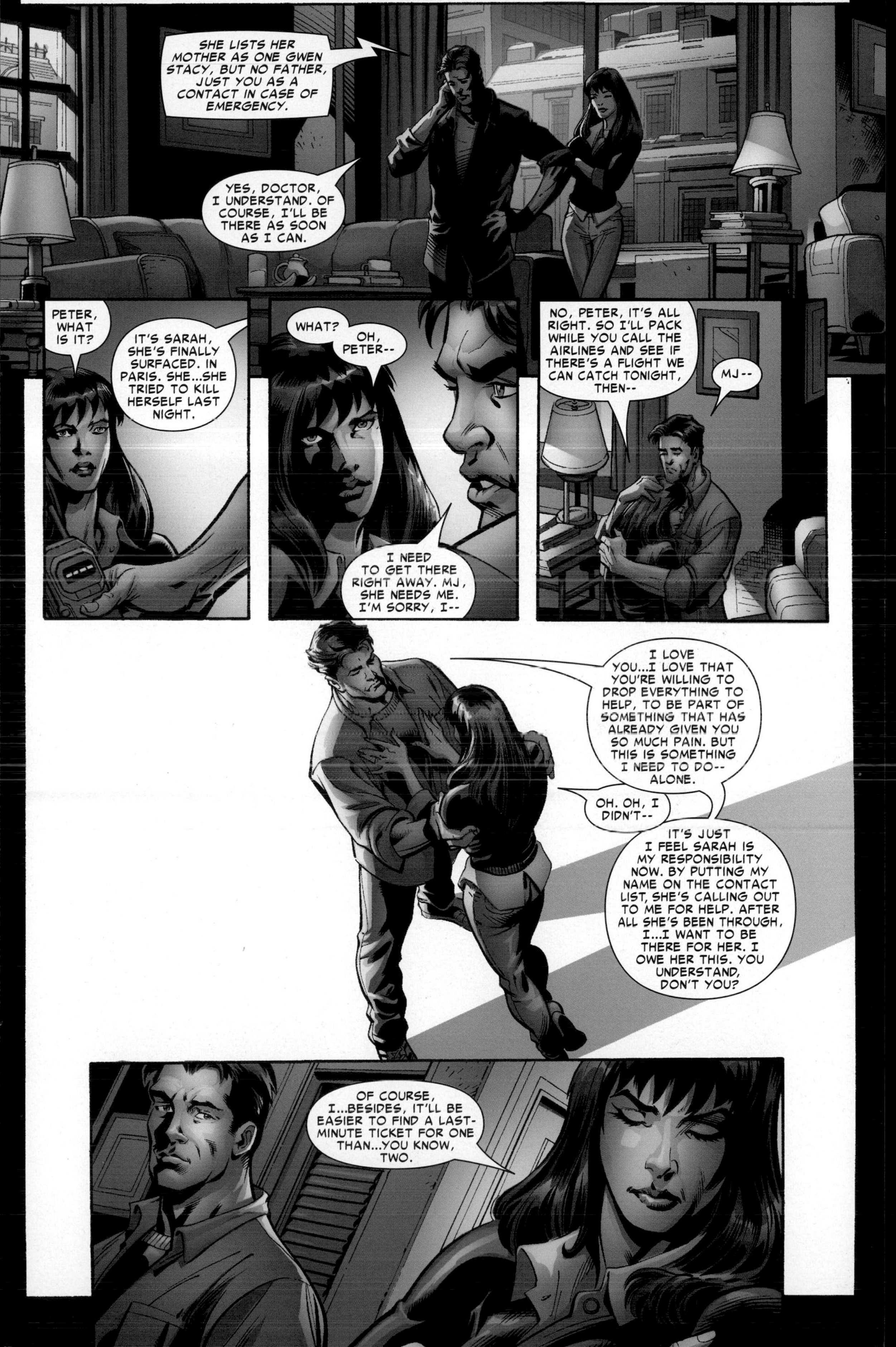
SHE LISTS HER MOTHER AS ONE GWEN STACY, BUT NO FATHER, JUST YOU AS A CONTACT IN CASE OF EMERGENCY.
YES, DOCTOR, I UNDERSTAND. OF COURSE, I'LL BE THERE AS SOON AS I CAN.
PETER, WHAT IS IT?
IT'S SARAH, SHE'S FINALLY SURFACED. IN PARIS. SHE...SHE TRIED TO KILL HERSELF LAST NIGHT.
WHAT?
OH, PETER--
I NEED TO GET THERE RIGHT AWAY. MJ, SHE NEEDS ME. I'M SORRY, I--
NO, PETER, IT'S ALL RIGHT. SO I'LL PACK WHILE YOU CALL THE AIRLINES AND SEE IF THERE'S A FLIGHT WE CAN CATCH TONIGHT, THEN--
MJ--
I LOVE YOU...I LOVE THAT YOU'RE WILLING TO DROP EVERYTHING TO HELP, TO BE PART OF SOMETHING THAT HAS ALREADY GIVEN YOU SO MUCH PAIN. BUT THIS IS SOMETHING I NEED TO DO-- ALONE.
OH. OH, I DIDN'T--
IT'S JUST I FEEL SARAH IS MY RESPONSIBILITY NOW. BY PUTTING MY NAME ON THE CONTACT LIST, SHE'S CALLING OUT TO ME FOR HELP. AFTER ALL SHE'S BEEN THROUGH, I...I WANT TO BE THERE FOR HER. I OWE HER THIS. YOU UNDERSTAND, DON'T YOU?
OF COURSE, I...BESIDES, IT'LL BE EASIER TO FIND A LAST-MINUTE TICKET FOR ONE THAN...YOU KNOW, TWO.

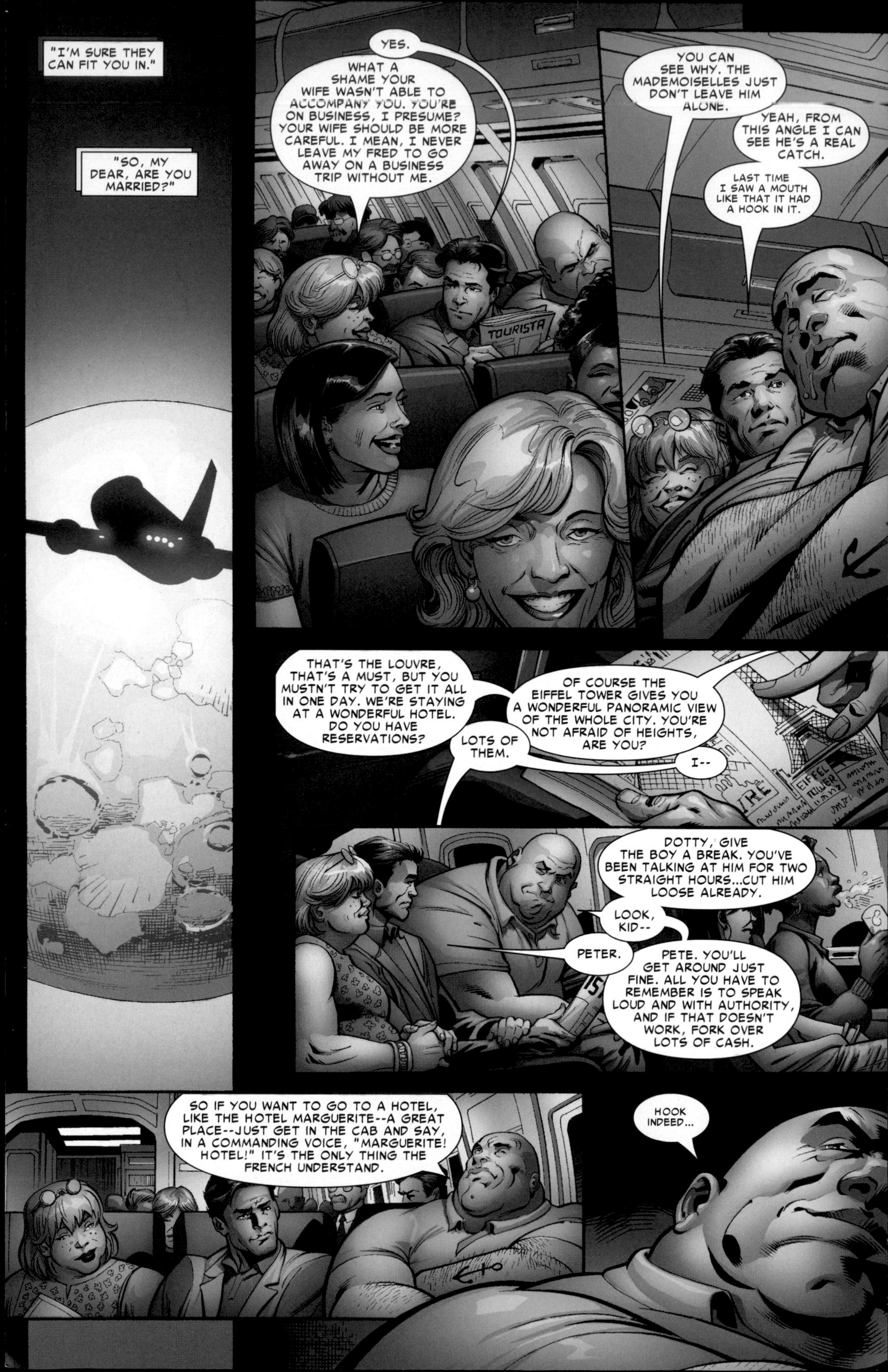
"I'M SURE THEY CAN FIT YOU IN."
"SO, MY DEAR, ARE YOU MARRIED?"
YES.
WHAT A SHAME YOUR WIFE WASN'T ABLE TO ACCOMPANY YOU. YOU'RE ON BUSINESS, I PRESUME? YOUR WIFE SHOULD BE MORE CAREFUL. I MEAN, I NEVER LEAVE MY FRED TO GO AWAY ON A BUSINESS TRIP WITHOUT ME.
TOURISTA
YOU CAN SEE WHY. THE MADEMOISELLES JUST DON'T LEAVE HIM ALONE.
YEAH, FROM THIS ANGLE I CAN SEE HE'S A REAL CATCH.
LAST TIME I SAW A MOUTH LIKE THAT IT HAD A HOOK IN IT.
THAT'S THE LOUVRE, THAT'S A MUST, BUT YOU MUSTN'T TRY TO GET IT ALL IN ONE DAY. WE'RE STAYING AT A WONDERFUL HOTEL. DO YOU HAVE RESERVATIONS?
LOTS OF THEM.
OF COURSE THE EIFFEL TOWER GIVES YOU A WONDERFUL PANORAMIC VIEW OF THE WHOLE CITY. YOU'RE NOT AFRAID OF HEIGHTS, ARE YOU?
I--
EIFFEL TOWER
DOTTY, GIVE THE BOY A BREAK. YOU'VE BEEN TALKING AT HIM FOR TWO STRAIGHT HOURS...CUT HIM LOOSE ALREADY.
LOOK, KID--
PETER.
PETE. YOU'LL GET AROUND JUST FINE. ALL YOU HAVE TO REMEMBER IS TO SPEAK LOUD AND WITH AUTHORITY, AND IF THAT DOESN'T WORK, FORK OVER LOTS OF CASH.
SO IF YOU WANT TO GO TO A HOTEL, LIKE THE HOTEL MARGUERITE--A GREAT PLACE--JUST GET IN THE CAB AND SAY, IN A COMMANDING VOICE, "MARGUERITE! HOTEL!" IT'S THE ONLY THING THE FRENCH UNDERSTAND.
HOOK INDEED...

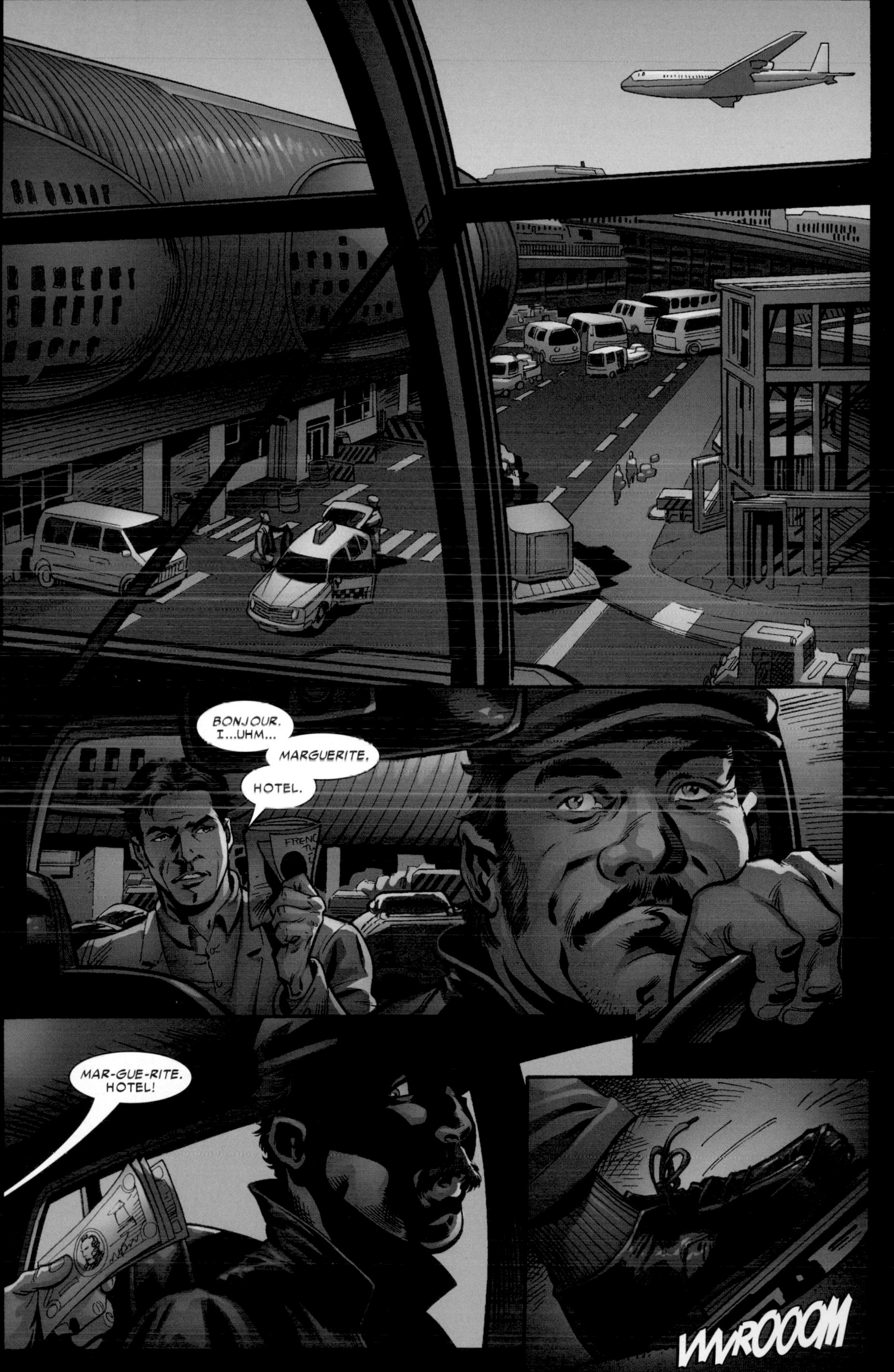
BONJOUR. I...UHM...
MARGUERITE.
HOTEL.
MAR-GUE-RITE. HOTEL!
VVVROOOM

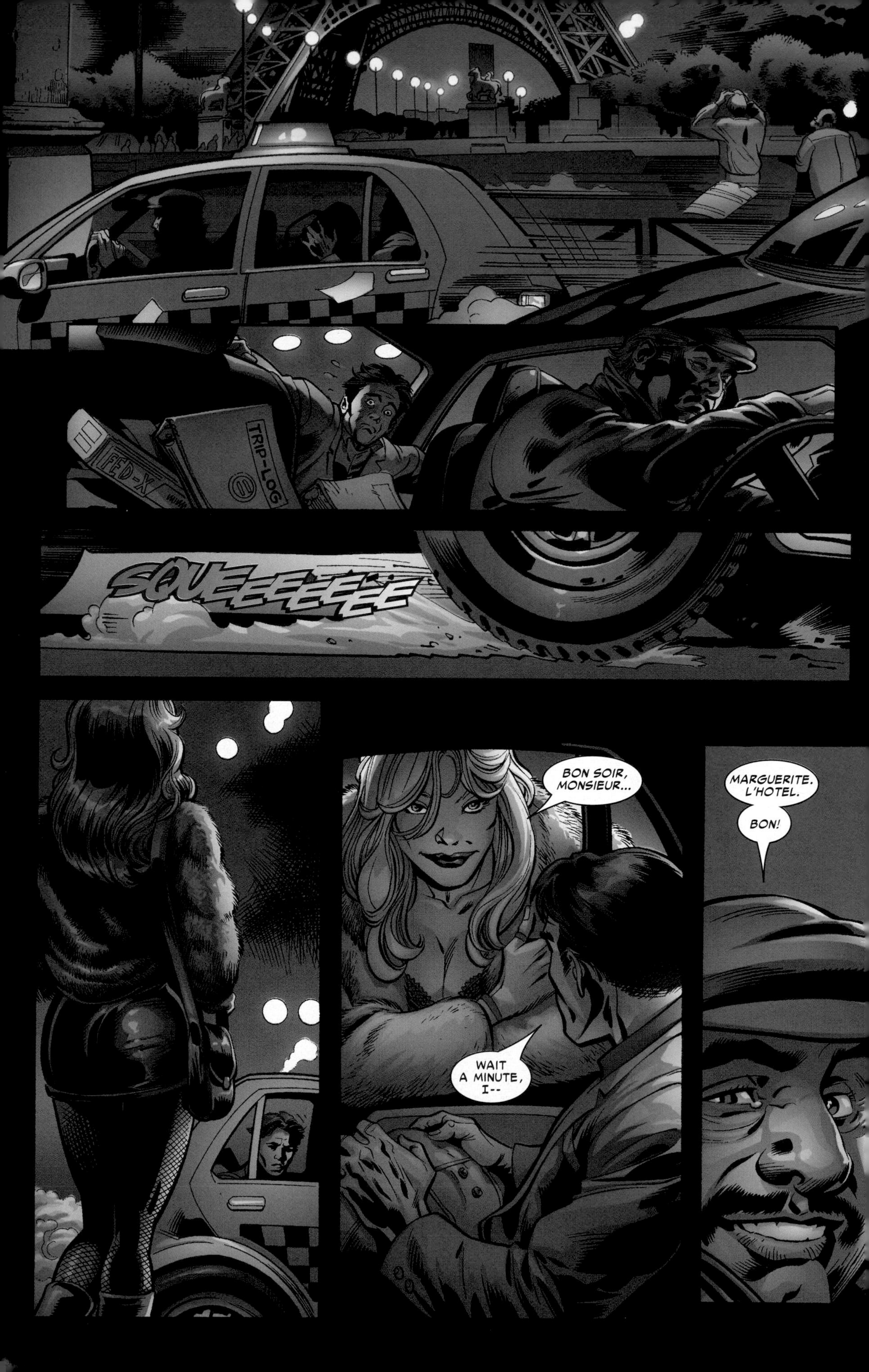
TRIP-LOG
FED-X
SQUEEEEEEEEE
BON SOIR, MONSIEUR...
WAIT A MINUTE, I--
MARGUERITE. L'HOTEL.
BON!

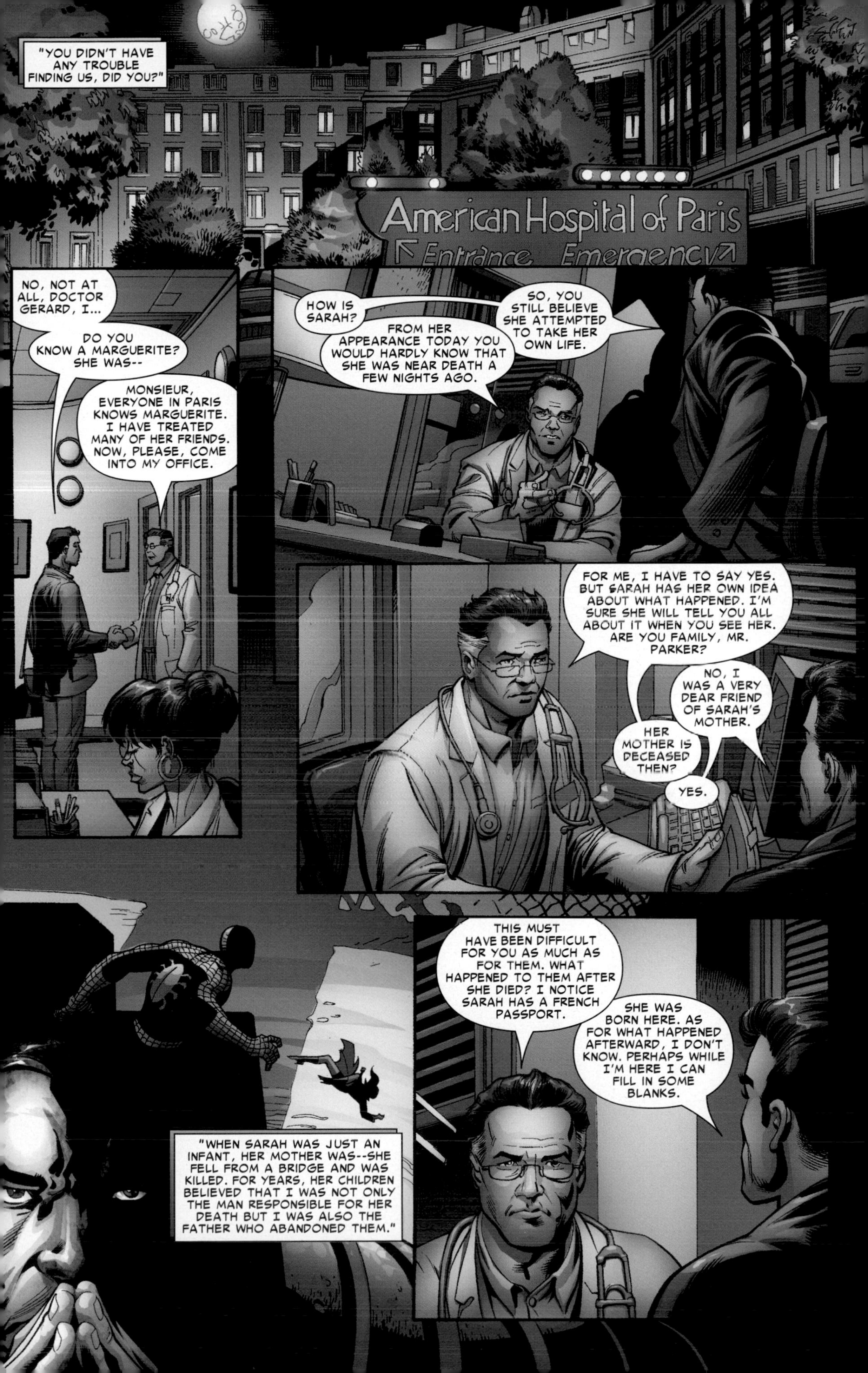
"YOU DIDN'T HAVE ANY TROUBLE FINDING US, DID YOU?"
American Hospital of Paris
Entrance Emergency
NO, NOT AT ALL, DOCTOR GERARD, I...
DO YOU KNOW A MARGUERITE? SHE WAS--
MONSIEUR, EVERYONE IN PARIS KNOWS MARGUERITE. I HAVE TREATED MANY OF HER FRIENDS. NOW, PLEASE, COME INTO MY OFFICE.
HOW IS SARAH?
FROM HER APPEARANCE TODAY YOU WOULD HARDLY KNOW THAT SHE WAS NEAR DEATH A FEW NIGHTS AGO.
SO, YOU STILL BELIEVE SHE ATTEMPTED TO TAKE HER OWN LIFE.
FOR ME, I HAVE TO SAY YES. BUT SARAH HAS HER OWN IDEA ABOUT WHAT HAPPENED. I'M SURE SHE WILL TELL YOU ALL ABOUT IT WHEN YOU SEE HER. ARE YOU FAMILY, MR. PARKER?
NO, I WAS A VERY DEAR FRIEND OF SARAH'S MOTHER.
HER MOTHER IS DECEASED THEN?
YES.
THIS MUST HAVE BEEN DIFFICULT FOR YOU AS MUCH AS FOR THEM. WHAT HAPPENED TO THEM AFTER SHE DIED? I NOTICE SARAH HAS A FRENCH PASSPORT.
SHE WAS BORN HERE. AS FOR WHAT HAPPENED AFTERWARD, I DON'T KNOW. PERHAPS WHILE I'M HERE I CAN FILL IN SOME BLANKS.
"WHEN SARAH WAS JUST AN INFANT, HER MOTHER WAS--SHE FELL FROM A BRIDGE AND WAS KILLED. FOR YEARS, HER CHILDREN BELIEVED THAT I WAS NOT ONLY THE MAN RESPONSIBLE FOR HER DEATH BUT I WAS ALSO THE FATHER WHO ABANDONED THEM."

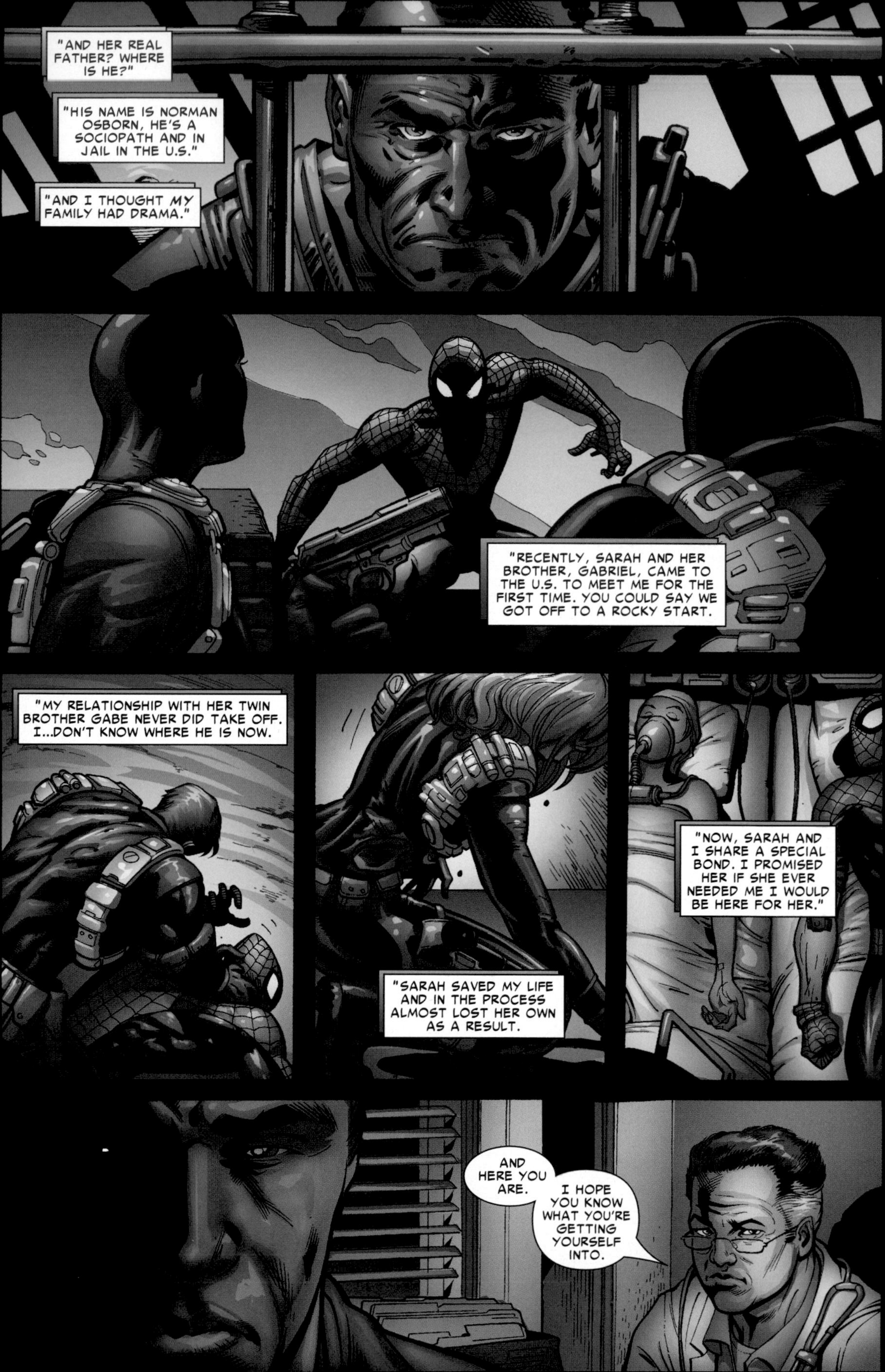
"AND HER REAL FATHER? WHERE IS HE?"
"HIS NAME IS NORMAN OSBORN, HE'S A SOCIOPATH AND IN JAIL IN THE U.S."
"AND I THOUGHT *MY* FAMILY HAD DRAMA."
"RECENTLY, SARAH AND HER BROTHER, GABRIEL, CAME TO THE U.S. TO MEET ME FOR THE FIRST TIME. YOU COULD SAY WE GOT OFF TO A ROCKY START.
"MY RELATIONSHIP WITH HER TWIN BROTHER GABE NEVER DID TAKE OFF. I...DON'T KNOW WHERE HE IS NOW.
"SARAH SAVED MY LIFE AND IN THE PROCESS ALMOST LOST HER OWN AS A RESULT.
"NOW, SARAH AND I SHARE A SPECIAL BOND. I PROMISED HER IF SHE EVER NEEDED ME I WOULD BE HERE FOR HER."
AND HERE YOU ARE.
I HOPE YOU KNOW WHAT YOU'RE GETTING YOURSELF INTO.

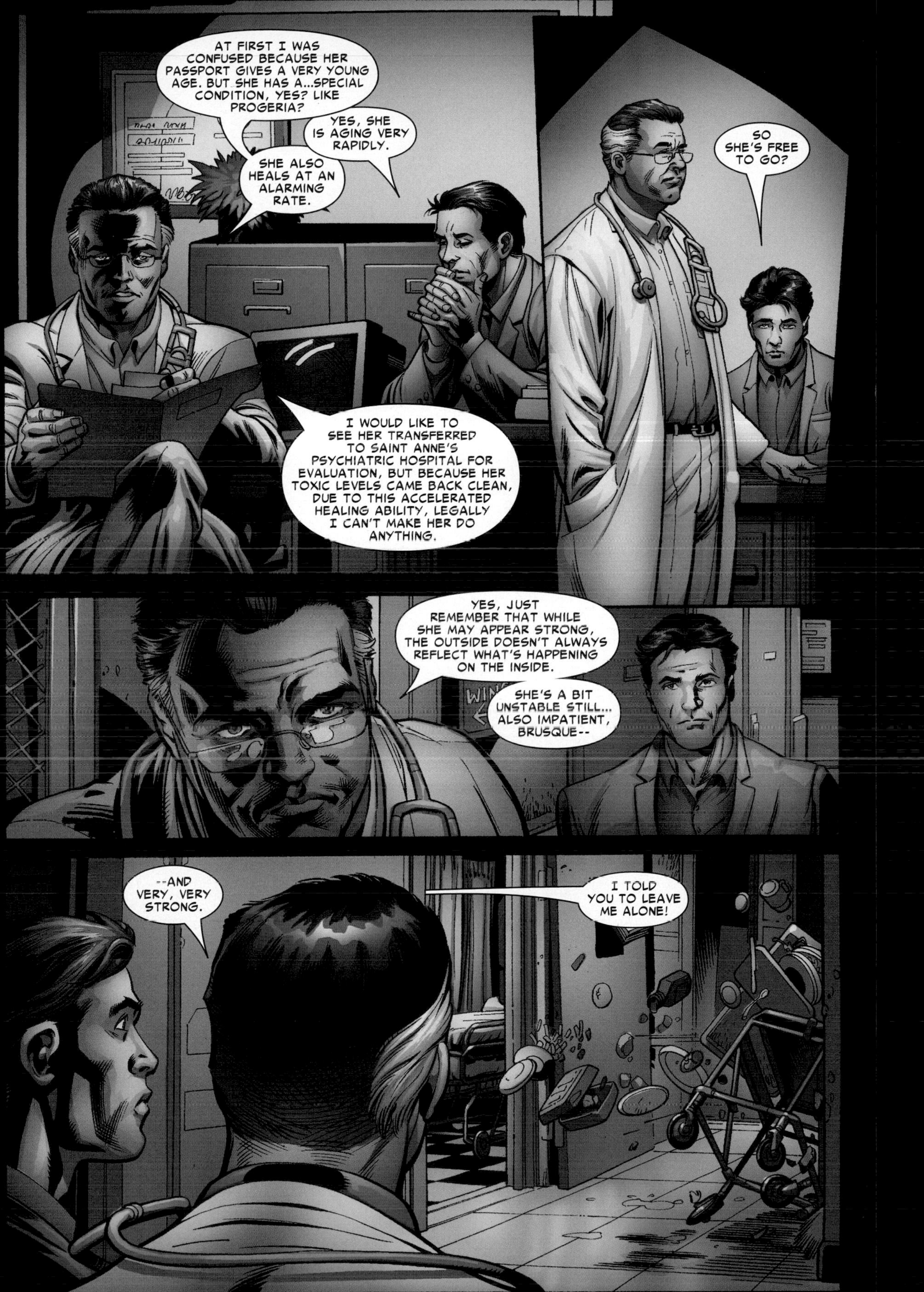
AT FIRST I WAS CONFUSED BECAUSE HER PASSPORT GIVES A VERY YOUNG AGE. BUT SHE HAS A...SPECIAL CONDITION, YES? LIKE PROGERIA?
YES, SHE IS AGING VERY RAPIDLY.
SHE ALSO HEALS AT AN ALARMING RATE.
I WOULD LIKE TO SEE HER TRANSFERRED TO SAINT ANNE'S PSYCHIATRIC HOSPITAL FOR EVALUATION, BUT BECAUSE HER TOXIC LEVELS CAME BACK CLEAN, DUE TO THIS ACCELERATED HEALING ABILITY, LEGALLY I CAN'T MAKE HER DO ANYTHING.
SO SHE'S FREE TO GO?
YES, JUST REMEMBER THAT WHILE SHE MAY APPEAR STRONG, THE OUTSIDE DOESN'T ALWAYS REFLECT WHAT'S HAPPENING ON THE INSIDE.
SHE'S A BIT UNSTABLE STILL... ALSO IMPATIENT, BRUSQUE--
--AND VERY, VERY STRONG.
I TOLD YOU TO LEAVE ME ALONE!

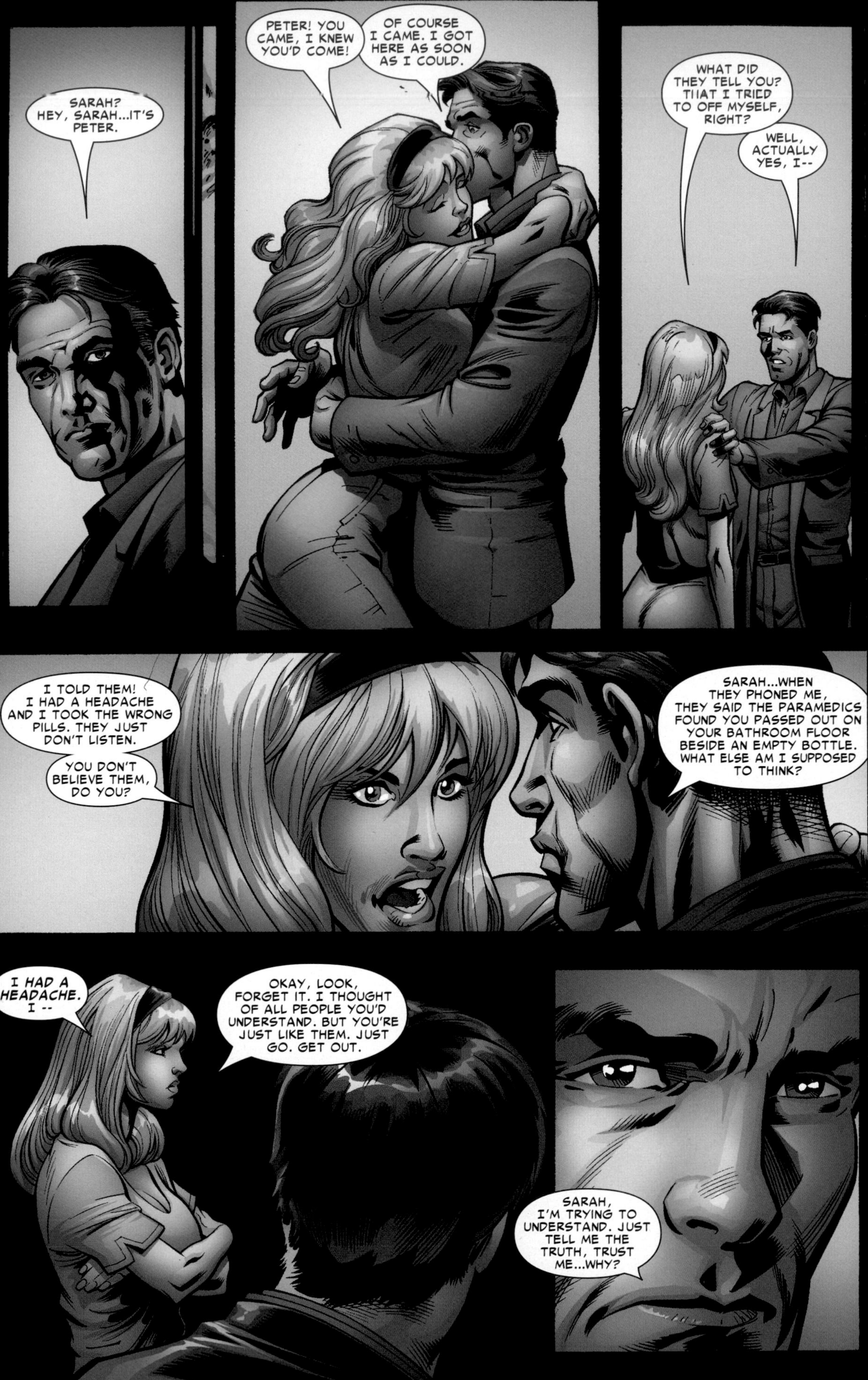
SARAH? HEY, SARAH...IT'S PETER.
PETER! YOU CAME, I KNEW YOU'D COME!
OF COURSE I CAME. I GOT HERE AS SOON AS I COULD.
WHAT DID THEY TELL YOU? THAT I TRIED TO OFF MYSELF, RIGHT?
WELL, ACTUALLY YES, I--
I TOLD THEM! I HAD A HEADACHE AND I TOOK THE WRONG PILLS. THEY JUST DON'T LISTEN.
YOU DON'T BELIEVE THEM, DO YOU?
SARAH...WHEN THEY PHONED ME, THEY SAID THE PARAMEDICS FOUND YOU PASSED OUT ON YOUR BATHROOM FLOOR BESIDE AN EMPTY BOTTLE. WHAT ELSE AM I SUPPOSED TO THINK?
I HAD A HEADACHE. I --
OKAY, LOOK, FORGET IT. I THOUGHT OF ALL PEOPLE YOU'D UNDERSTAND. BUT YOU'RE JUST LIKE THEM. JUST GO. GET OUT.
SARAH, I'M TRYING TO UNDERSTAND. JUST TELL ME THE TRUTH, TRUST ME...WHY?

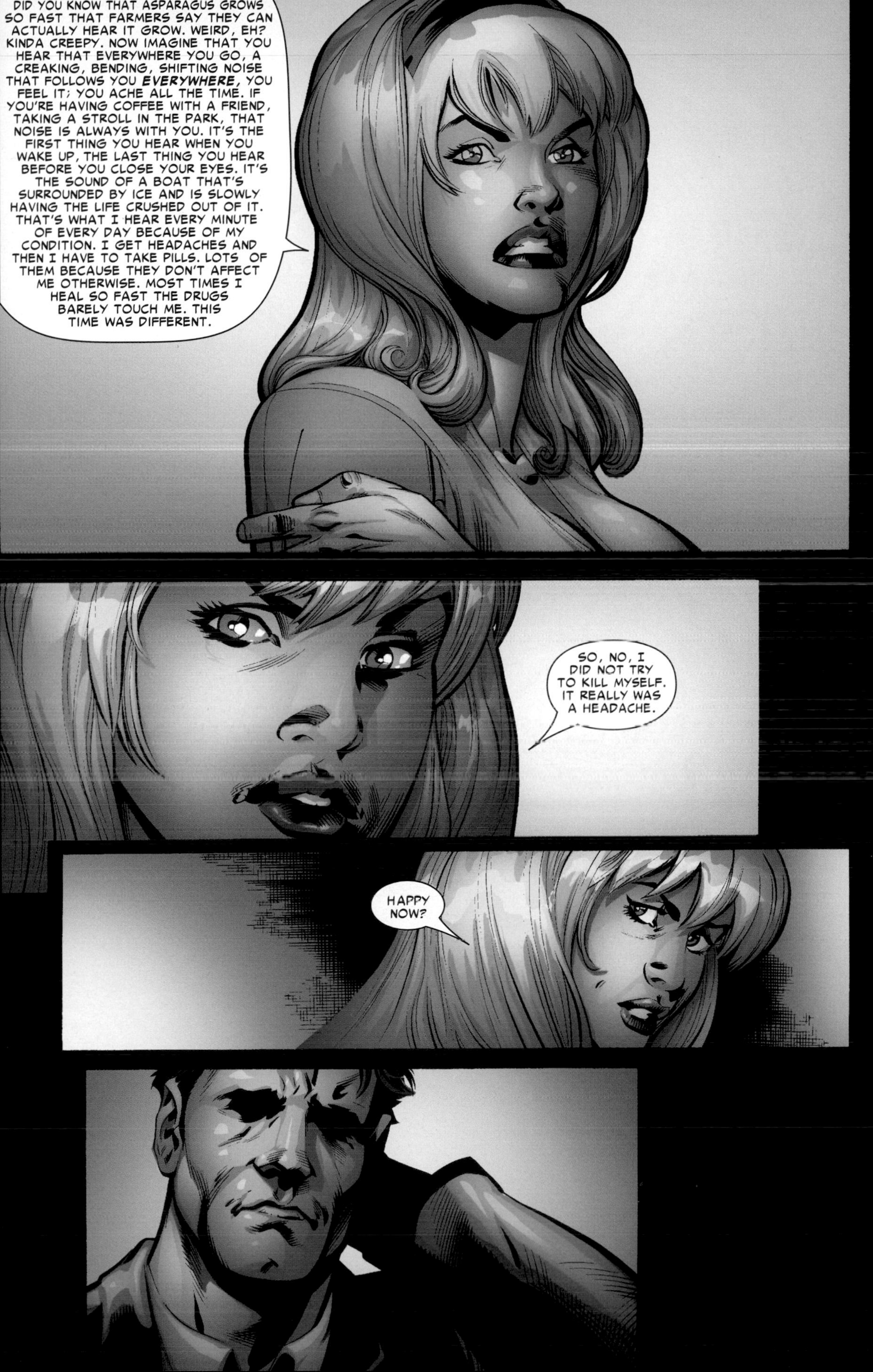
DID YOU KNOW THAT ASPARAGUS GROWS SO FAST THAT FARMERS SAY THEY CAN ACTUALLY HEAR IT GROW. WEIRD, EH? KINDA CREEPY. NOW IMAGINE THAT YOU HEAR THAT EVERYWHERE YOU GO, A CREAKING, BENDING, SHIFTING NOISE THAT FOLLOWS YOU EVERYWHERE, YOU FEEL IT; YOU ACHE ALL THE TIME. IF YOU'RE HAVING COFFEE WITH A FRIEND, TAKING A STROLL IN THE PARK, THAT NOISE IS ALWAYS WITH YOU. IT'S THE FIRST THING YOU HEAR WHEN YOU WAKE UP, THE LAST THING YOU HEAR BEFORE YOU CLOSE YOUR EYES. IT'S THE SOUND OF A BOAT THAT'S SURROUNDED BY ICE AND IS SLOWLY HAVING THE LIFE CRUSHED OUT OF IT. THAT'S WHAT I HEAR EVERY MINUTE OF EVERY DAY BECAUSE OF MY CONDITION. I GET HEADACHES AND THEN I HAVE TO TAKE PILLS. LOTS OF THEM BECAUSE THEY DON'T AFFECT ME OTHERWISE. MOST TIMES I HEAL SO FAST THE DRUGS BARELY TOUCH ME. THIS TIME WAS DIFFERENT.
SO, NO, I DID NOT TRY TO KILL MYSELF. IT REALLY WAS A HEADACHE.
HAPPY NOW?

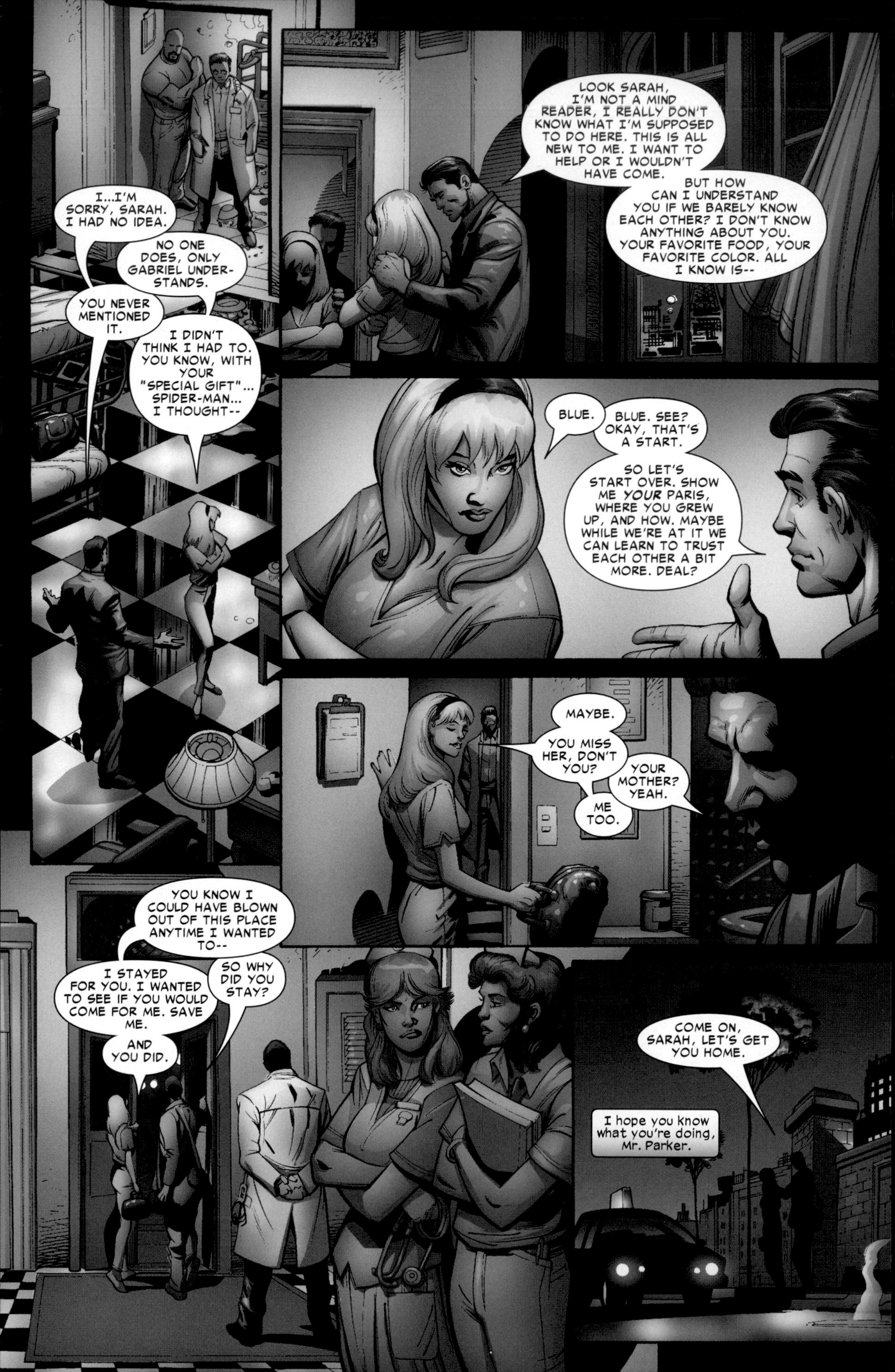
I...I'M SORRY, SARAH. I HAD NO IDEA.
NO ONE DOES, ONLY GABRIEL UNDER-STANDS.
YOU NEVER MENTIONED IT.
I DIDN'T THINK I HAD TO. YOU KNOW, WITH YOUR "SPECIAL GIFT"... SPIDER-MAN... I THOUGHT--
LOOK SARAH, I'M NOT A MIND READER, I REALLY DON'T KNOW WHAT I'M SUPPOSED TO DO HERE. THIS IS ALL NEW TO ME. I WANT TO HELP OR I WOULDN'T HAVE COME.
BUT HOW CAN I UNDERSTAND YOU IF WE BARELY KNOW EACH OTHER? I DON'T KNOW ANYTHING ABOUT YOU. YOUR FAVORITE FOOD, YOUR FAVORITE COLOR. ALL I KNOW IS--
BLUE.
BLUE. SEE? OKAY, THAT'S A START.
SO LET'S START OVER. SHOW ME YOUR PARIS, WHERE YOU GREW UP, AND HOW. MAYBE WHILE WE'RE AT IT WE CAN LEARN TO TRUST EACH OTHER A BIT MORE. DEAL?
MAYBE.
YOU MISS HER, DON'T YOU?
YOUR MOTHER? YEAH.
ME TOO.
YOU KNOW I COULD HAVE BLOWN OUT OF THIS PLACE ANYTIME I WANTED TO--
SO WHY DID YOU STAY?
I STAYED FOR YOU. I WANTED TO SEE IF YOU WOULD COME FOR ME. SAVE ME.
AND YOU DID.
COME ON, SARAH, LET'S GET YOU HOME.
I hope you know what you're doing, Mr. Parker.

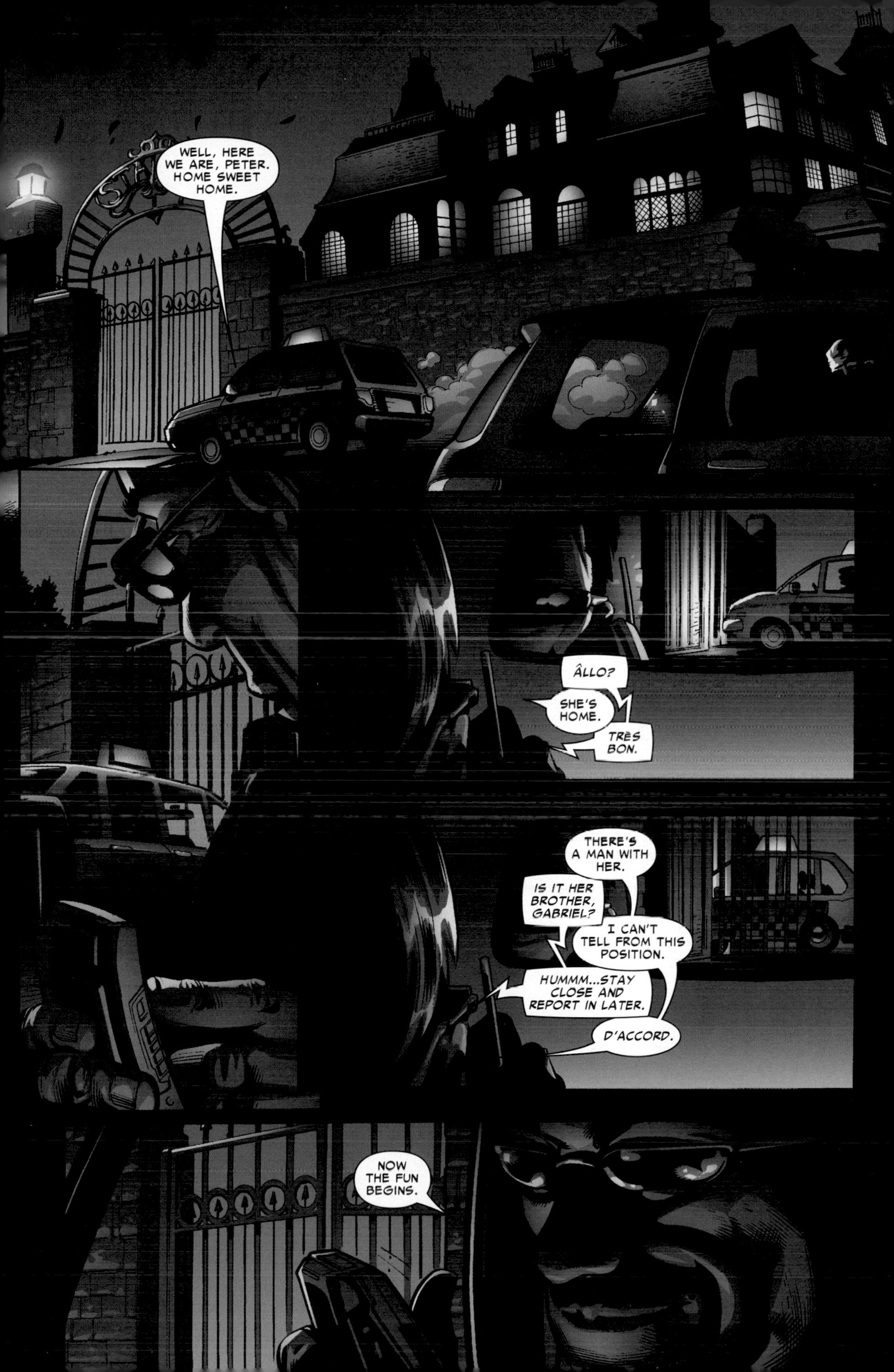
WELL, HERE WE ARE, PETER. HOME SWEET HOME.
ÂLLO?
SHE'S HOME.
TRÈS BON.
THERE'S A MAN WITH HER.
IS IT HER BROTHER, GABRIEL?
I CAN'T TELL FROM THIS POSITION.
HUMMM...STAY CLOSE AND REPORT IN LATER.
D'ACCORD.
NOW THE FUN BEGINS.

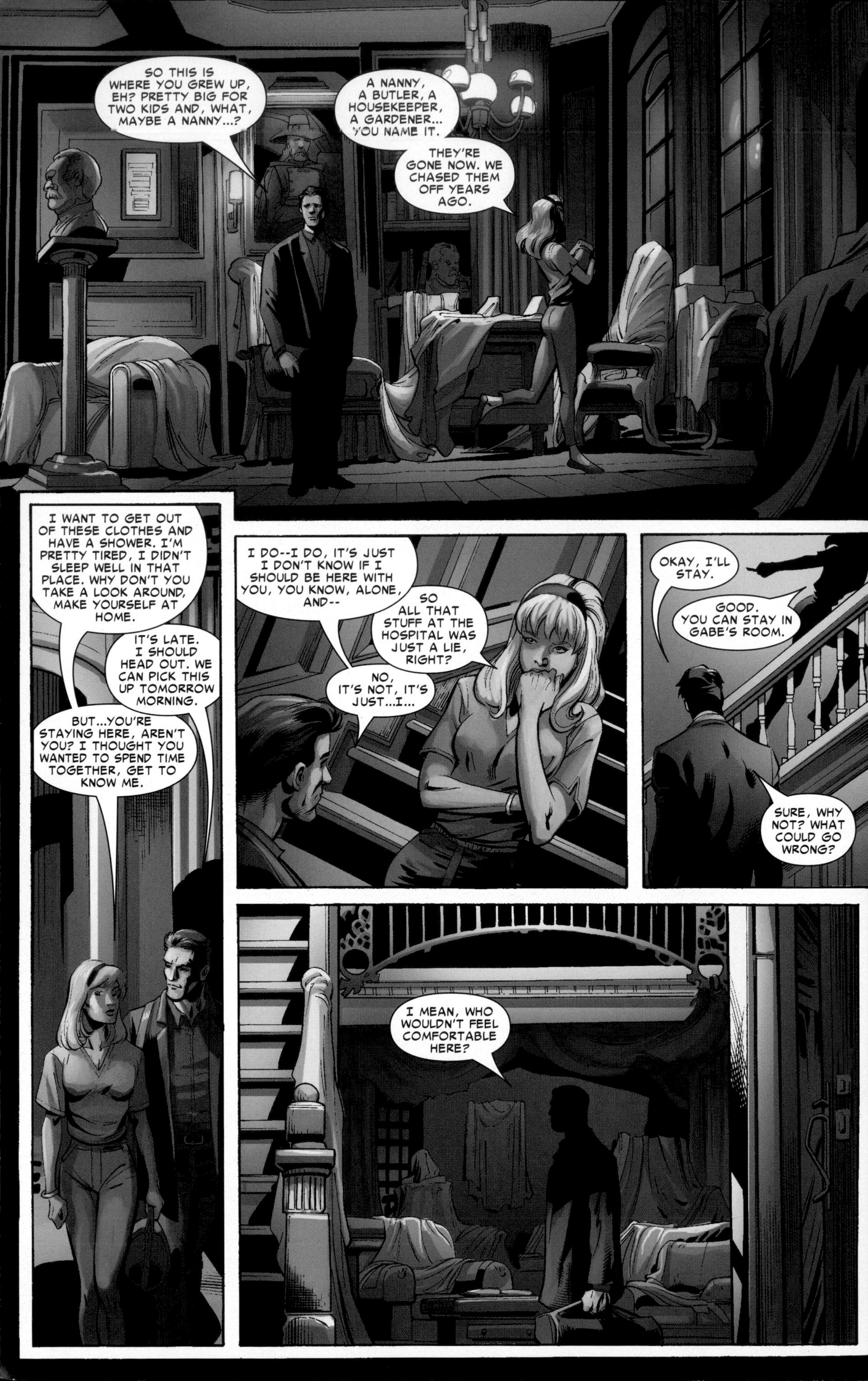
SO THIS IS WHERE YOU GREW UP, EH? PRETTY BIG FOR TWO KIDS AND, WHAT, MAYBE A NANNY...?
A NANNY, A BUTLER, A HOUSEKEEPER, A GARDENER... YOU NAME IT.
THEY'RE GONE NOW. WE CHASED THEM OFF YEARS AGO.
I WANT TO GET OUT OF THESE CLOTHES AND HAVE A SHOWER. I'M PRETTY TIRED, I DIDN'T SLEEP WELL IN THAT PLACE. WHY DON'T YOU TAKE A LOOK AROUND, MAKE YOURSELF AT HOME.
IT'S LATE. I SHOULD HEAD OUT. WE CAN PICK THIS UP TOMORROW MORNING.
BUT...YOU'RE STAYING HERE, AREN'T YOU? I THOUGHT YOU WANTED TO SPEND TIME TOGETHER, GET TO KNOW ME.
I DO--I DO, IT'S JUST I DON'T KNOW IF I SHOULD BE HERE WITH YOU, YOU KNOW, ALONE, AND--
SO ALL THAT STUFF AT THE HOSPITAL WAS JUST A LIE, RIGHT?
NO, IT'S NOT, IT'S JUST...I...
OKAY, I'LL STAY.
GOOD. YOU CAN STAY IN GABE'S ROOM.
SURE, WHY NOT? WHAT COULD GO WRONG?
I MEAN, WHO WOULDN'T FEEL COMFORTABLE HERE?

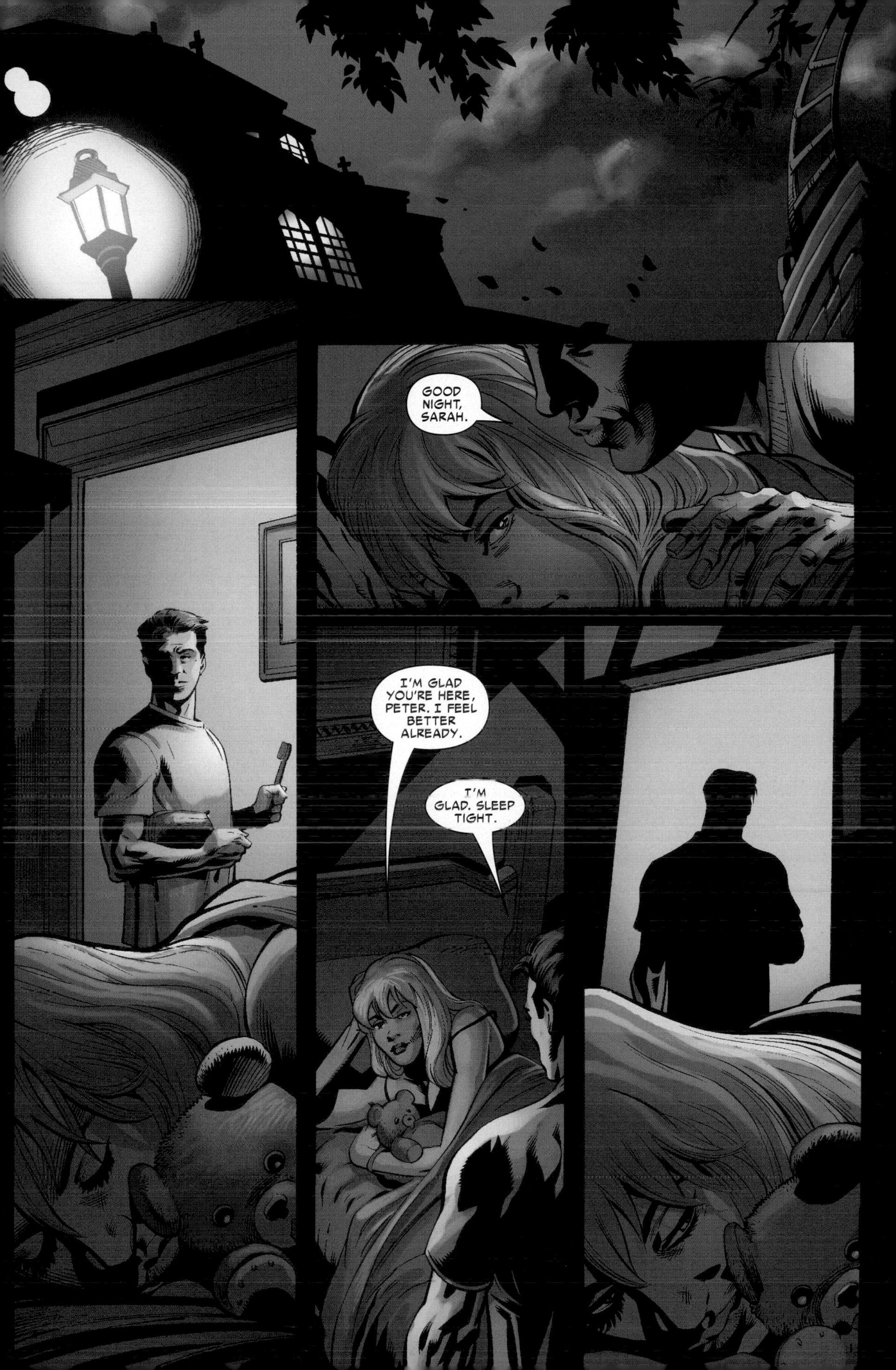
GOOD NIGHT, SARAH.
I'M GLAD YOU'RE HERE, PETER. I FEEL BETTER ALREADY.
I'M GLAD. SLEEP TIGHT.

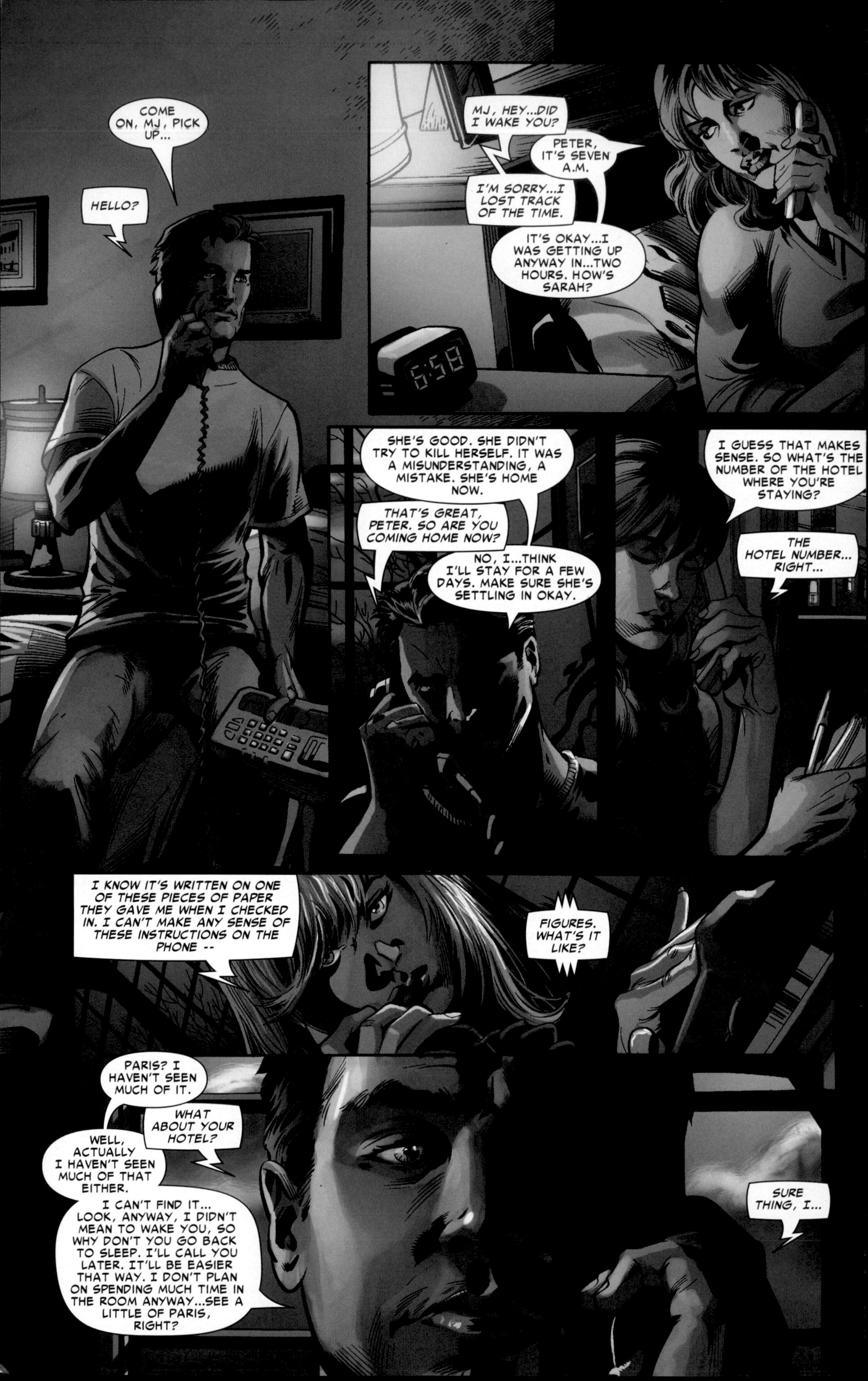
COME ON, MJ, PICK UP...
HELLO?
MJ, HEY...DID I WAKE YOU?
PETER, IT'S SEVEN A.M.
I'M SORRY...I LOST TRACK OF THE TIME.
IT'S OKAY...I WAS GETTING UP ANYWAY IN...TWO HOURS. HOW'S SARAH?
SHE'S GOOD. SHE DIDN'T TRY TO KILL HERSELF. IT WAS A MISUNDERSTANDING, A MISTAKE. SHE'S HOME NOW.
THAT'S GREAT, PETER. SO ARE YOU COMING HOME NOW?
NO, I...THINK I'LL STAY FOR A FEW DAYS. MAKE SURE SHE'S SETTLING IN OKAY.
I GUESS THAT MAKES SENSE. SO WHAT'S THE NUMBER OF THE HOTEL WHERE YOU'RE STAYING?
THE HOTEL NUMBER... RIGHT...
I KNOW IT'S WRITTEN ON ONE OF THESE PIECES OF PAPER THEY GAVE ME WHEN I CHECKED IN. I CAN'T MAKE ANY SENSE OF THESE INSTRUCTIONS ON THE PHONE --
FIGURES. WHAT'S IT LIKE?
PARIS? I HAVEN'T SEEN MUCH OF IT.
WHAT ABOUT YOUR HOTEL?
WELL, ACTUALLY I HAVEN'T SEEN MUCH OF THAT EITHER.
I CAN'T FIND IT... LOOK, ANYWAY, I DIDN'T MEAN TO WAKE YOU, SO WHY DON'T YOU GO BACK TO SLEEP. I'LL CALL YOU LATER. IT'LL BE EASIER THAT WAY. I DON'T PLAN ON SPENDING MUCH TIME IN THE ROOM ANYWAY...SEE A LITTLE OF PARIS, RIGHT?
SURE THING, I...

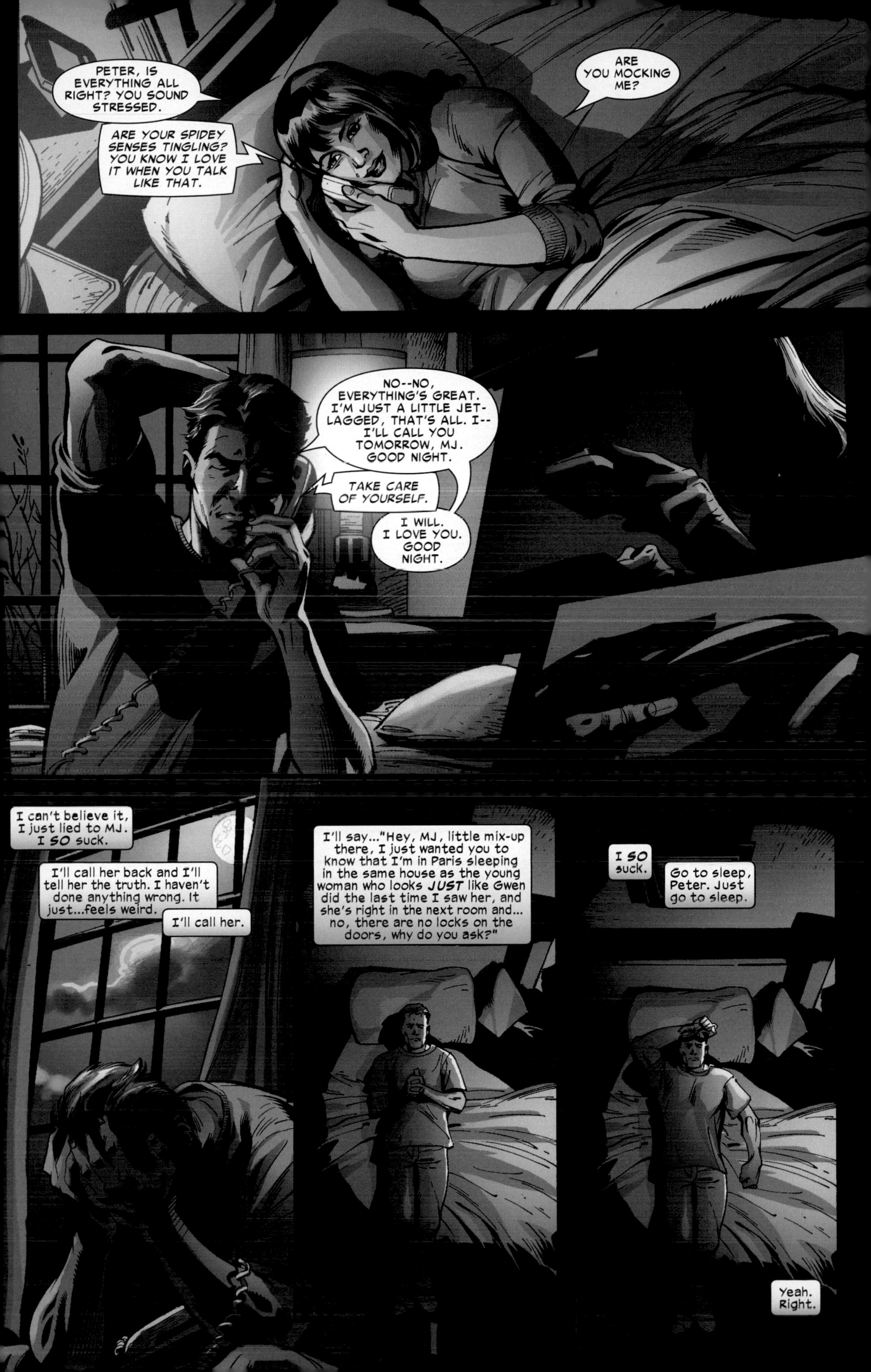

PETER, IS EVERYTHING ALL RIGHT? YOU SOUND STRESSED.
ARE YOUR SPIDEY SENSES TINGLING? YOU KNOW I LOVE IT WHEN YOU TALK LIKE THAT.
ARE YOU MOCKING ME?
NO--NO, EVERYTHING'S GREAT. I'M JUST A LITTLE JET-LAGGED, THAT'S ALL. I--I'LL CALL YOU TOMORROW, MJ. GOOD NIGHT.
TAKE CARE OF YOURSELF.
I WILL. I LOVE YOU. GOOD NIGHT.
I can't believe it, I just lied to MJ. I SO suck.
I'll call her back and I'll tell her the truth. I haven't done anything wrong. It just...feels weird.
I'll call her.
I'll say..."Hey, MJ, little mix-up there, I just wanted you to know that I'm in Paris sleeping in the same house as the young woman who looks JUST like Gwen did the last time I saw her, and she's right in the next room and... no, there are no locks on the doors, why do you ask?"
I SO suck.
Go to sleep, Peter. Just go to sleep.
Yeah. Right.

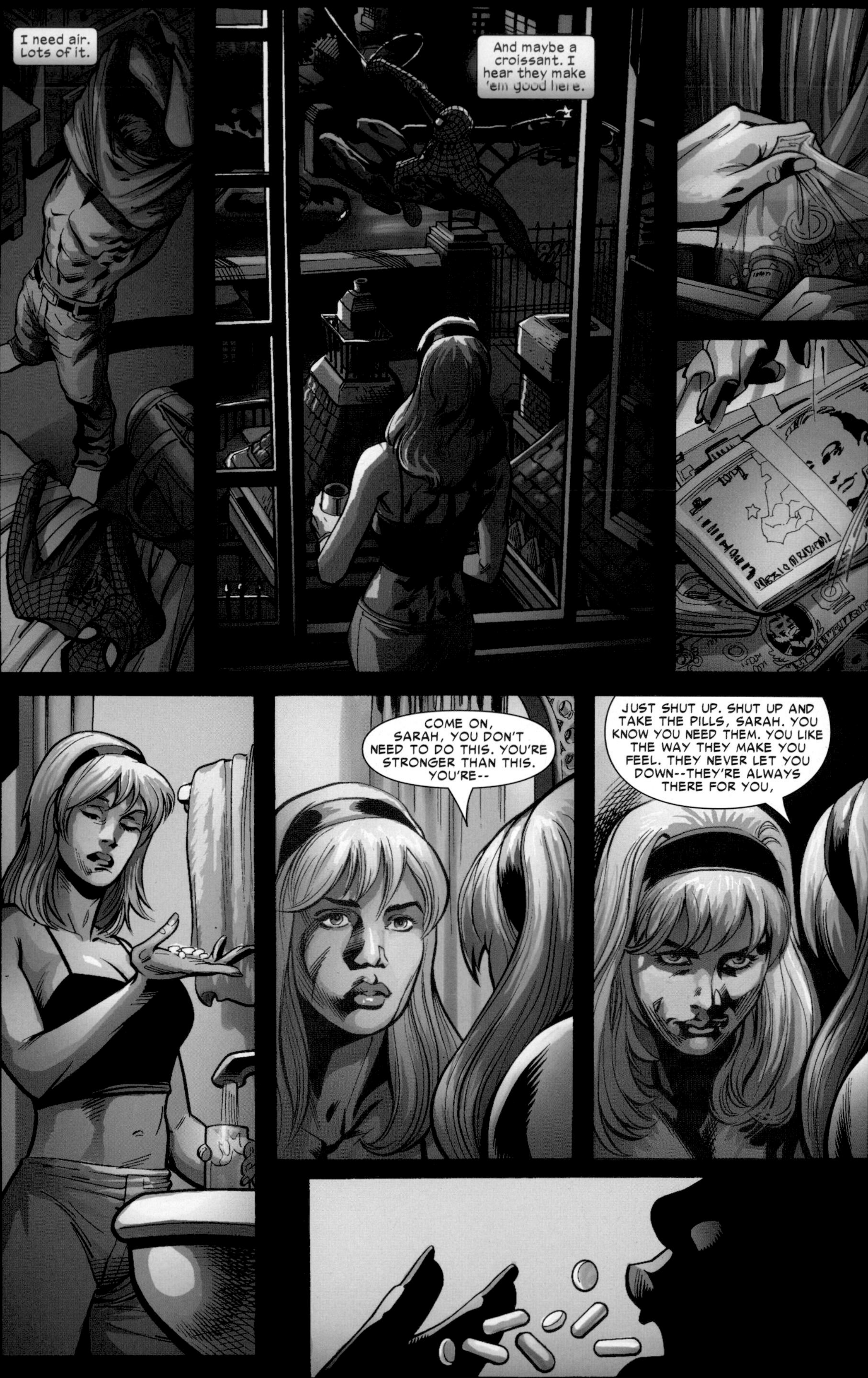
I need air. Lots of it.
And maybe a croissant. I hear they make 'em good here.
COME ON, SARAH, YOU DON'T NEED TO DO THIS. YOU'RE STRONGER THAN THIS. YOU'RE--
JUST SHUT UP. SHUT UP AND TAKE THE PILLS, SARAH. YOU KNOW YOU NEED THEM. YOU LIKE THE WAY THEY MAKE YOU FEEL. THEY NEVER LET YOU DOWN--THEY'RE ALWAYS THERE FOR YOU,

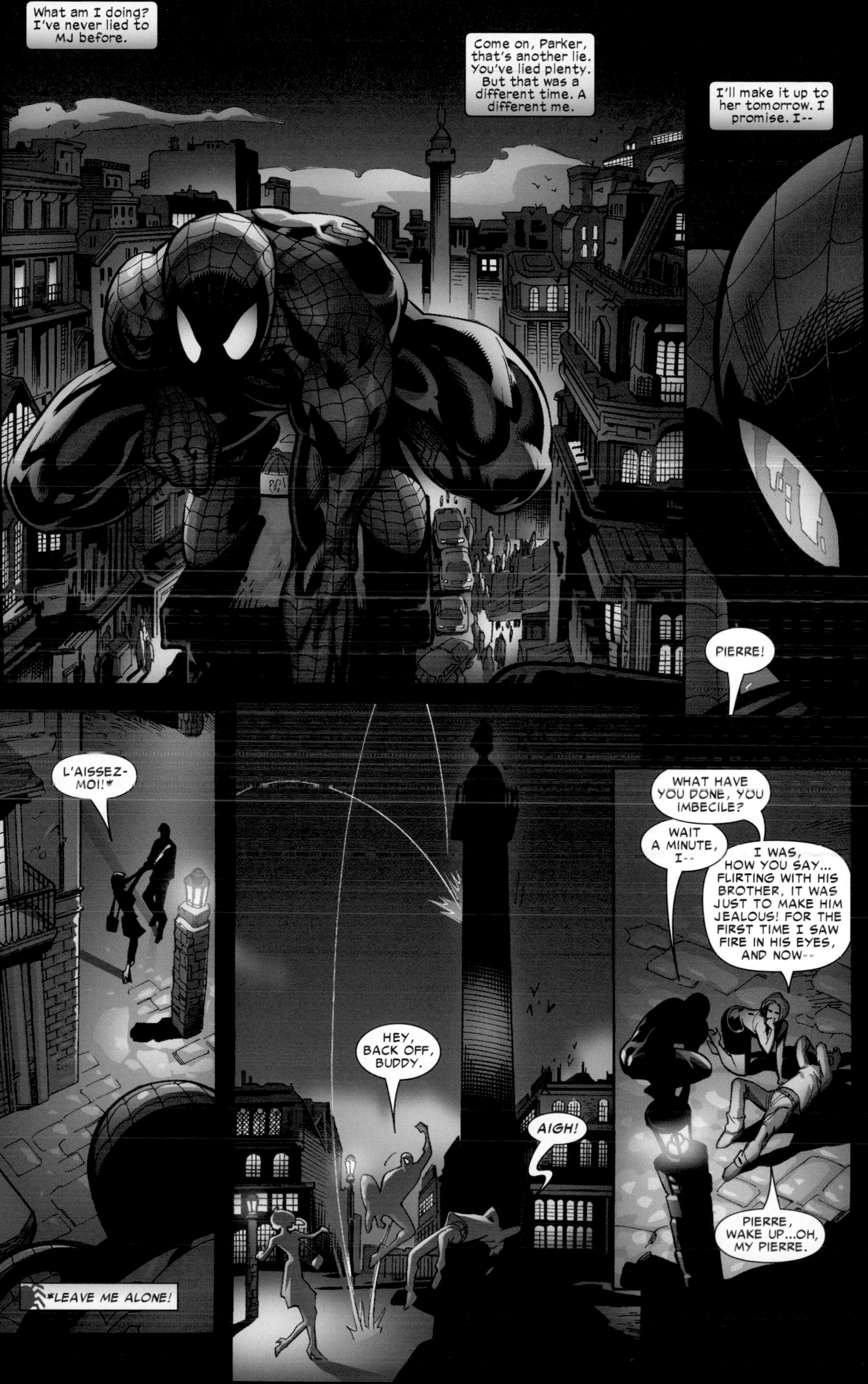
What am I doing? I've never lied to MJ before.
Come on, Parker, that's another lie. You've lied plenty. But that was a different time. A different me.
I'll make it up to her tomorrow. I promise. I--
PIERRE!
L'AISSEZ-MOI!*
HEY, BACK OFF, BUDDY.
AIGH!
WHAT HAVE YOU DONE, YOU IMBECILE?
WAIT A MINUTE, I--
I WAS, HOW YOU SAY... FLIRTING WITH HIS BROTHER, IT WAS JUST TO MAKE HIM JEALOUS! FOR THE FIRST TIME I SAW FIRE IN HIS EYES, AND NOW--
PIERRE, WAKE UP...OH, MY PIERRE.
*LEAVE ME ALONE!

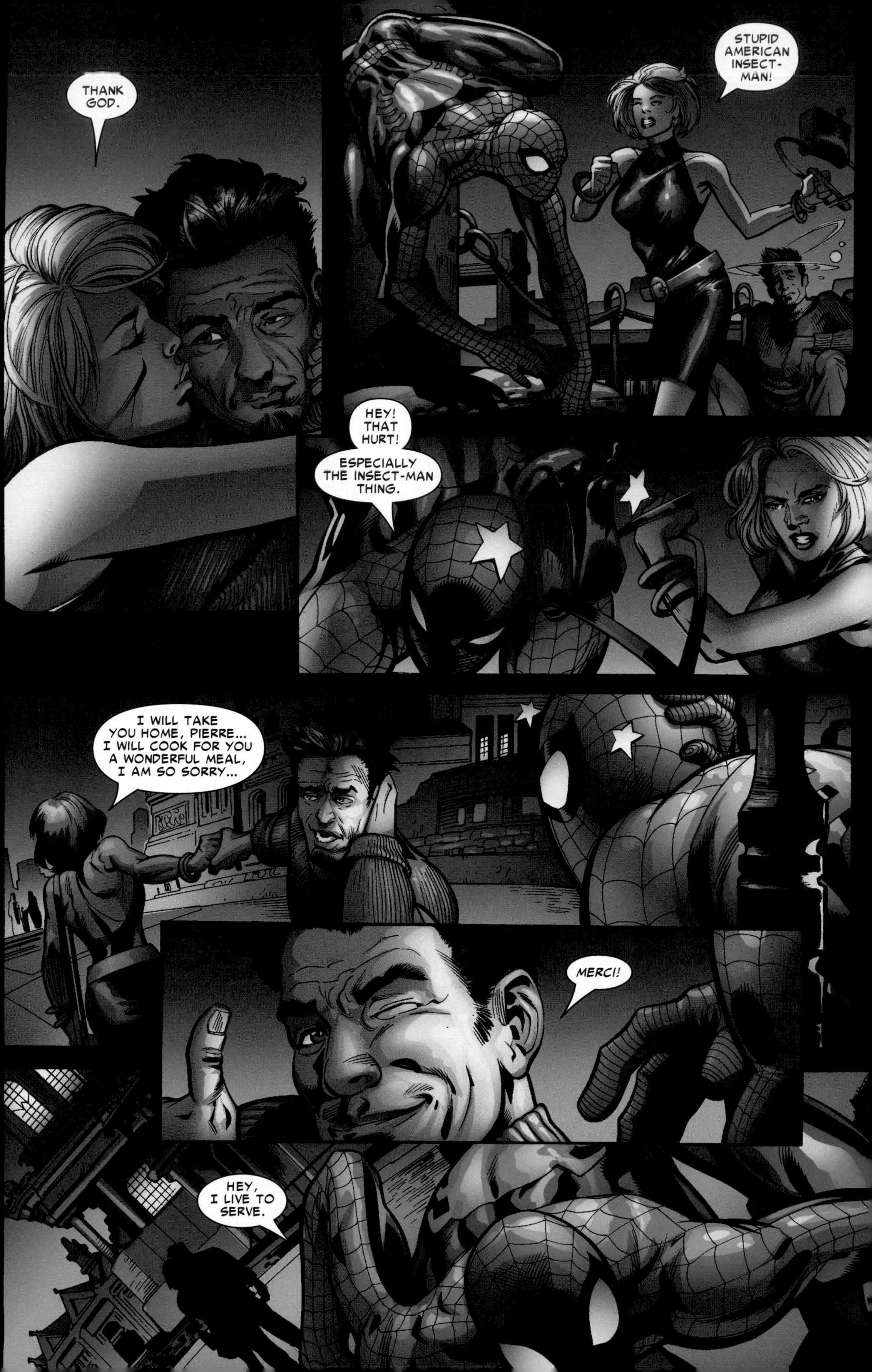
THANK GOD.
STUPID AMERICAN INSECT-MAN!
HEY! THAT HURT!
ESPECIALLY THE INSECT-MAN THING.
I WILL TAKE YOU HOME, PIERRE... I WILL COOK FOR YOU A WONDERFUL MEAL, I AM SO SORRY...
MERCI!
HEY, I LIVE TO SERVE.

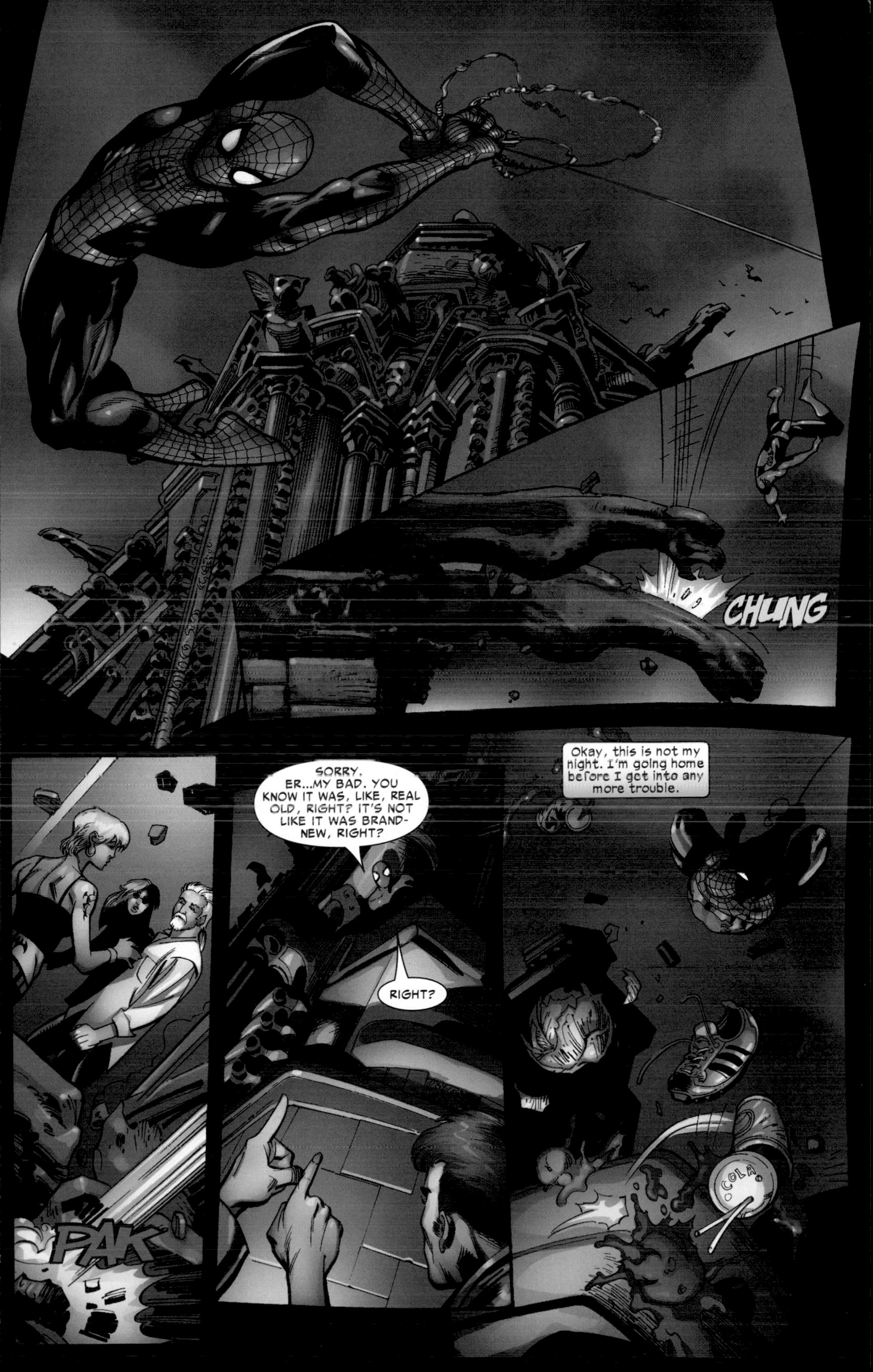
CHUNG
PAK
SORRY. ER...MY BAD. YOU KNOW IT WAS, LIKE, REAL OLD, RIGHT? IT'S NOT LIKE IT WAS BRAND-NEW, RIGHT?
RIGHT?
Okay, this is not my night. I'm going home before I get into any more trouble.
COLA

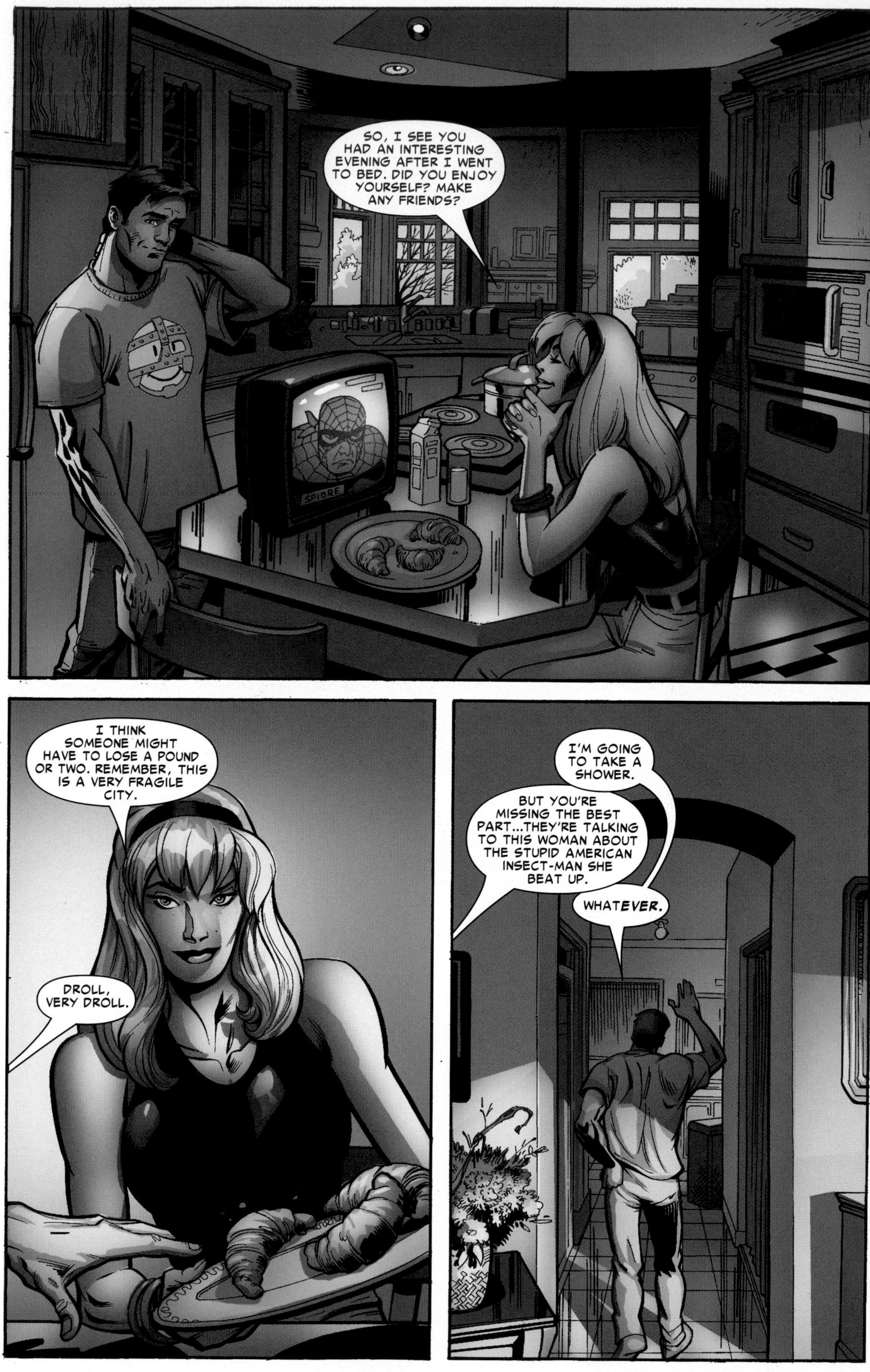
SO, I SEE YOU HAD AN INTERESTING EVENING AFTER I WENT TO BED. DID YOU ENJOY YOURSELF? MAKE ANY FRIENDS?
SPIDRE
I THINK SOMEONE MIGHT HAVE TO LOSE A POUND OR TWO. REMEMBER, THIS IS A VERY FRAGILE CITY.
DROLL, VERY DROLL.
I'M GOING TO TAKE A SHOWER.
BUT YOU'RE MISSING THE BEST PART...THEY'RE TALKING TO THIS WOMAN ABOUT THE STUPID AMERICAN INSECT-MAN SHE BEAT UP.
WHATEVER.

IT'S ME. EVERYTHING IS GOING AS I HAD HOPED.

I'LL MAKE THE DROP, YOU JUST KEEP YOUR END OF THE BARGAIN. WHO KNOWS, IF WE'RE LUCKY--

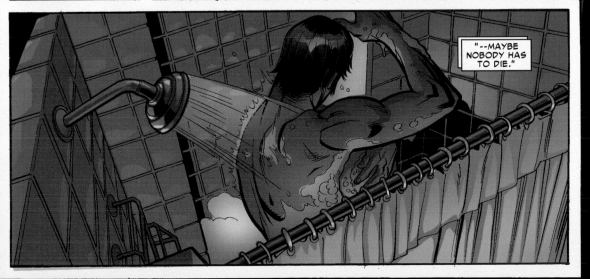

"--MAYBE NOBODY HAS TO DIE."

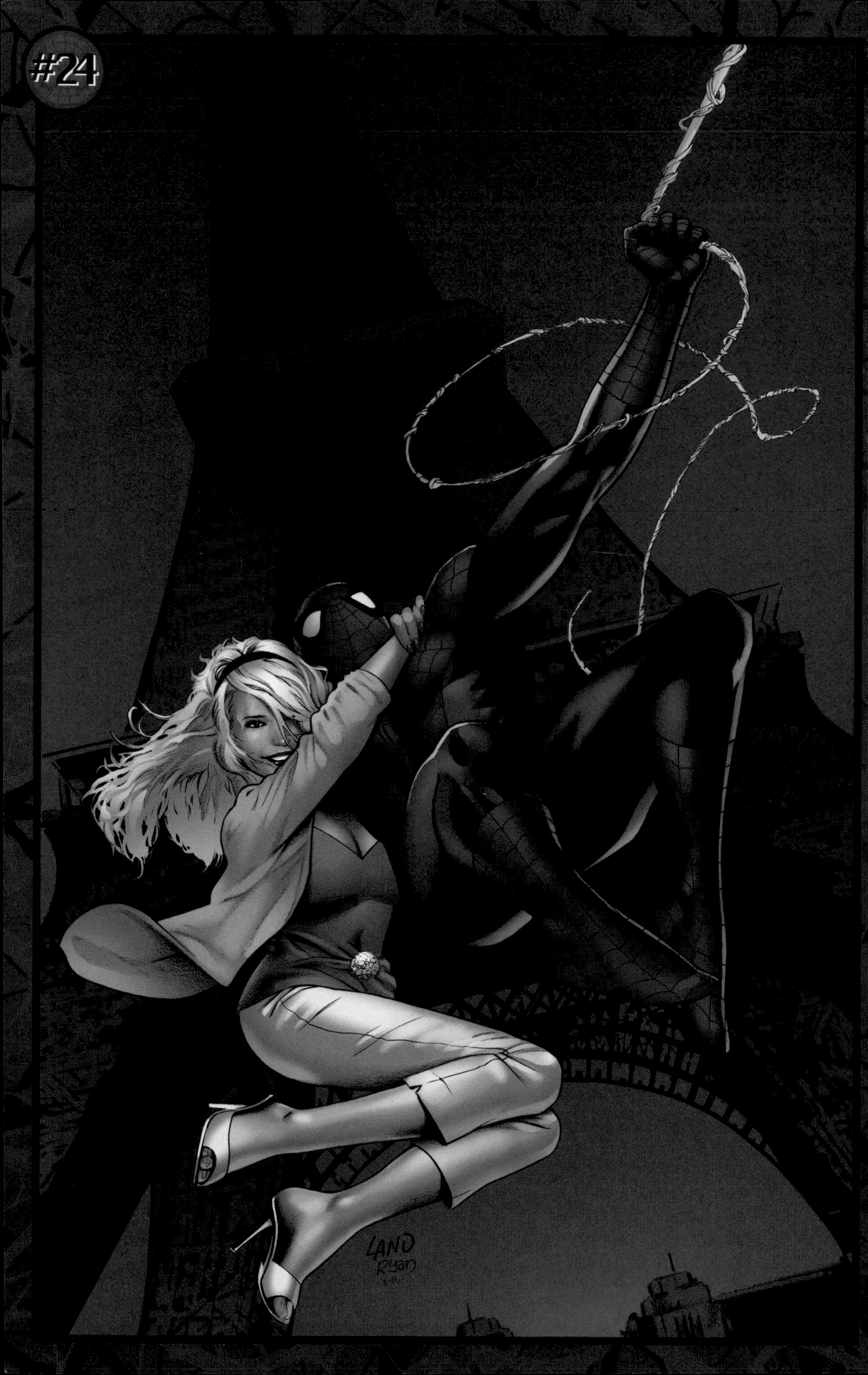
#24
LAND
Ryan

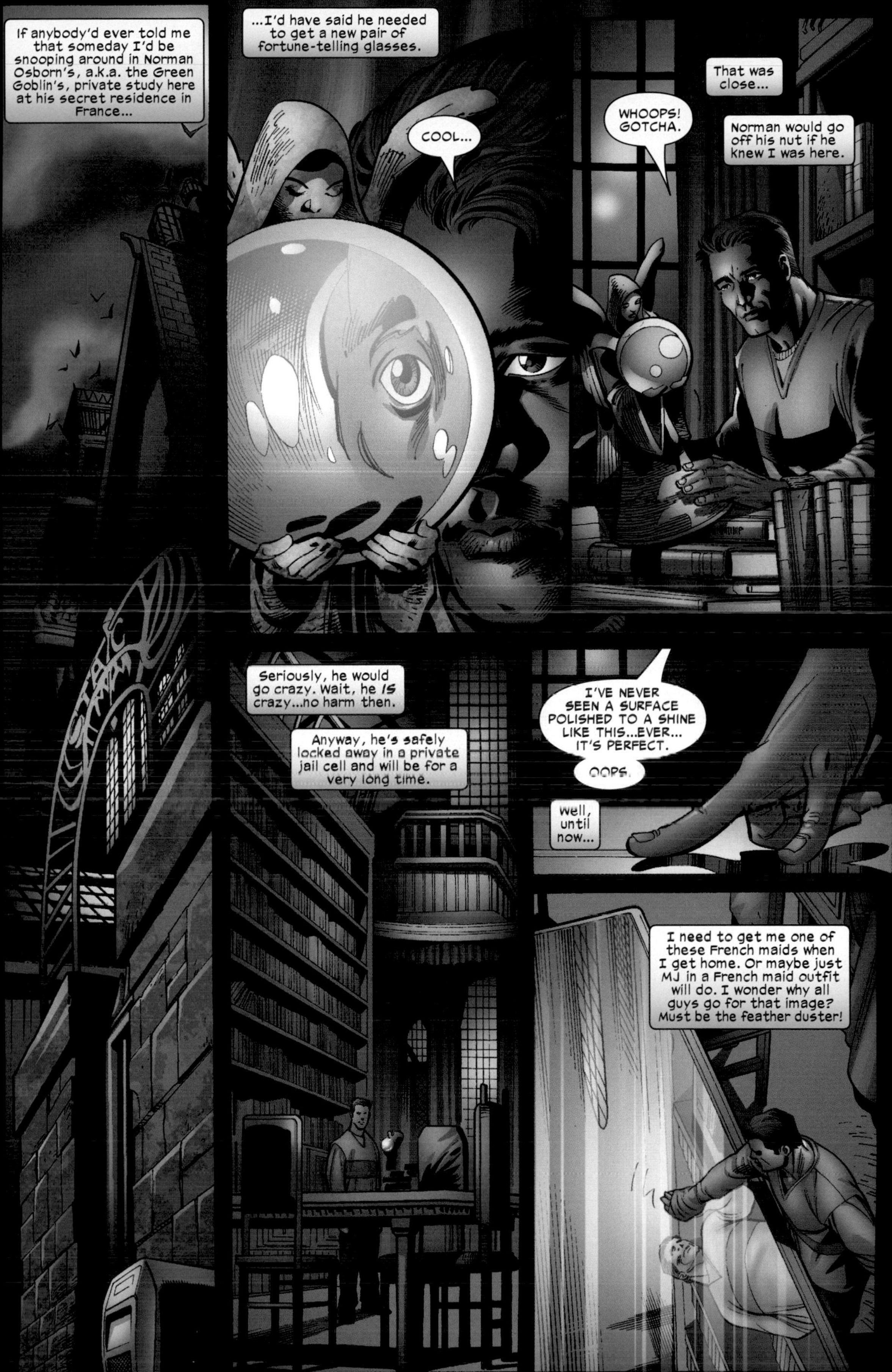
If anybody'd ever told me that someday I'd be snooping around in Norman Osborn's, a.k.a. the Green Goblin's, private study here at his secret residence in France...
...I'd have said he needed to get a new pair of fortune-telling glasses.
COOL...
WHOOPS! GOTCHA.
That was close...
Norman would go off his nut if he knew I was here.
Seriously, he would go crazy. Wait, he *IS* crazy...no harm then.
Anyway, he's safely locked away in a private jail cell and will be for a very long time.
I'VE NEVER SEEN A SURFACE POLISHED TO A SHINE LIKE THIS...EVER... IT'S PERFECT.
OOPS.
Well, until now...
I need to get me one of these French maids when I get home. Or maybe just MJ in a French maid outfit will do. I wonder why all guys go for that image? Must be the feather duster!

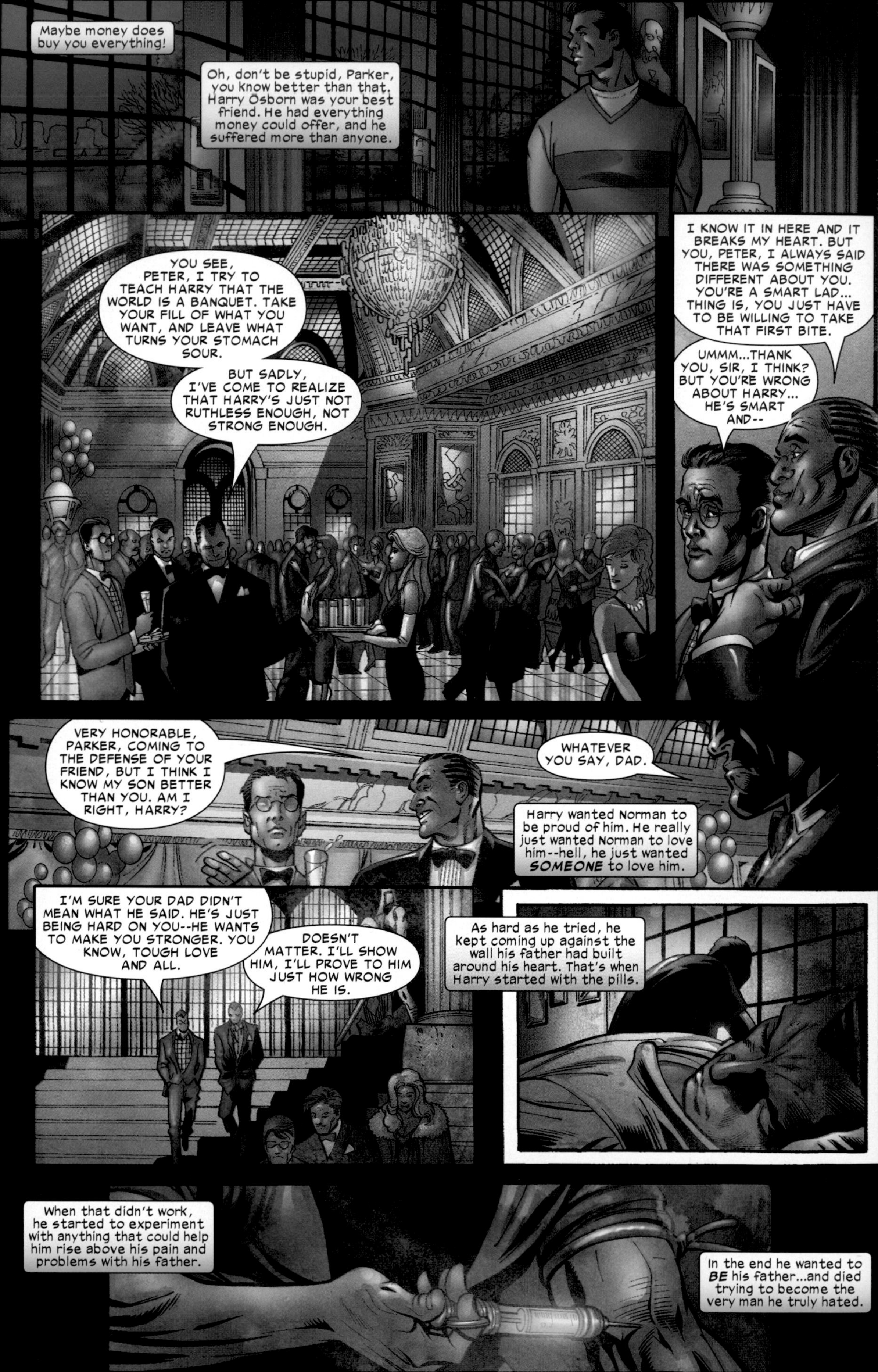

Maybe money does buy you everything!
Oh, don't be stupid, Parker, you know better than that. Harry Osborn was your best friend. He had everything money could offer, and he suffered more than anyone.
YOU SEE, PETER, I TRY TO TEACH HARRY THAT THE WORLD IS A BANQUET. TAKE YOUR FILL OF WHAT YOU WANT, AND LEAVE WHAT TURNS YOUR STOMACH SOUR.
BUT SADLY, I'VE COME TO REALIZE THAT HARRY'S JUST NOT RUTHLESS ENOUGH, NOT STRONG ENOUGH.
I KNOW IT IN HERE AND IT BREAKS MY HEART. BUT YOU, PETER, I ALWAYS SAID THERE WAS SOMETHING DIFFERENT ABOUT YOU. YOU'RE A SMART LAD... THING IS, YOU JUST HAVE TO BE WILLING TO TAKE THAT FIRST BITE.
UMMM...THANK YOU, SIR, I THINK? BUT YOU'RE WRONG ABOUT HARRY... HE'S SMART AND--
VERY HONORABLE, PARKER, COMING TO THE DEFENSE OF YOUR FRIEND, BUT I THINK I KNOW MY SON BETTER THAN YOU. AM I RIGHT, HARRY?
WHATEVER YOU SAY, DAD.
Harry wanted Norman to be proud of him. He really just wanted Norman to love him--hell, he just wanted SOMEONE to love him.
I'M SURE YOUR DAD DIDN'T MEAN WHAT HE SAID. HE'S JUST BEING HARD ON YOU--HE WANTS TO MAKE YOU STRONGER. YOU KNOW, TOUGH LOVE AND ALL.
DOESN'T MATTER. I'LL SHOW HIM, I'LL PROVE TO HIM JUST HOW WRONG HE IS.
As hard as he tried, he kept coming up against the wall his father had built around his heart. That's when Harry started with the pills.
When that didn't work, he started to experiment with anything that could help him rise above his pain and problems with his father.
In the end he wanted to BE his father...and died trying to become the very man he truly hated.

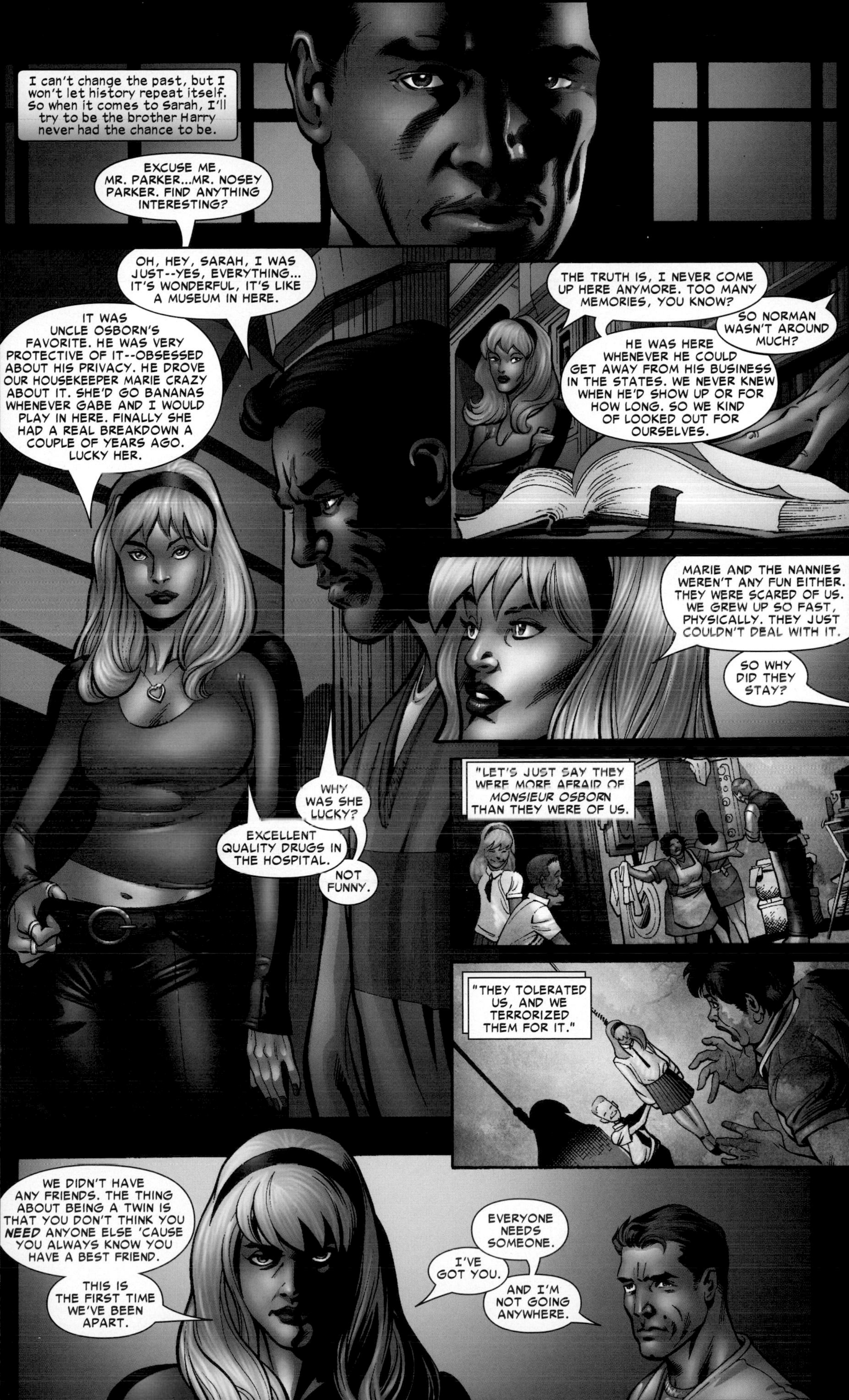
I can't change the past, but I won't let history repeat itself. So when it comes to Sarah, I'll try to be the brother Harry never had the chance to be.
EXCUSE ME, MR. PARKER...MR. NOSEY PARKER. FIND ANYTHING INTERESTING?
OH, HEY, SARAH, I WAS JUST--YES, EVERYTHING... IT'S WONDERFUL, IT'S LIKE A MUSEUM IN HERE.
IT WAS UNCLE OSBORN'S FAVORITE. HE WAS VERY PROTECTIVE OF IT--OBSESSED ABOUT HIS PRIVACY. HE DROVE OUR HOUSEKEEPER MARIE CRAZY ABOUT IT. SHE'D GO BANANAS WHENEVER GABE AND I WOULD PLAY IN HERE. FINALLY SHE HAD A REAL BREAKDOWN A COUPLE OF YEARS AGO. LUCKY HER.
WHY WAS SHE LUCKY?
EXCELLENT QUALITY DRUGS IN THE HOSPITAL.
NOT FUNNY.
THE TRUTH IS, I NEVER COME UP HERE ANYMORE. TOO MANY MEMORIES, YOU KNOW?
SO NORMAN WASN'T AROUND MUCH?
HE WAS HERE WHENEVER HE COULD GET AWAY FROM HIS BUSINESS IN THE STATES. WE NEVER KNEW WHEN HE'D SHOW UP OR FOR HOW LONG. SO WE KIND OF LOOKED OUT FOR OURSELVES.
MARIE AND THE NANNIES WEREN'T ANY FUN EITHER. THEY WERE SCARED OF US. WE GREW UP SO FAST, PHYSICALLY. THEY JUST COULDN'T DEAL WITH IT.
SO WHY DID THEY STAY?
"LET'S JUST SAY THEY WERE MORE AFRAID OF *MONSIEUR OSBORN* THAN THEY WERE OF US.
"THEY TOLERATED US, AND WE TERRORIZED THEM FOR IT."
WE DIDN'T HAVE ANY FRIENDS. THE THING ABOUT BEING A TWIN IS THAT YOU DON'T THINK YOU ***NEED*** ANYONE ELSE 'CAUSE YOU ALWAYS KNOW YOU HAVE A BEST FRIEND.
THIS IS THE FIRST TIME WE'VE BEEN APART.
EVERYONE NEEDS SOMEONE.
I'VE GOT YOU.
AND I'M NOT GOING ANYWHERE.

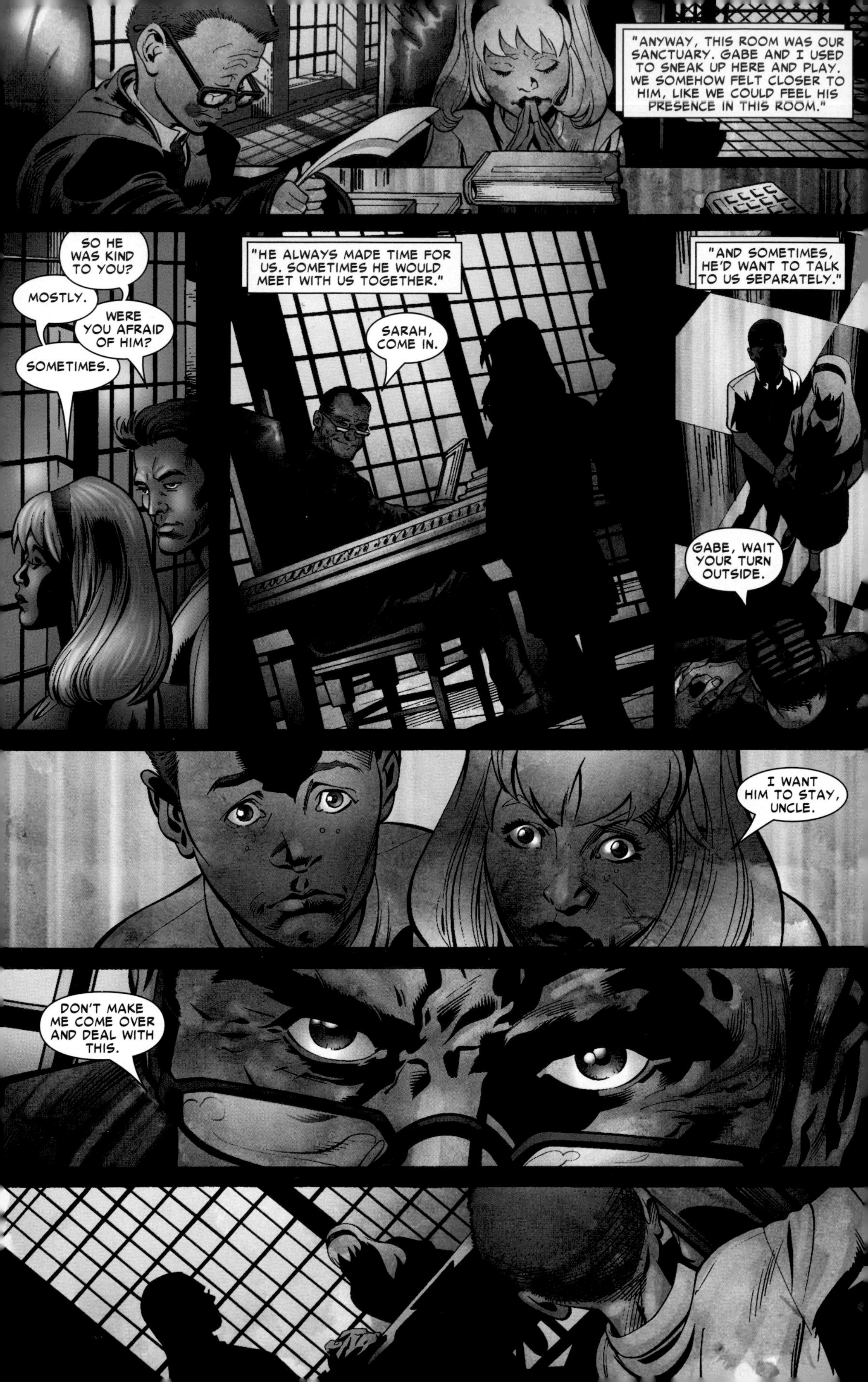
"ANYWAY, THIS ROOM WAS OUR SANCTUARY. GABE AND I USED TO SNEAK UP HERE AND PLAY. WE SOMEHOW FELT CLOSER TO HIM, LIKE WE COULD FEEL HIS PRESENCE IN THIS ROOM."
SO HE WAS KIND TO YOU?
MOSTLY.
WERE YOU AFRAID OF HIM?
SOMETIMES.
"HE ALWAYS MADE TIME FOR US. SOMETIMES HE WOULD MEET WITH US TOGETHER."
SARAH, COME IN.
"AND SOMETIMES, HE'D WANT TO TALK TO US SEPARATELY."
GABE, WAIT YOUR TURN OUTSIDE.
I WANT HIM TO STAY, UNCLE.
DON'T MAKE ME COME OVER AND DEAL WITH THIS.

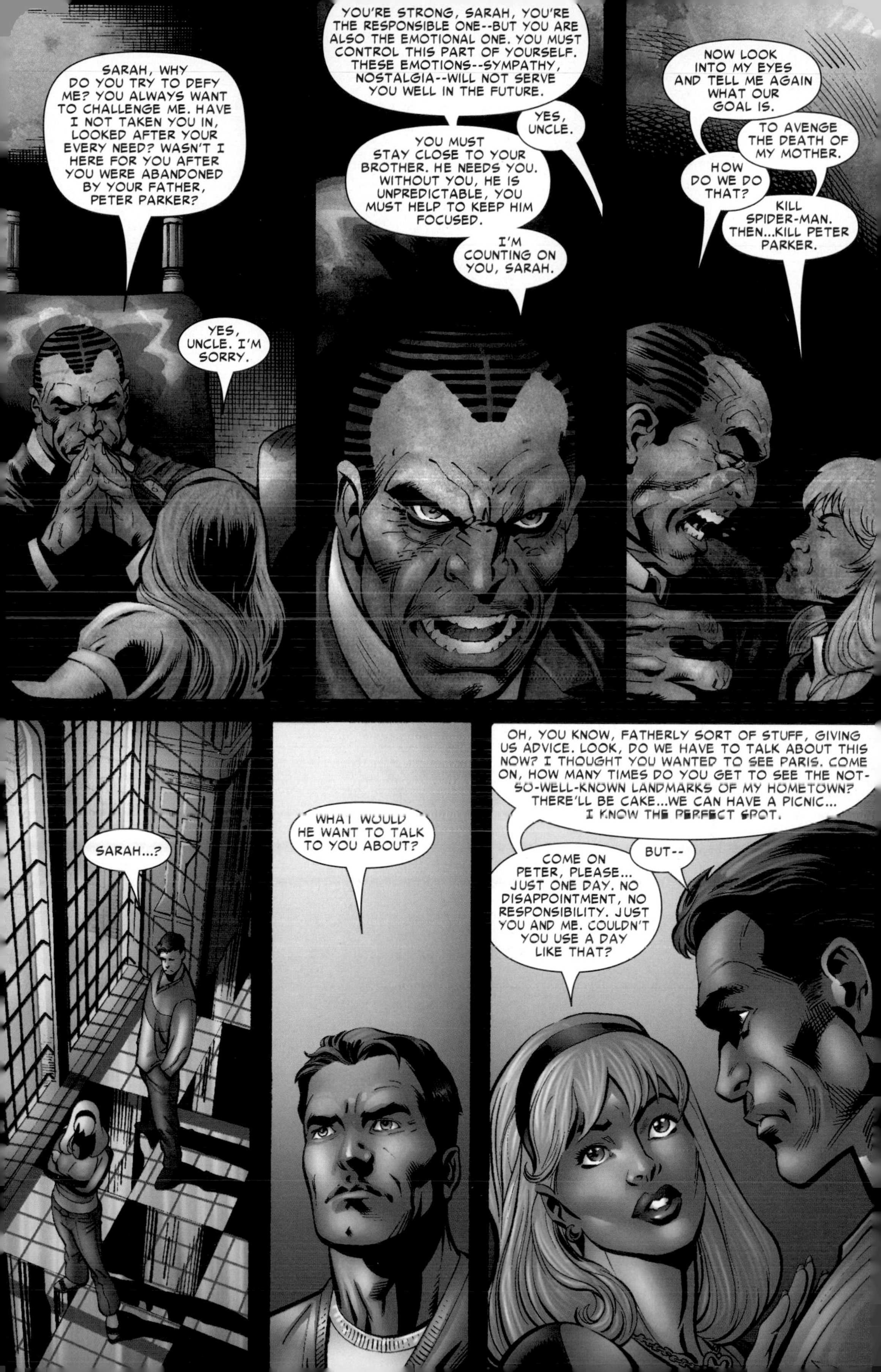
SARAH, WHY DO YOU TRY TO DEFY ME? YOU ALWAYS WANT TO CHALLENGE ME. HAVE I NOT TAKEN YOU IN, LOOKED AFTER YOUR EVERY NEED? WASN'T I HERE FOR YOU AFTER YOU WERE ABANDONED BY YOUR FATHER, PETER PARKER?
YES, UNCLE. I'M SORRY.
YOU'RE STRONG, SARAH, YOU'RE THE RESPONSIBLE ONE--BUT YOU ARE ALSO THE EMOTIONAL ONE. YOU MUST CONTROL THIS PART OF YOURSELF. THESE EMOTIONS--SYMPATHY, NOSTALGIA--WILL NOT SERVE YOU WELL IN THE FUTURE.
YES, UNCLE.
YOU MUST STAY CLOSE TO YOUR BROTHER. HE NEEDS YOU. WITHOUT YOU, HE IS UNPREDICTABLE, YOU MUST HELP TO KEEP HIM FOCUSED.
I'M COUNTING ON YOU, SARAH.
NOW LOOK INTO MY EYES AND TELL ME AGAIN WHAT OUR GOAL IS.
TO AVENGE THE DEATH OF MY MOTHER.
HOW DO WE DO THAT?
KILL SPIDER-MAN. THEN...KILL PETER PARKER.
SARAH...?
WHAT WOULD HE WANT TO TALK TO YOU ABOUT?
OH, YOU KNOW, FATHERLY SORT OF STUFF, GIVING US ADVICE. LOOK, DO WE HAVE TO TALK ABOUT THIS NOW? I THOUGHT YOU WANTED TO SEE PARIS. COME ON, HOW MANY TIMES DO YOU GET TO SEE THE NOT-SO-WELL-KNOWN LANDMARKS OF MY HOMETOWN? THERE'LL BE CAKE...WE CAN HAVE A PICNIC... I KNOW THE PERFECT SPOT.
BUT--
COME ON PETER, PLEASE... JUST ONE DAY. NO DISAPPOINTMENT, NO RESPONSIBILITY. JUST YOU AND ME. COULDN'T YOU USE A DAY LIKE THAT?

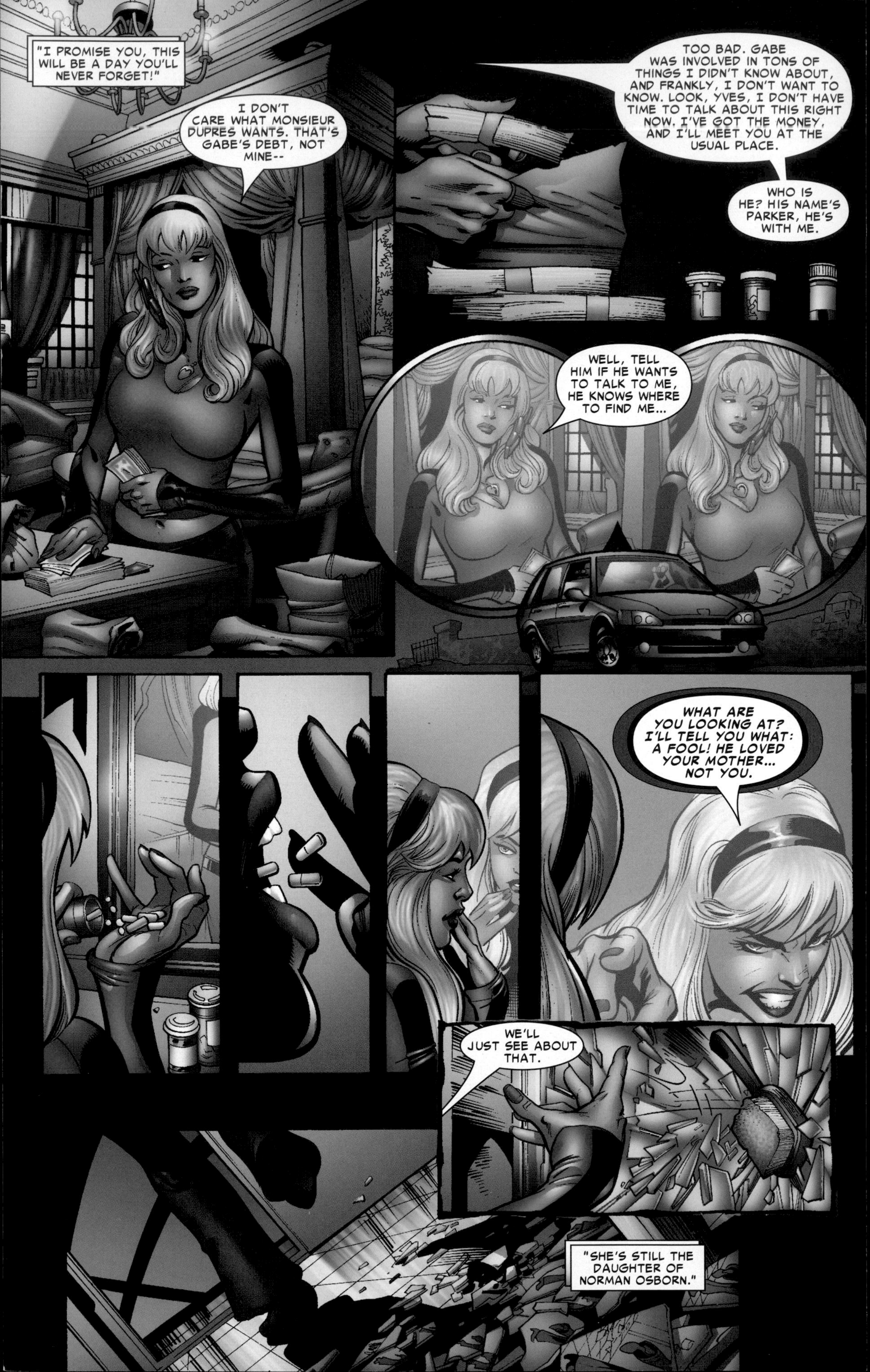
"I PROMISE YOU, THIS WILL BE A DAY YOU'LL NEVER FORGET!"
I DON'T CARE WHAT MONSIEUR DUPRES WANTS. THAT'S GABE'S DEBT, NOT MINE--
TOO BAD. GABE WAS INVOLVED IN TONS OF THINGS I DIDN'T KNOW ABOUT, AND FRANKLY, I DON'T WANT TO KNOW. LOOK, YVES, I DON'T HAVE TIME TO TALK ABOUT THIS RIGHT NOW. I'VE GOT THE MONEY, AND I'LL MEET YOU AT THE USUAL PLACE.
WHO IS HE? HIS NAME'S PARKER, HE'S WITH ME.
WELL, TELL HIM IF HE WANTS TO TALK TO ME, HE KNOWS WHERE TO FIND ME...
WHAT ARE YOU LOOKING AT? I'LL TELL YOU WHAT: A FOOL! HE LOVED YOUR MOTHER... NOT YOU.
WE'LL JUST SEE ABOUT THAT.
"SHE'S STILL THE DAUGHTER OF NORMAN OSBORN."

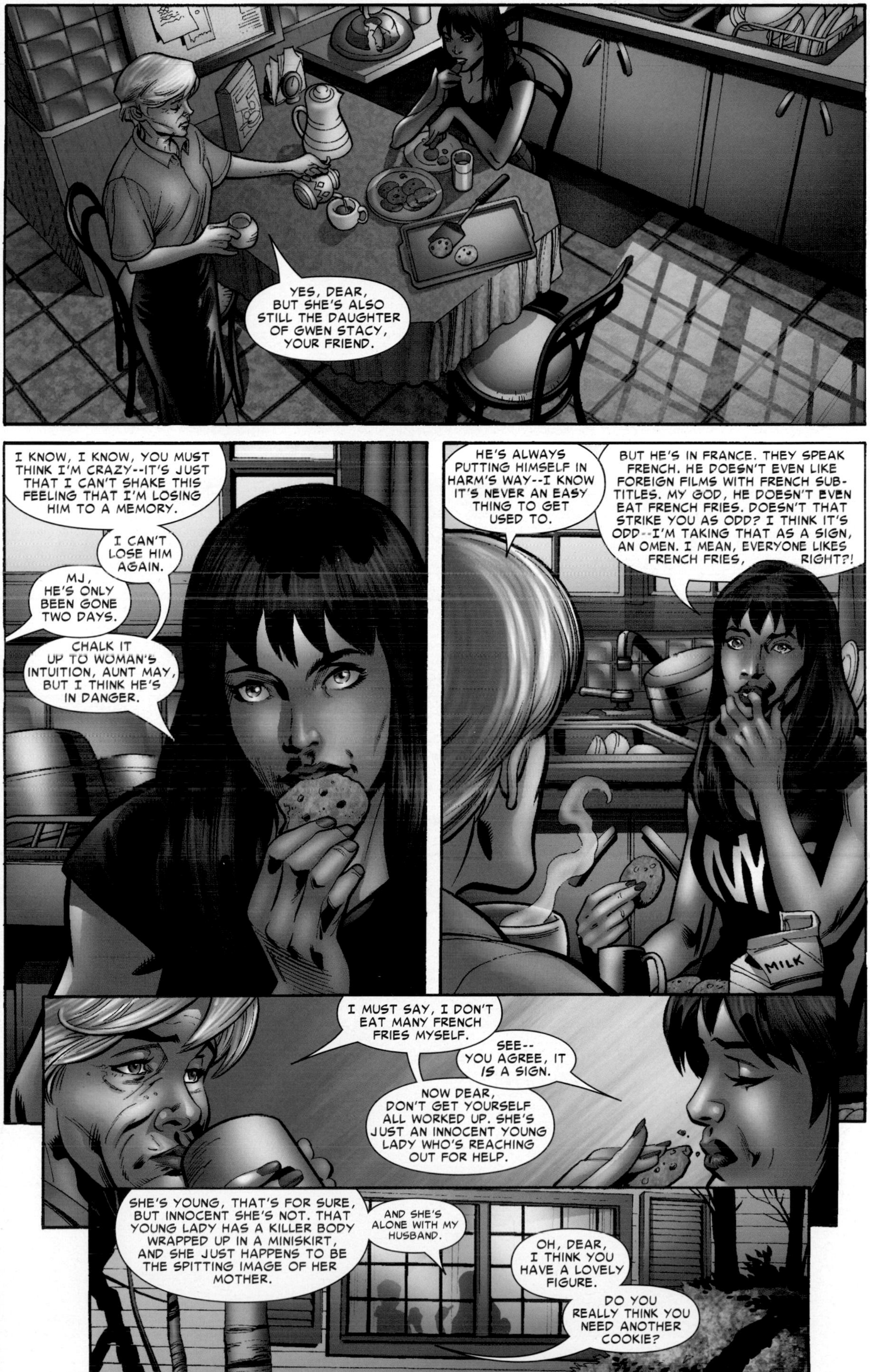
YES, DEAR, BUT SHE'S ALSO STILL THE DAUGHTER OF GWEN STACY, YOUR FRIEND.
I KNOW, I KNOW, YOU MUST THINK I'M CRAZY--IT'S JUST THAT I CAN'T SHAKE THIS FEELING THAT I'M LOSING HIM TO A MEMORY.
I CAN'T LOSE HIM AGAIN.
MJ, HE'S ONLY BEEN GONE TWO DAYS.
CHALK IT UP TO WOMAN'S INTUITION, AUNT MAY, BUT I THINK HE'S IN DANGER.
HE'S ALWAYS PUTTING HIMSELF IN HARM'S WAY--I KNOW IT'S NEVER AN EASY THING TO GET USED TO.
BUT HE'S IN FRANCE. THEY SPEAK FRENCH. HE DOESN'T EVEN LIKE FOREIGN FILMS WITH FRENCH SUB-TITLES. MY GOD, HE DOESN'T EVEN EAT FRENCH FRIES. DOESN'T THAT STRIKE YOU AS ODD? I THINK IT'S ODD--I'M TAKING THAT AS A SIGN, AN OMEN. I MEAN, EVERYONE LIKES FRENCH FRIES, RIGHT?!
MILK
I MUST SAY, I DON'T EAT MANY FRENCH FRIES MYSELF.
SEE-- YOU AGREE, IT IS A SIGN.
NOW DEAR, DON'T GET YOURSELF ALL WORKED UP. SHE'S JUST AN INNOCENT YOUNG LADY WHO'S REACHING OUT FOR HELP.
SHE'S YOUNG, THAT'S FOR SURE, BUT INNOCENT SHE'S NOT. THAT YOUNG LADY HAS A KILLER BODY WRAPPED UP IN A MINISKIRT, AND SHE JUST HAPPENS TO BE THE SPITTING IMAGE OF HER MOTHER.
AND SHE'S ALONE WITH MY HUSBAND.
OH, DEAR, I THINK YOU HAVE A LOVELY FIGURE.
DO YOU REALLY THINK YOU NEED ANOTHER COOKIE?

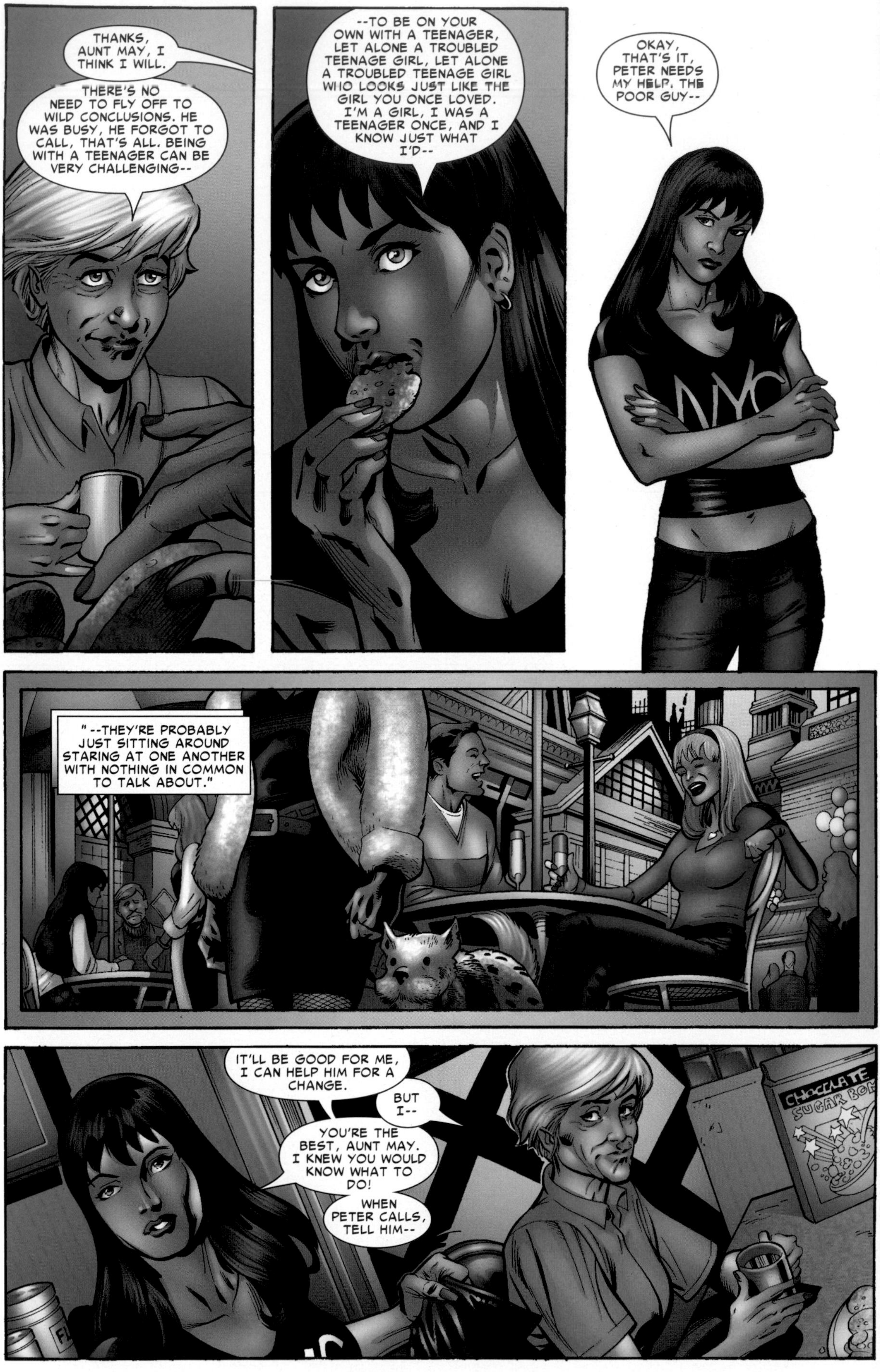
THANKS, AUNT MAY, I THINK I WILL.
THERE'S NO NEED TO FLY OFF TO WILD CONCLUSIONS. HE WAS BUSY, HE FORGOT TO CALL, THAT'S ALL. BEING WITH A TEENAGER CAN BE VERY CHALLENGING--
--TO BE ON YOUR OWN WITH A TEENAGER, LET ALONE A TROUBLED TEENAGE GIRL, LET ALONE A TROUBLED TEENAGE GIRL WHO LOOKS JUST LIKE THE GIRL YOU ONCE LOVED. I'M A GIRL, I WAS A TEENAGER ONCE, AND I KNOW JUST WHAT I'D--
OKAY, THAT'S IT, PETER NEEDS MY HELP. THE POOR GUY--
" --THEY'RE PROBABLY JUST SITTING AROUND STARING AT ONE ANOTHER WITH NOTHING IN COMMON TO TALK ABOUT."
IT'LL BE GOOD FOR ME, I CAN HELP HIM FOR A CHANGE.
BUT I--
YOU'RE THE BEST, AUNT MAY. I KNEW YOU WOULD KNOW WHAT TO DO!
WHEN PETER CALLS, TELL HIM--
CHOCOLATE SUGAR BOM

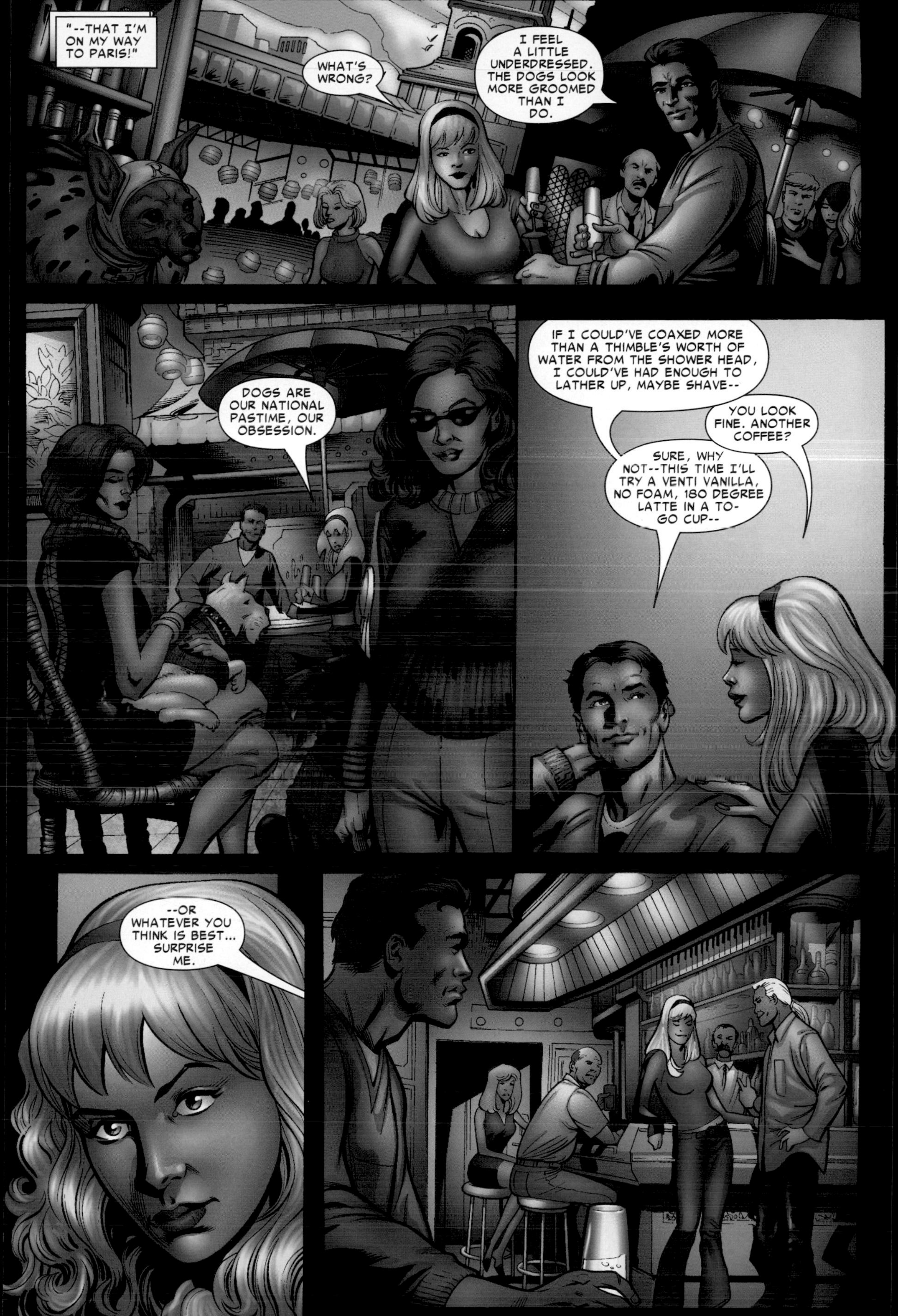
"--THAT I'M ON MY WAY TO PARIS!"
WHAT'S WRONG?
I FEEL A LITTLE UNDERDRESSED. THE DOGS LOOK MORE GROOMED THAN I DO.
DOGS ARE OUR NATIONAL PASTIME, OUR OBSESSION.
IF I COULD'VE COAXED MORE THAN A THIMBLE'S WORTH OF WATER FROM THE SHOWER HEAD, I COULD'VE HAD ENOUGH TO LATHER UP, MAYBE SHAVE--
YOU LOOK FINE. ANOTHER COFFEE?
SURE, WHY NOT--THIS TIME I'LL TRY A VENTI VANILLA, NO FOAM, 180 DEGREE LATTE IN A TO-GO CUP--
--OR WHATEVER YOU THINK IS BEST... SURPRISE ME.

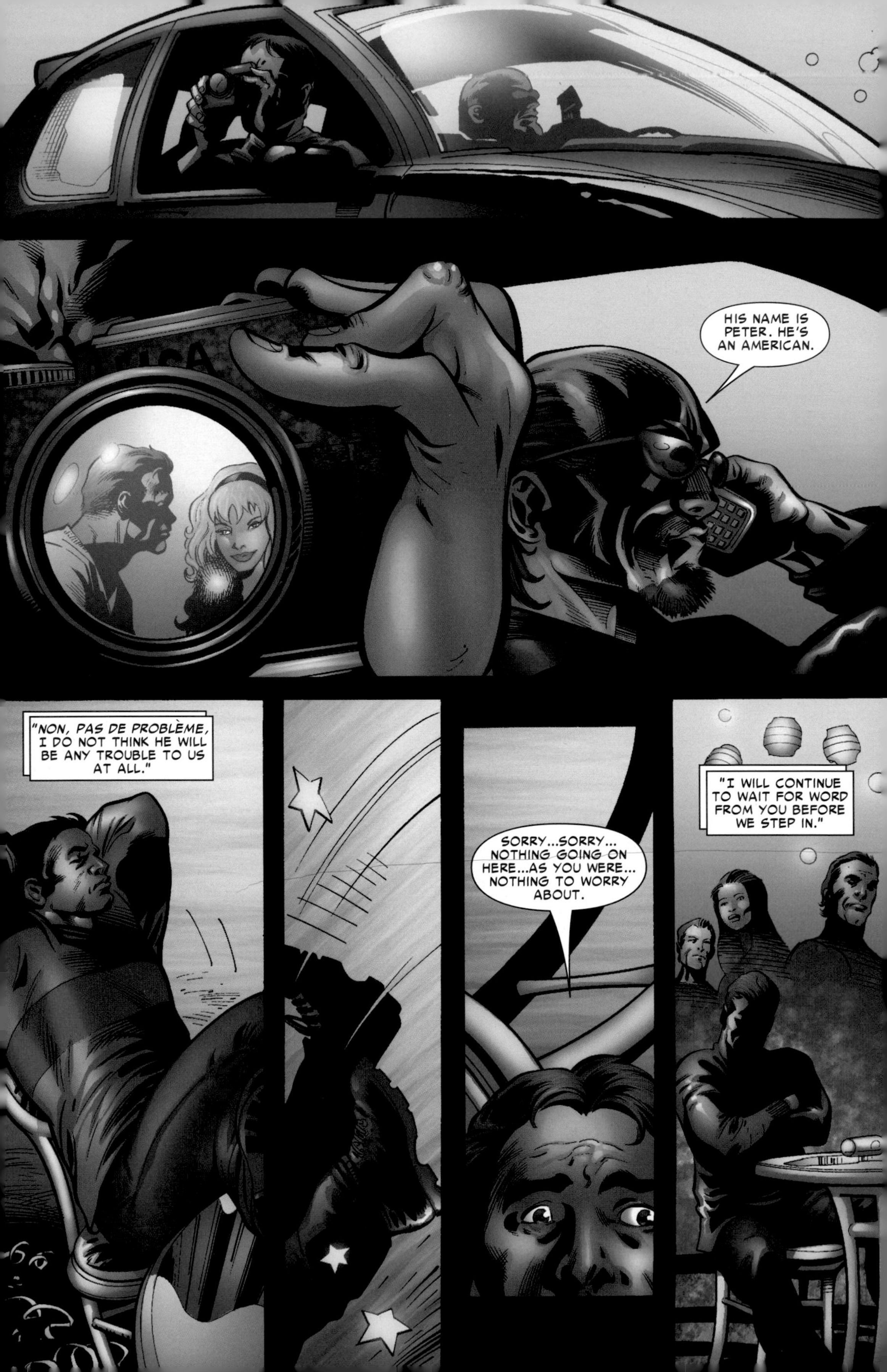
HIS NAME IS PETER. HE'S AN AMERICAN.
"NON, PAS DE PROBLÈME, I DO NOT THINK HE WILL BE ANY TROUBLE TO US AT ALL."
SORRY...SORRY... NOTHING GOING ON HERE...AS YOU WERE... NOTHING TO WORRY ABOUT.
"I WILL CONTINUE TO WAIT FOR WORD FROM YOU BEFORE WE STEP IN."

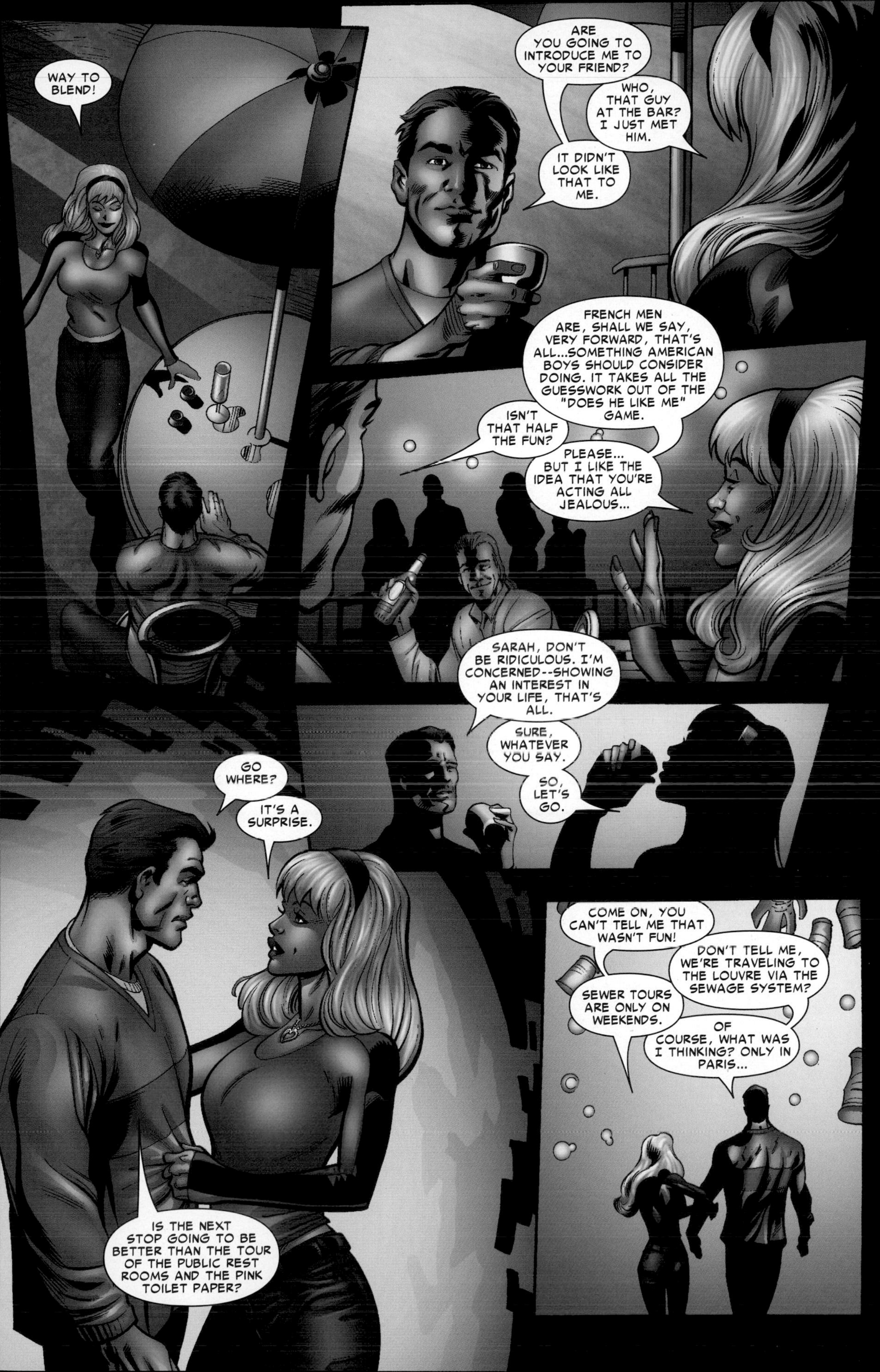
WAY TO BLEND!
ARE YOU GOING TO INTRODUCE ME TO YOUR FRIEND?
WHO, THAT GUY AT THE BAR? I JUST MET HIM.
IT DIDN'T LOOK LIKE THAT TO ME.
FRENCH MEN ARE, SHALL WE SAY, VERY FORWARD, THAT'S ALL...SOMETHING AMERICAN BOYS SHOULD CONSIDER DOING. IT TAKES ALL THE GUESSWORK OUT OF THE "DOES HE LIKE ME" GAME.
ISN'T THAT HALF THE FUN?
PLEASE... BUT I LIKE THE IDEA THAT YOU'RE ACTING ALL JEALOUS...
SARAH, DON'T BE RIDICULOUS. I'M CONCERNED--SHOWING AN INTEREST IN YOUR LIFE, THAT'S ALL.
SURE, WHATEVER YOU SAY.
SO, LET'S GO.
GO WHERE?
IT'S A SURPRISE.
IS THE NEXT STOP GOING TO BE BETTER THAN THE TOUR OF THE PUBLIC REST ROOMS AND THE PINK TOILET PAPER?
COME ON, YOU CAN'T TELL ME THAT WASN'T FUN!
DON'T TELL ME, WE'RE TRAVELING TO THE LOUVRE VIA THE SEWAGE SYSTEM?
SEWER TOURS ARE ONLY ON WEEKENDS.
OF COURSE, WHAT WAS I THINKING? ONLY IN PARIS...

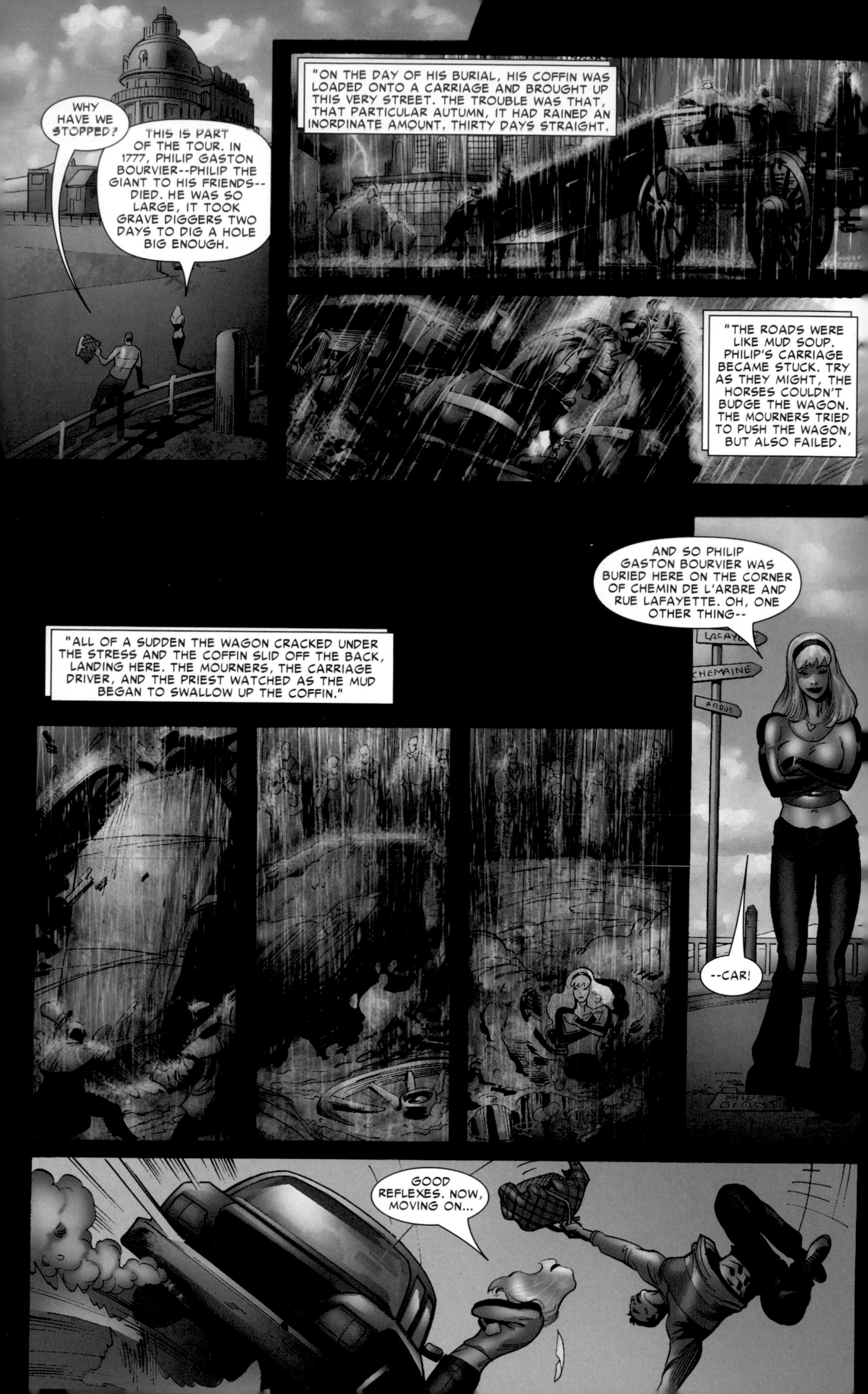
WHY HAVE WE STOPPED?
THIS IS PART OF THE TOUR. IN 1777, PHILIP GASTON BOURVIER--PHILIP THE GIANT TO HIS FRIENDS--DIED. HE WAS SO LARGE, IT TOOK GRAVE DIGGERS TWO DAYS TO DIG A HOLE BIG ENOUGH.
"ON THE DAY OF HIS BURIAL, HIS COFFIN WAS LOADED ONTO A CARRIAGE AND BROUGHT UP THIS VERY STREET. THE TROUBLE WAS THAT, THAT PARTICULAR AUTUMN, IT HAD RAINED AN INORDINATE AMOUNT. THIRTY DAYS STRAIGHT.
"THE ROADS WERE LIKE MUD SOUP. PHILIP'S CARRIAGE BECAME STUCK. TRY AS THEY MIGHT, THE HORSES COULDN'T BUDGE THE WAGON. THE MOURNERS TRIED TO PUSH THE WAGON, BUT ALSO FAILED.
"ALL OF A SUDDEN THE WAGON CRACKED UNDER THE STRESS AND THE COFFIN SLID OFF THE BACK, LANDING HERE. THE MOURNERS, THE CARRIAGE DRIVER, AND THE PRIEST WATCHED AS THE MUD BEGAN TO SWALLOW UP THE COFFIN."
AND SO PHILIP GASTON BOURVIER WAS BURIED HERE ON THE CORNER OF CHEMIN DE L'ARBRE AND RUE LAFAYETTE. OH, ONE OTHER THING--
CHEMAINE
--CAR!
GOOD REFLEXES. NOW, MOVING ON...

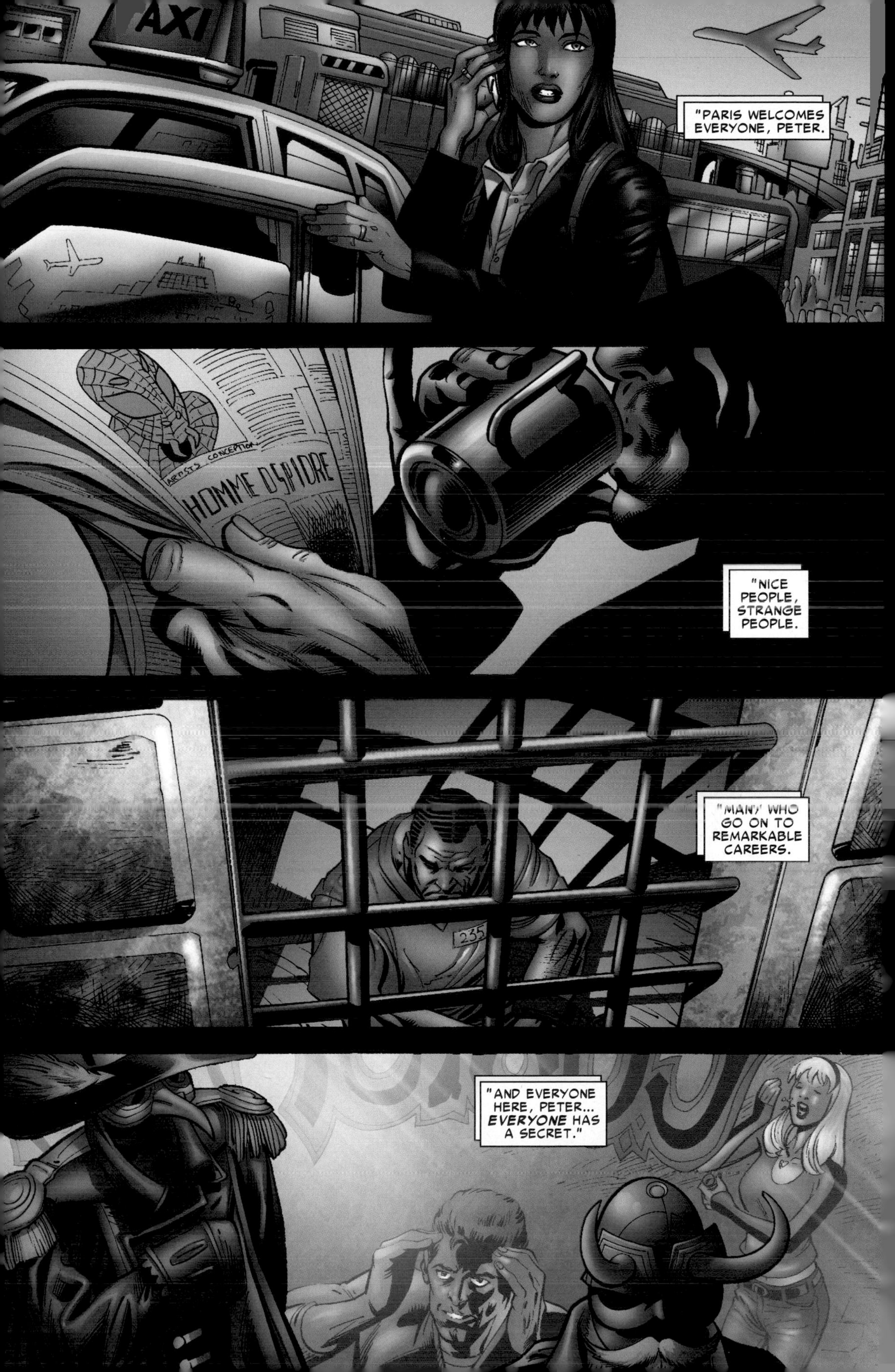
"PARIS WELCOMES EVERYONE, PETER.
"NICE PEOPLE, STRANGE PEOPLE.
"MANY WHO GO ON TO REMARKABLE CAREERS.
"AND EVERYONE HERE, PETER... *EVERYONE* HAS A SECRET."

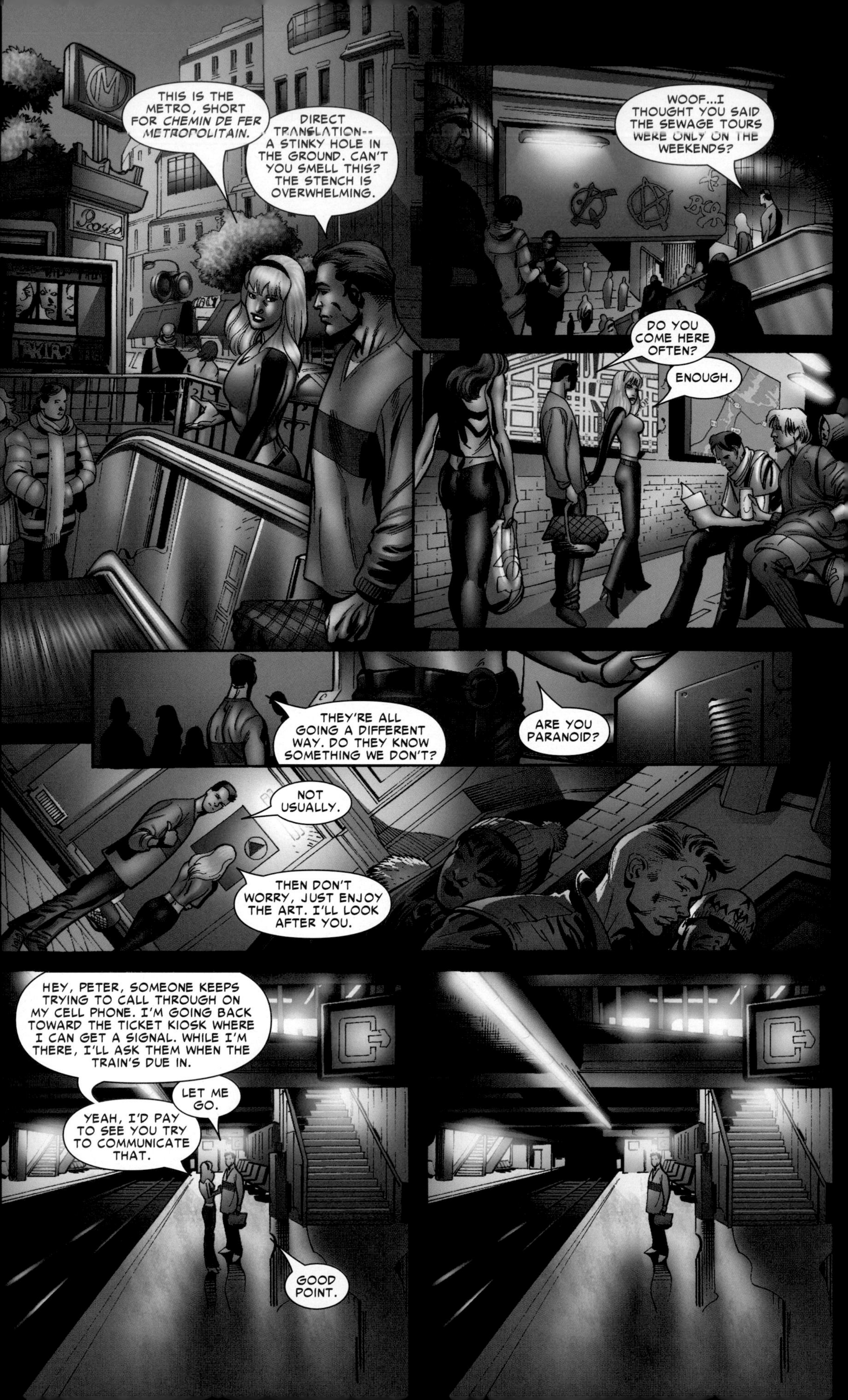
THIS IS THE METRO, SHORT FOR CHEMIN DE FER METROPOLITAIN.
DIRECT TRANSLATION-- A STINKY HOLE IN THE GROUND. CAN'T YOU SMELL THIS? THE STENCH IS OVERWHELMING.
WOOF...I THOUGHT YOU SAID THE SEWAGE TOURS WERE ONLY ON THE WEEKENDS?
DO YOU COME HERE OFTEN?
ENOUGH.
THEY'RE ALL GOING A DIFFERENT WAY. DO THEY KNOW SOMETHING WE DON'T?
ARE YOU PARANOID?
NOT USUALLY.
THEN DON'T WORRY, JUST ENJOY THE ART. I'LL LOOK AFTER YOU.
HEY, PETER, SOMEONE KEEPS TRYING TO CALL THROUGH ON MY CELL PHONE. I'M GOING BACK TOWARD THE TICKET KIOSK WHERE I CAN GET A SIGNAL. WHILE I'M THERE, I'LL ASK THEM WHEN THE TRAIN'S DUE IN.
LET ME GO.
YEAH, I'D PAY TO SEE YOU TRY TO COMMUNICATE THAT.
GOOD POINT.

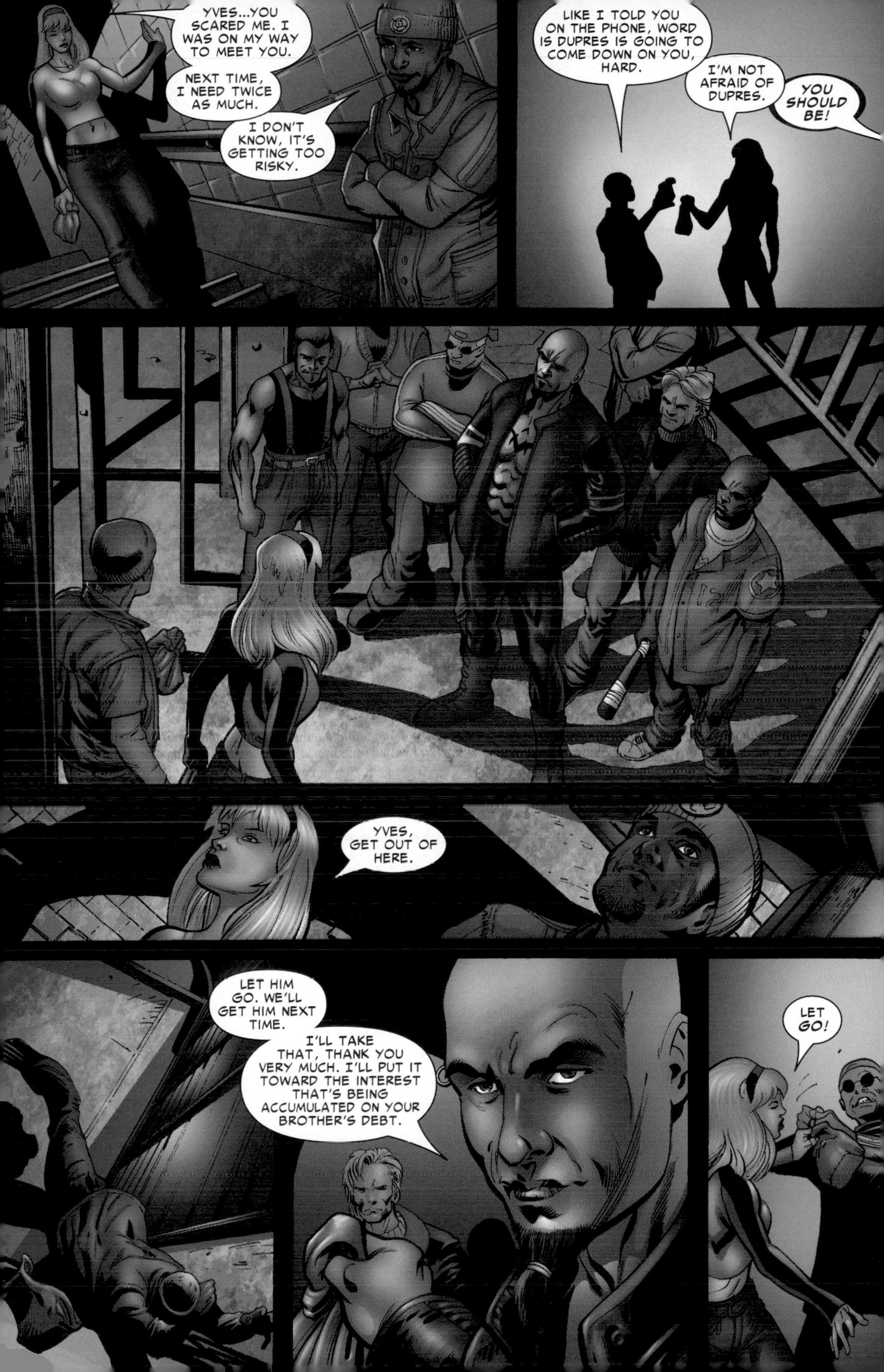
YVES...YOU SCARED ME. I WAS ON MY WAY TO MEET YOU.
NEXT TIME, I NEED TWICE AS MUCH.
I DON'T KNOW, IT'S GETTING TOO RISKY.
LIKE I TOLD YOU ON THE PHONE, WORD IS DUPRES IS GOING TO COME DOWN ON YOU, HARD.
I'M NOT AFRAID OF DUPRES.
YOU SHOULD BE!
YVES, GET OUT OF HERE.
LET HIM GO. WE'LL GET HIM NEXT TIME.
I'LL TAKE THAT, THANK YOU VERY MUCH. I'LL PUT IT TOWARD THE INTEREST THAT'S BEING ACCUMULATED ON YOUR BROTHER'S DEBT.
LET GO!

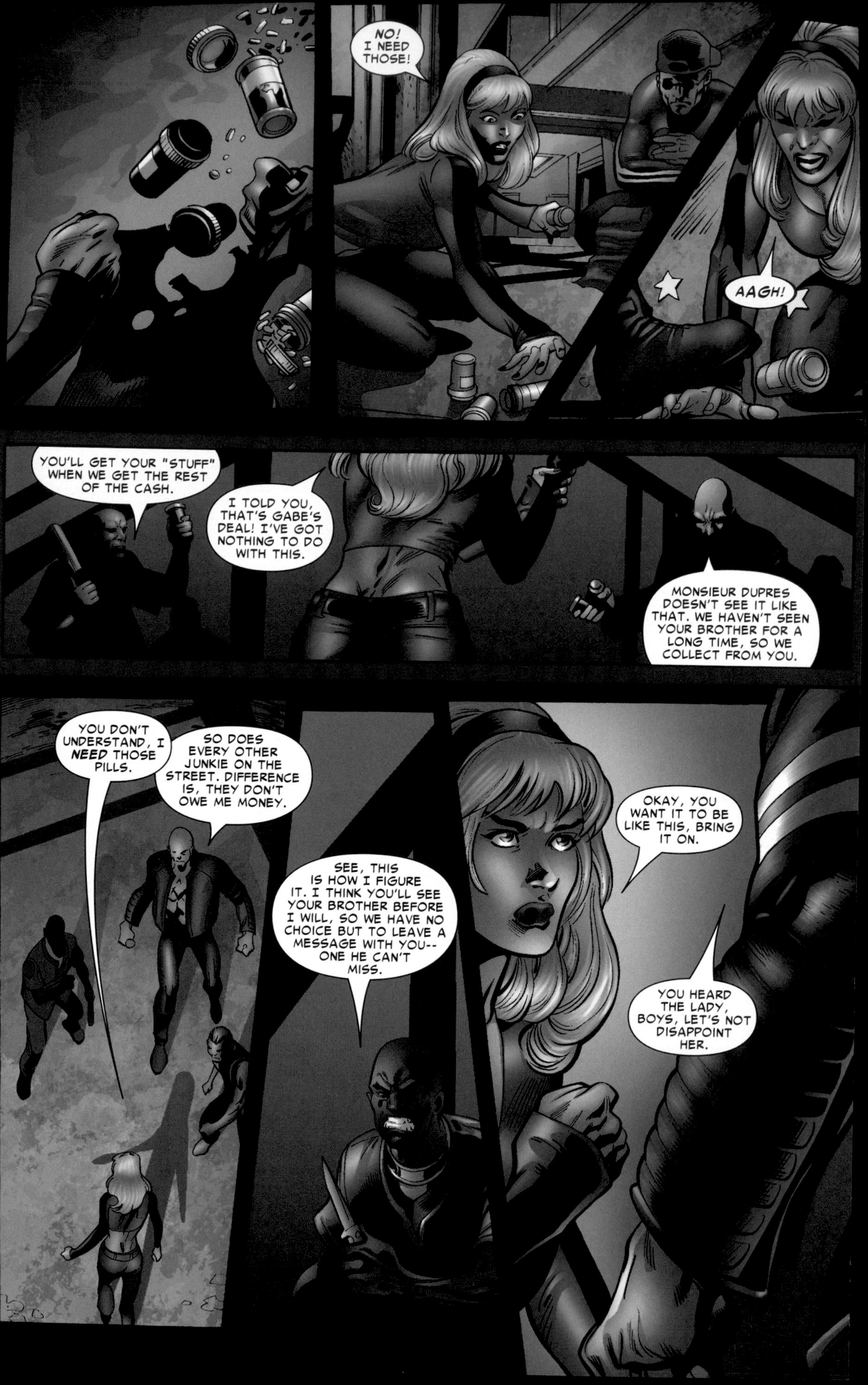
NO! I NEED THOSE!
AAGH!
YOU'LL GET YOUR "STUFF" WHEN WE GET THE REST OF THE CASH.
I TOLD YOU, THAT'S GABE'S DEAL! I'VE GOT NOTHING TO DO WITH THIS.
MONSIEUR DUPRES DOESN'T SEE IT LIKE THAT. WE HAVEN'T SEEN YOUR BROTHER FOR A LONG TIME, SO WE COLLECT FROM YOU.
YOU DON'T UNDERSTAND, I NEED THOSE PILLS.
SO DOES EVERY OTHER JUNKIE ON THE STREET. DIFFERENCE IS, THEY DON'T OWE ME MONEY.
SEE, THIS IS HOW I FIGURE IT. I THINK YOU'LL SEE YOUR BROTHER BEFORE I WILL, SO WE HAVE NO CHOICE BUT TO LEAVE A MESSAGE WITH YOU-- ONE HE CAN'T MISS.
OKAY, YOU WANT IT TO BE LIKE THIS, BRING IT ON.
YOU HEARD THE LADY, BOYS, LET'S NOT DISAPPOINT HER.

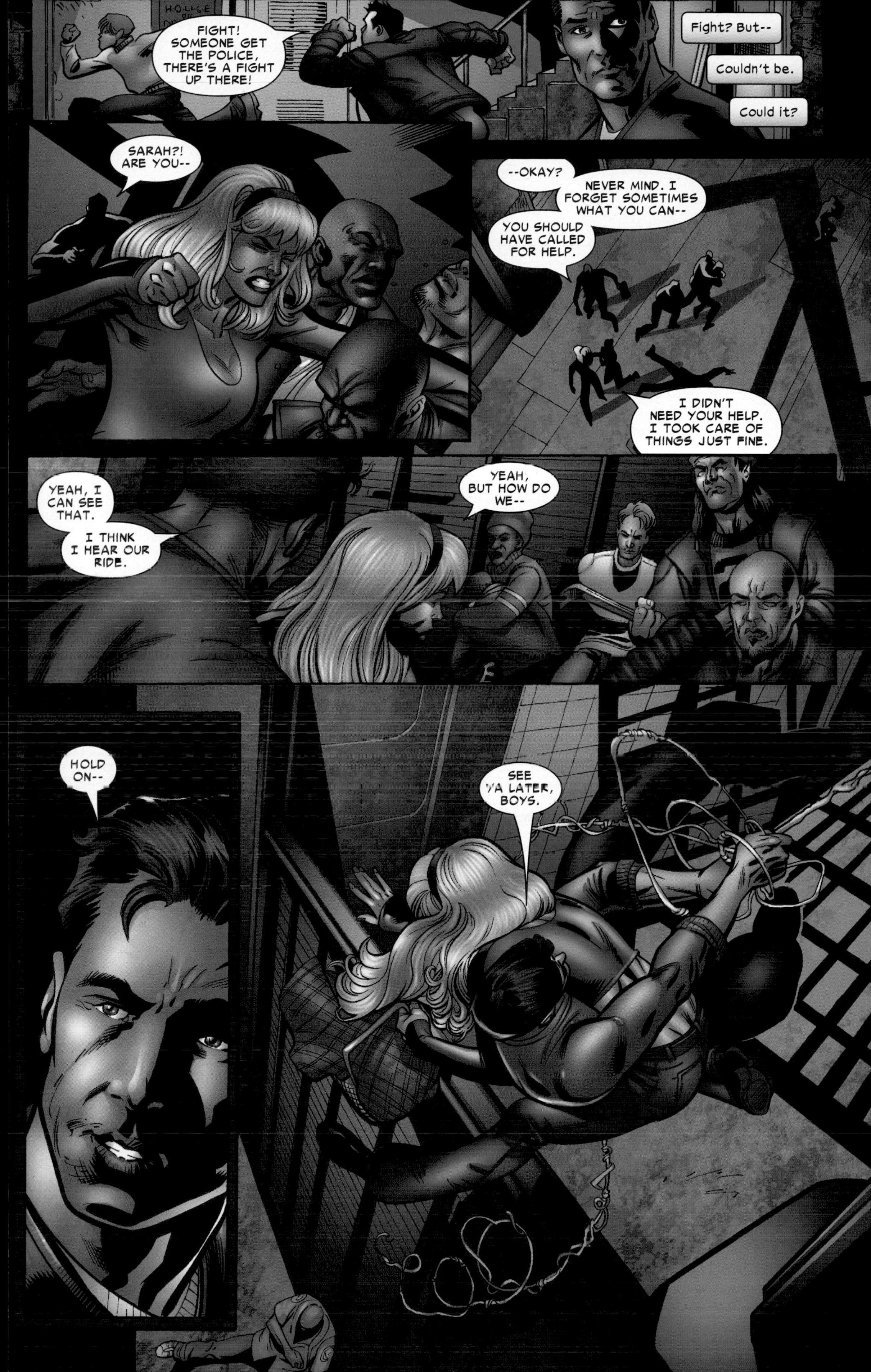
FIGHT! SOMEONE GET THE POLICE, THERE'S A FIGHT UP THERE!
Fight? But--
Couldn't be.
Could it?
SARAH?! ARE YOU--
--OKAY?
NEVER MIND. I FORGET SOMETIMES WHAT YOU CAN--
YOU SHOULD HAVE CALLED FOR HELP.
I DIDN'T NEED YOUR HELP. I TOOK CARE OF THINGS JUST FINE.
YEAH, I CAN SEE THAT.
I THINK I HEAR OUR RIDE.
YEAH, BUT HOW DO WE--
HOLD ON--
SEE YA LATER, BOYS.

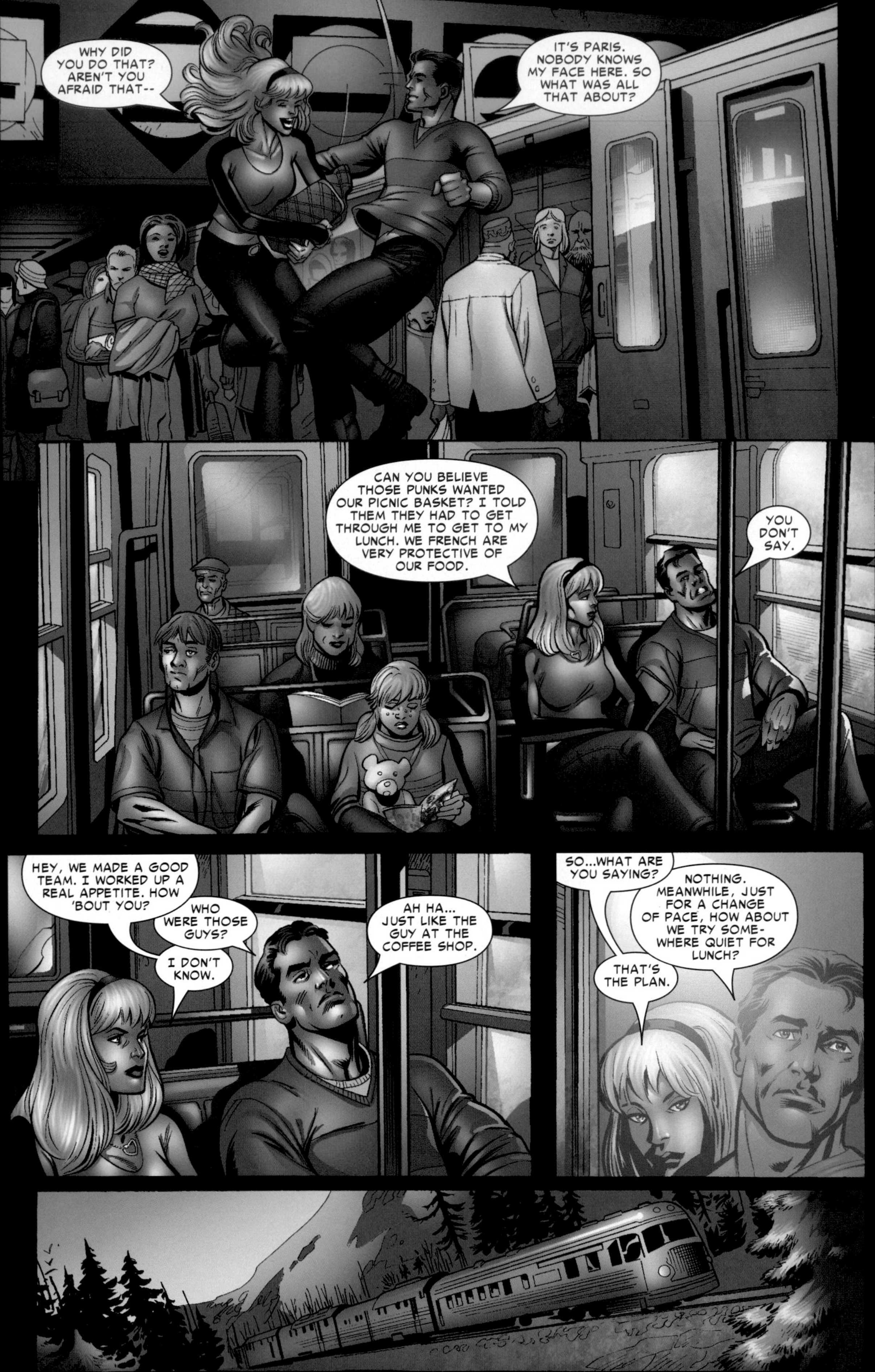
WHY DID YOU DO THAT? AREN'T YOU AFRAID THAT--
IT'S PARIS. NOBODY KNOWS MY FACE HERE. SO WHAT WAS ALL THAT ABOUT?
CAN YOU BELIEVE THOSE PUNKS WANTED OUR PICNIC BASKET? I TOLD THEM THEY HAD TO GET THROUGH ME TO GET TO MY LUNCH. WE FRENCH ARE VERY PROTECTIVE OF OUR FOOD.
YOU DON'T SAY.
HEY, WE MADE A GOOD TEAM. I WORKED UP A REAL APPETITE. HOW 'BOUT YOU?
WHO WERE THOSE GUYS?
I DON'T KNOW.
AH HA... JUST LIKE THE GUY AT THE COFFEE SHOP.
SO...WHAT ARE YOU SAYING?
NOTHING. MEANWHILE, JUST FOR A CHANGE OF PACE, HOW ABOUT WE TRY SOME-WHERE QUIET FOR LUNCH?
THAT'S THE PLAN.

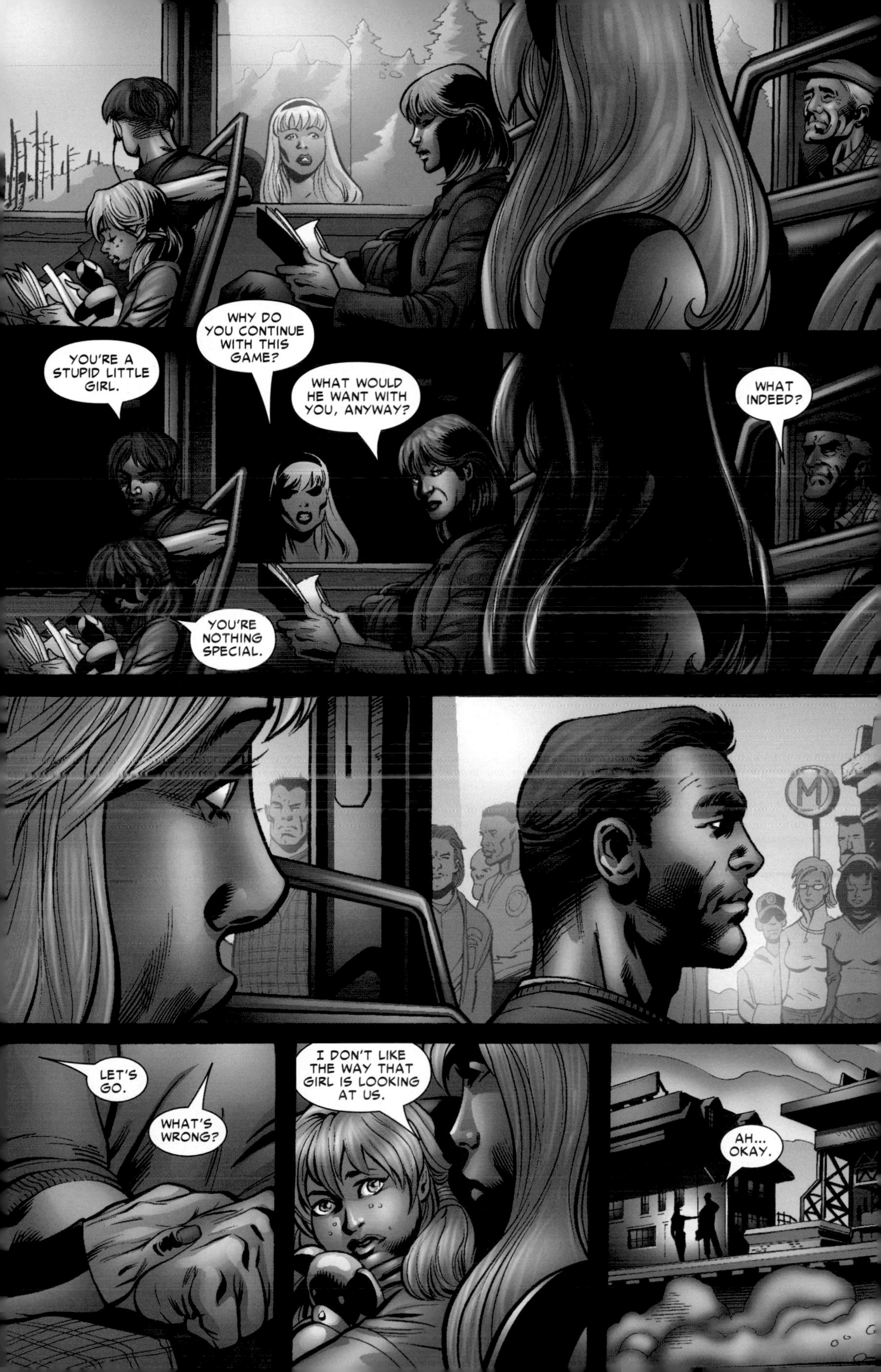
YOU'RE A STUPID LITTLE GIRL.
WHY DO YOU CONTINUE WITH THIS GAME?
WHAT WOULD HE WANT WITH YOU, ANYWAY?
WHAT INDEED?
YOU'RE NOTHING SPECIAL.
LET'S GO.
WHAT'S WRONG?
I DON'T LIKE THE WAY THAT GIRL IS LOOKING AT US.
AH... OKAY.

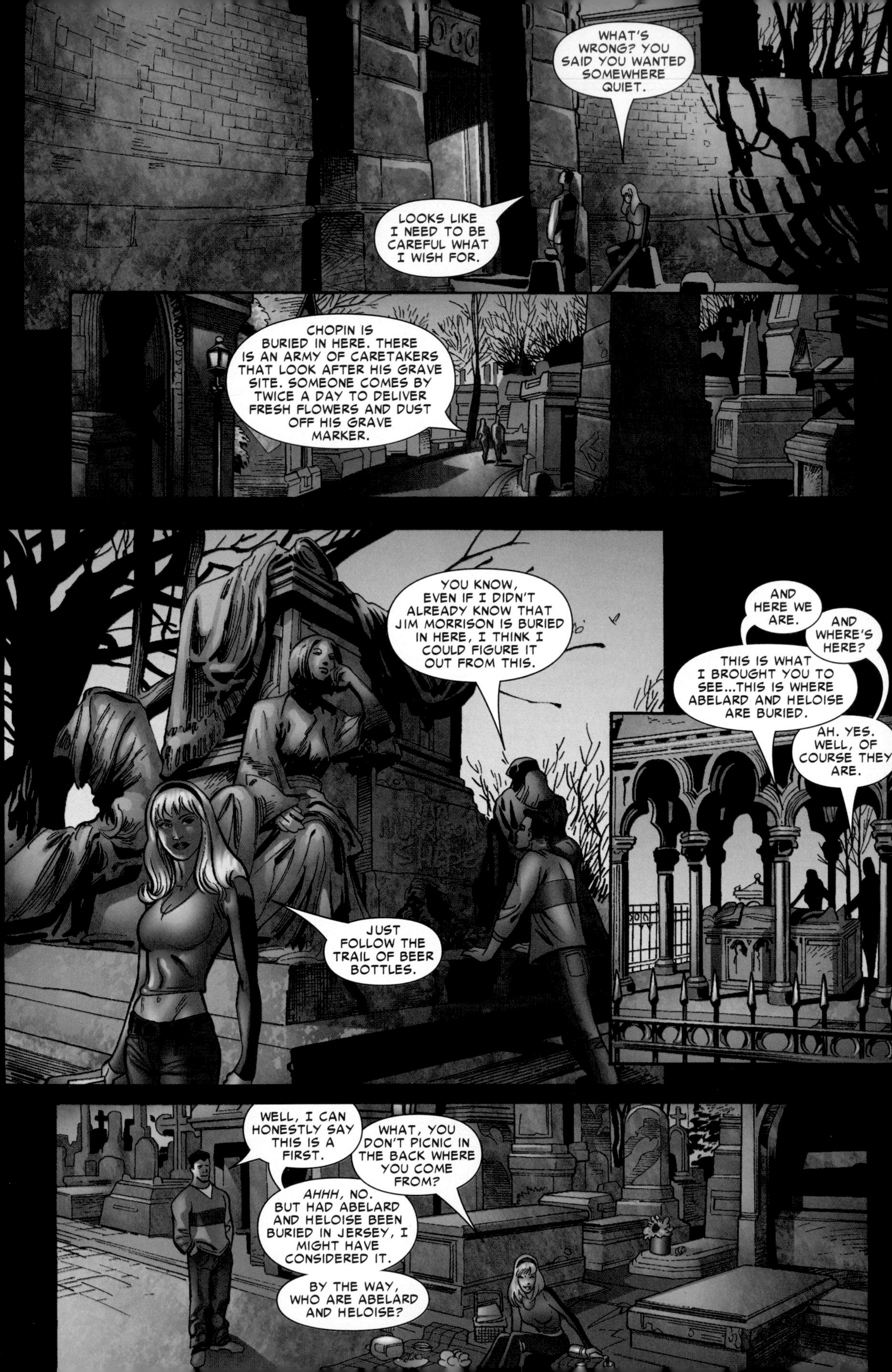

WHAT'S WRONG? YOU SAID YOU WANTED SOMEWHERE QUIET.
LOOKS LIKE I NEED TO BE CAREFUL WHAT I WISH FOR.
CHOPIN IS BURIED IN HERE. THERE IS AN ARMY OF CARETAKERS THAT LOOK AFTER HIS GRAVE SITE. SOMEONE COMES BY TWICE A DAY TO DELIVER FRESH FLOWERS AND DUST OFF HIS GRAVE MARKER.
YOU KNOW, EVEN IF I DIDN'T ALREADY KNOW THAT JIM MORRISON IS BURIED IN HERE, I THINK I COULD FIGURE IT OUT FROM THIS.
JUST FOLLOW THE TRAIL OF BEER BOTTLES.
AND HERE WE ARE.
AND WHERE'S HERE?
THIS IS WHAT I BROUGHT YOU TO SEE...THIS IS WHERE ABELARD AND HELOISE ARE BURIED.
AH. YES. WELL, OF COURSE THEY ARE.
WELL, I CAN HONESTLY SAY THIS IS A FIRST.
WHAT, YOU DON'T PICNIC IN THE BACK WHERE YOU COME FROM?
AHHH, NO. BUT HAD ABELARD AND HELOISE BEEN BURIED IN JERSEY, I MIGHT HAVE CONSIDERED IT.
BY THE WAY, WHO ARE ABELARD AND HELOISE?

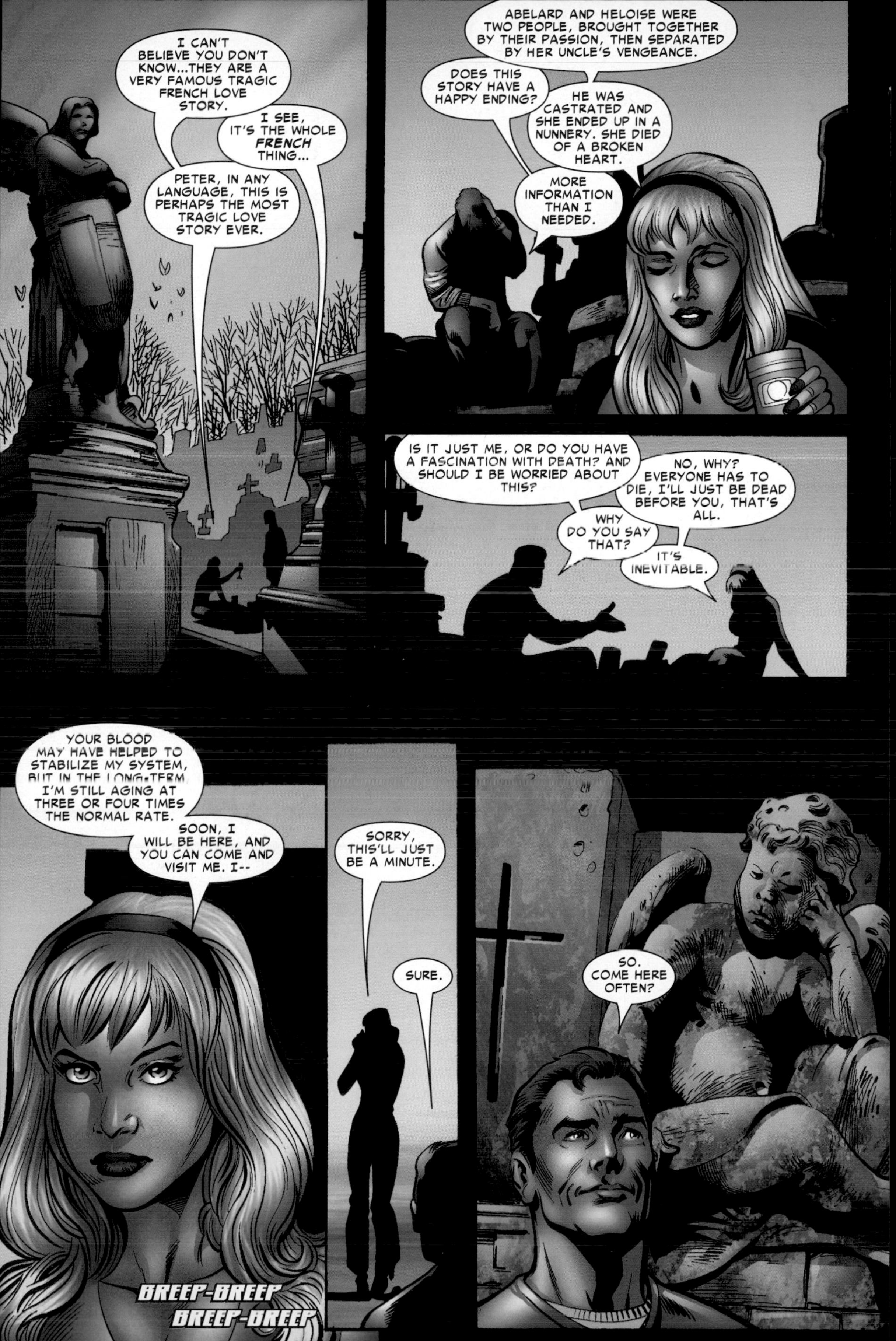
I CAN'T BELIEVE YOU DON'T KNOW...THEY ARE A VERY FAMOUS TRAGIC FRENCH LOVE STORY.
I SEE, IT'S THE WHOLE FRENCH THING...
PETER, IN ANY LANGUAGE, THIS IS PERHAPS THE MOST TRAGIC LOVE STORY EVER.
ABELARD AND HELOISE WERE TWO PEOPLE, BROUGHT TOGETHER BY THEIR PASSION, THEN SEPARATED BY HER UNCLE'S VENGEANCE.
DOES THIS STORY HAVE A HAPPY ENDING?
HE WAS CASTRATED AND SHE ENDED UP IN A NUNNERY. SHE DIED OF A BROKEN HEART.
MORE INFORMATION THAN I NEEDED.
IS IT JUST ME, OR DO YOU HAVE A FASCINATION WITH DEATH? AND SHOULD I BE WORRIED ABOUT THIS?
NO, WHY? EVERYONE HAS TO DIE, I'LL JUST BE DEAD BEFORE YOU, THAT'S ALL.
WHY DO YOU SAY THAT?
IT'S INEVITABLE.
YOUR BLOOD MAY HAVE HELPED TO STABILIZE MY SYSTEM, BUT IN THE LONG-TERM I'M STILL AGING AT THREE OR FOUR TIMES THE NORMAL RATE.
SOON, I WILL BE HERE, AND YOU CAN COME AND VISIT ME. I--
BREEP-BREEP
BREEP-BREEP
SORRY, THIS'LL JUST BE A MINUTE.
SURE.
SO. COME HERE OFTEN?

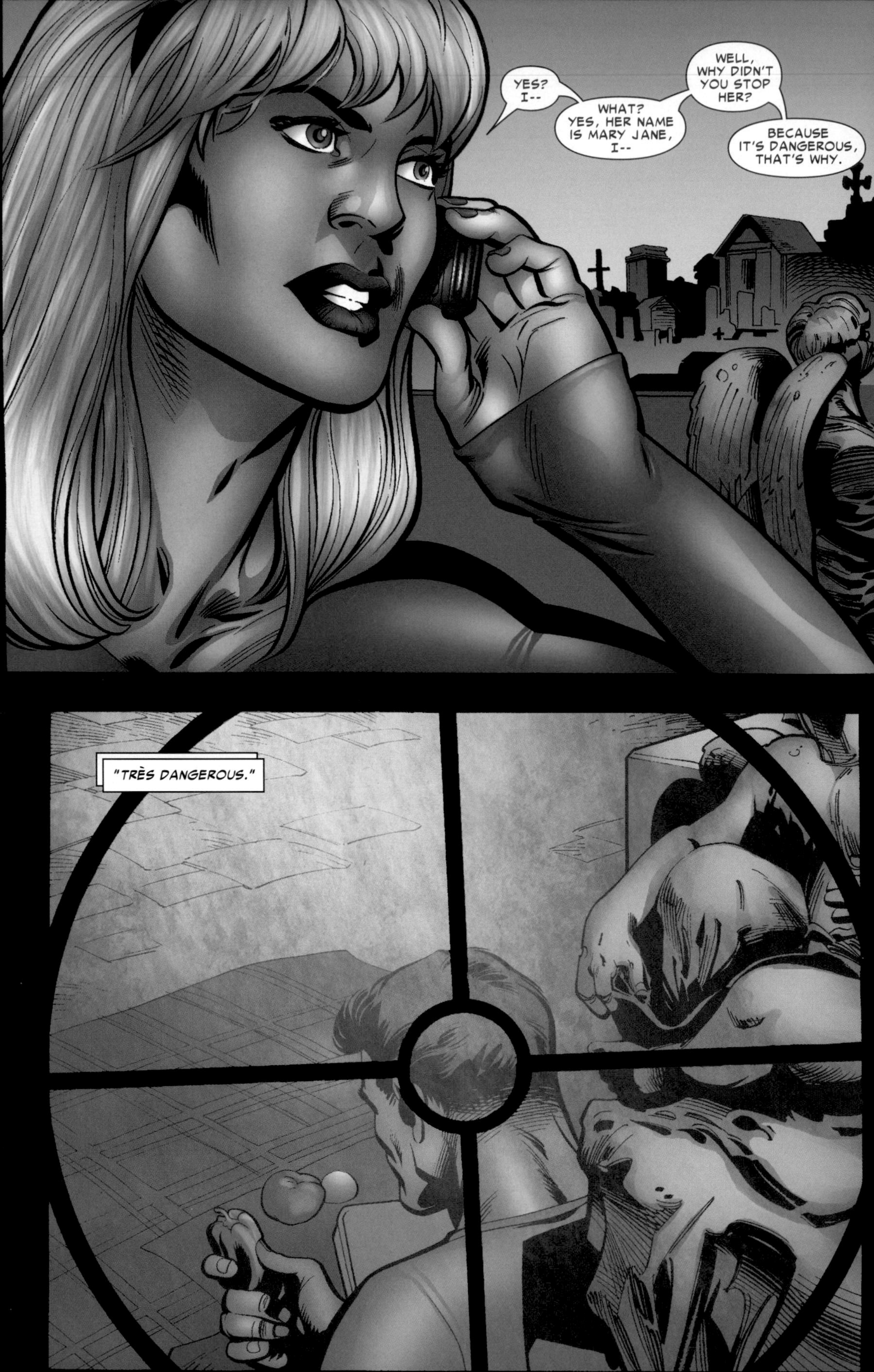
YES? I--
WHAT? YES, HER NAME IS MARY JANE, I--
WELL, WHY DIDN'T YOU STOP HER?
BECAUSE IT'S DANGEROUS, THAT'S WHY.
"TRÈS DANGEROUS."

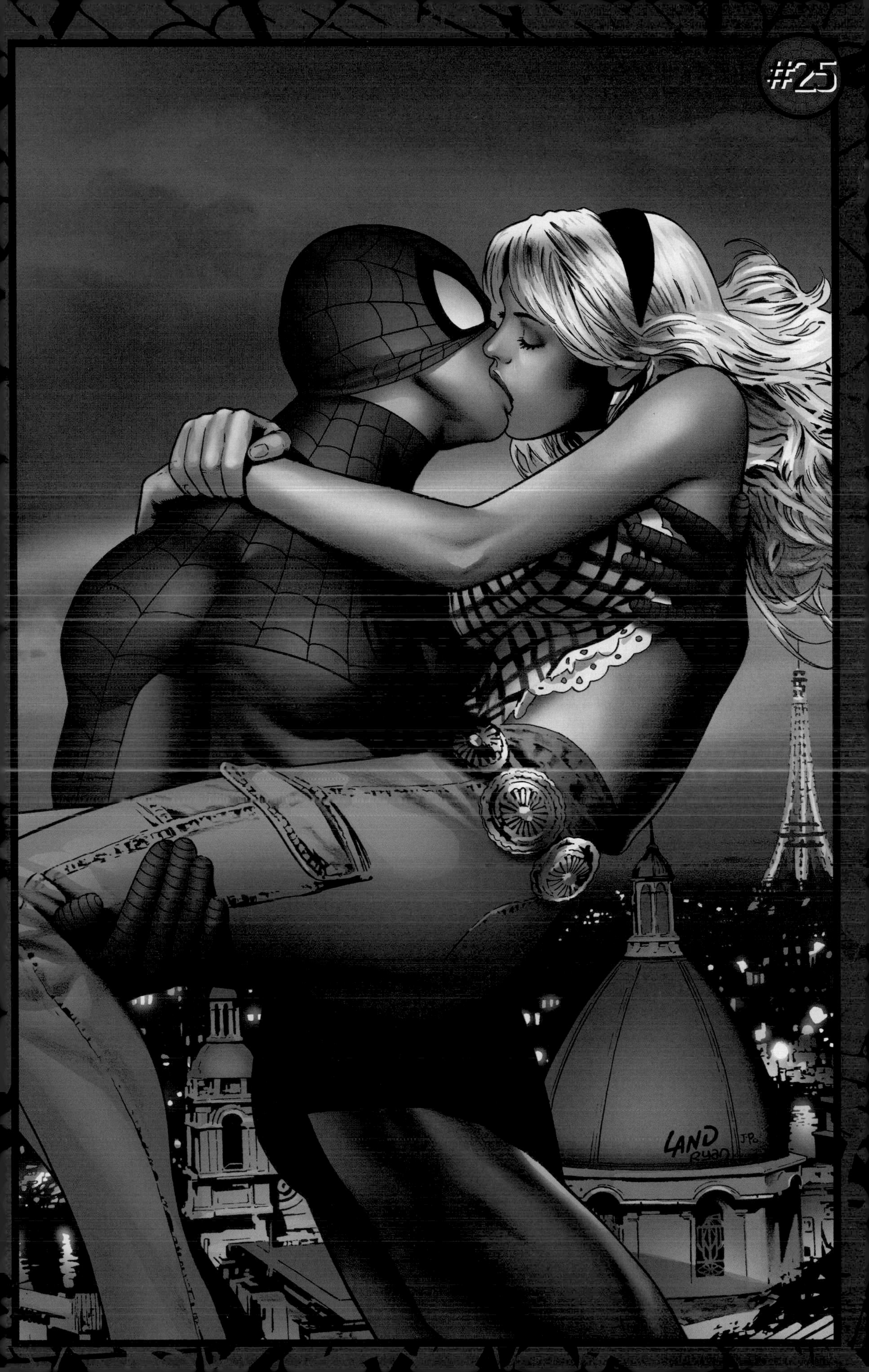
#25
LAND
RYAN
J-Po

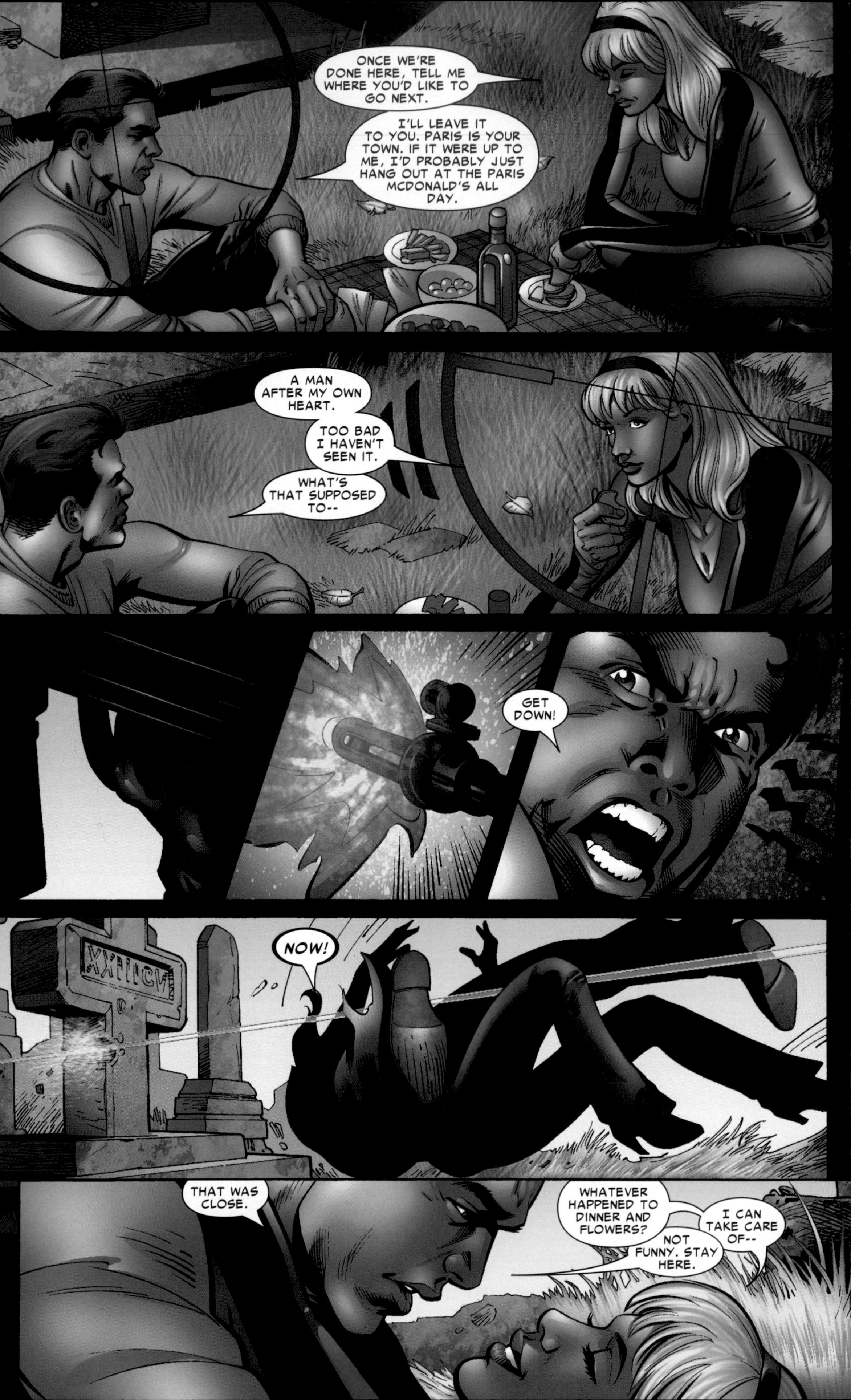
ONCE WE'RE DONE HERE, TELL ME WHERE YOU'D LIKE TO GO NEXT.
I'LL LEAVE IT TO YOU. PARIS IS YOUR TOWN. IF IT WERE UP TO ME, I'D PROBABLY JUST HANG OUT AT THE PARIS MCDONALD'S ALL DAY.
A MAN AFTER MY OWN HEART.
TOO BAD I HAVEN'T SEEN IT.
WHAT'S THAT SUPPOSED TO--
GET DOWN!
NOW!
THAT WAS CLOSE.
WHATEVER HAPPENED TO DINNER AND FLOWERS?
I CAN TAKE CARE OF--
NOT FUNNY. STAY HERE.

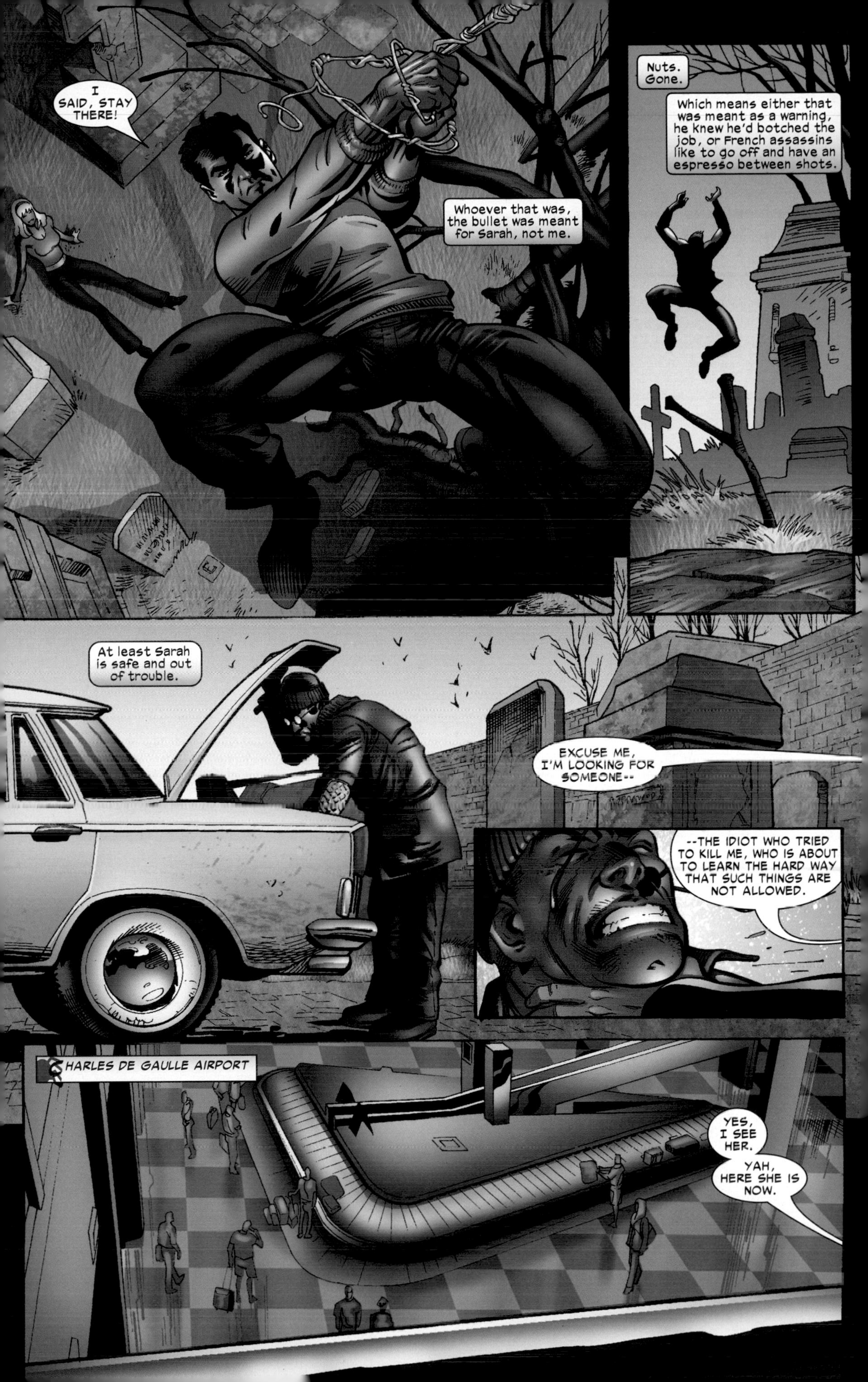
I SAID, STAY THERE!
Whoever that was, the bullet was meant for Sarah, not me.
Nuts. Gone.
Which means either that was meant as a warning, he knew he'd botched the job, or French assassins like to go off and have an espresso between shots.
At least Sarah is safe and out of trouble.
EXCUSE ME, I'M LOOKING FOR SOMEONE--
--THE IDIOT WHO TRIED TO KILL ME, WHO IS ABOUT TO LEARN THE HARD WAY THAT SUCH THINGS ARE NOT ALLOWED.
CHARLES DE GAULLE AIRPORT
YES, I SEE HER.
YAH, HERE SHE IS NOW.

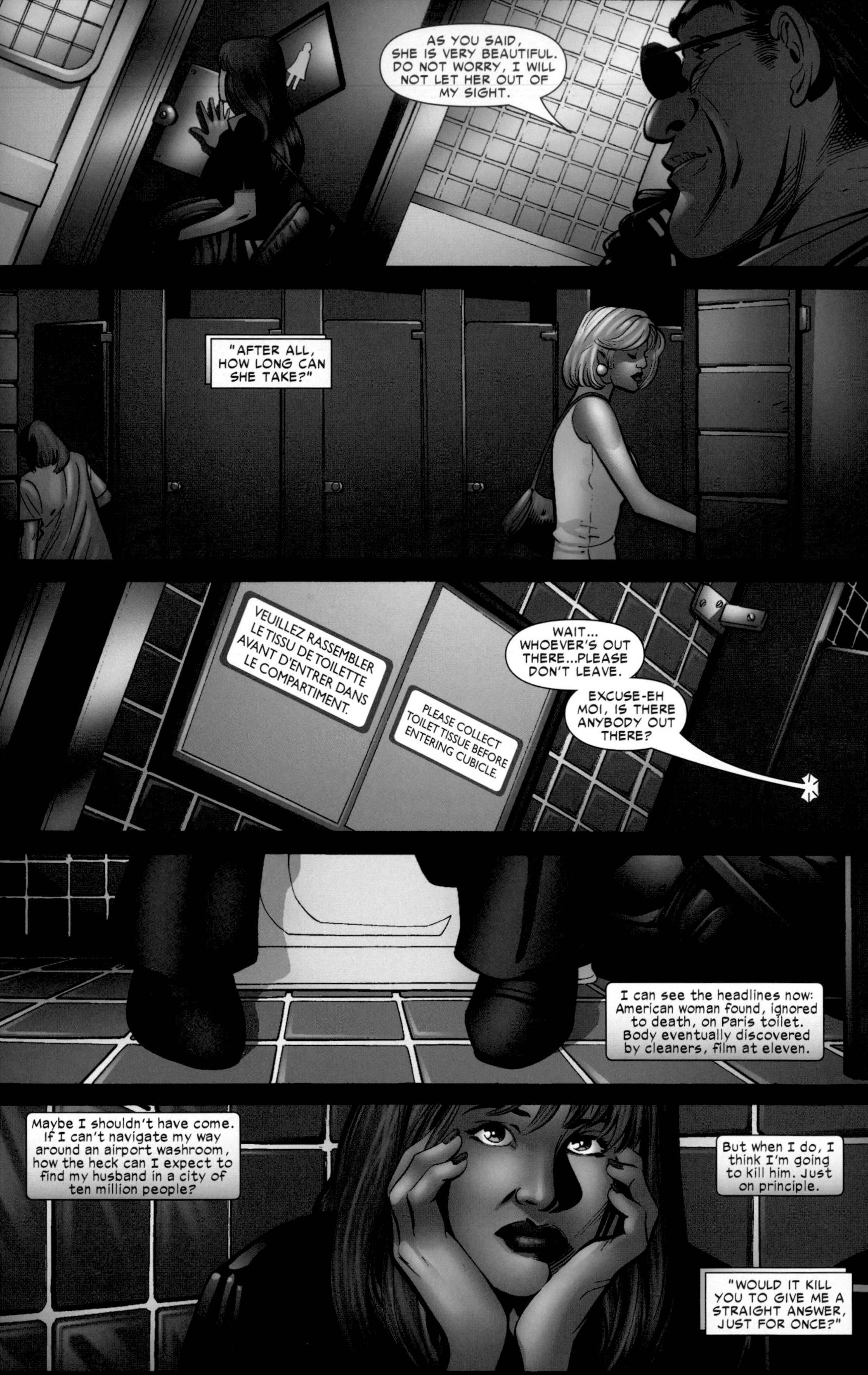
AS YOU SAID, SHE IS VERY BEAUTIFUL. DO NOT WORRY, I WILL NOT LET HER OUT OF MY SIGHT.
"AFTER ALL, HOW LONG CAN SHE TAKE?"
VEUILLEZ RASSEMBLER LE TISSU DE TOILETTE AVANT D'ENTRER DANS LE COMPARTIMENT.
PLEASE COLLECT TOILET TISSUE BEFORE ENTERING CUBICLE.
WAIT... WHOEVER'S OUT THERE...PLEASE DON'T LEAVE.
EXCUSE-EH MOI, IS THERE ANYBODY OUT THERE?
I can see the headlines now: American woman found, ignored to death, on Paris toilet. Body eventually discovered by cleaners, film at eleven.
Maybe I shouldn't have come. If I can't navigate my way around an airport washroom, how the heck can I expect to find my husband in a city of ten million people?
But when I do, I think I'm going to kill him. Just on principle.
"WOULD IT KILL YOU TO GIVE ME A STRAIGHT ANSWER, JUST FOR ONCE?"

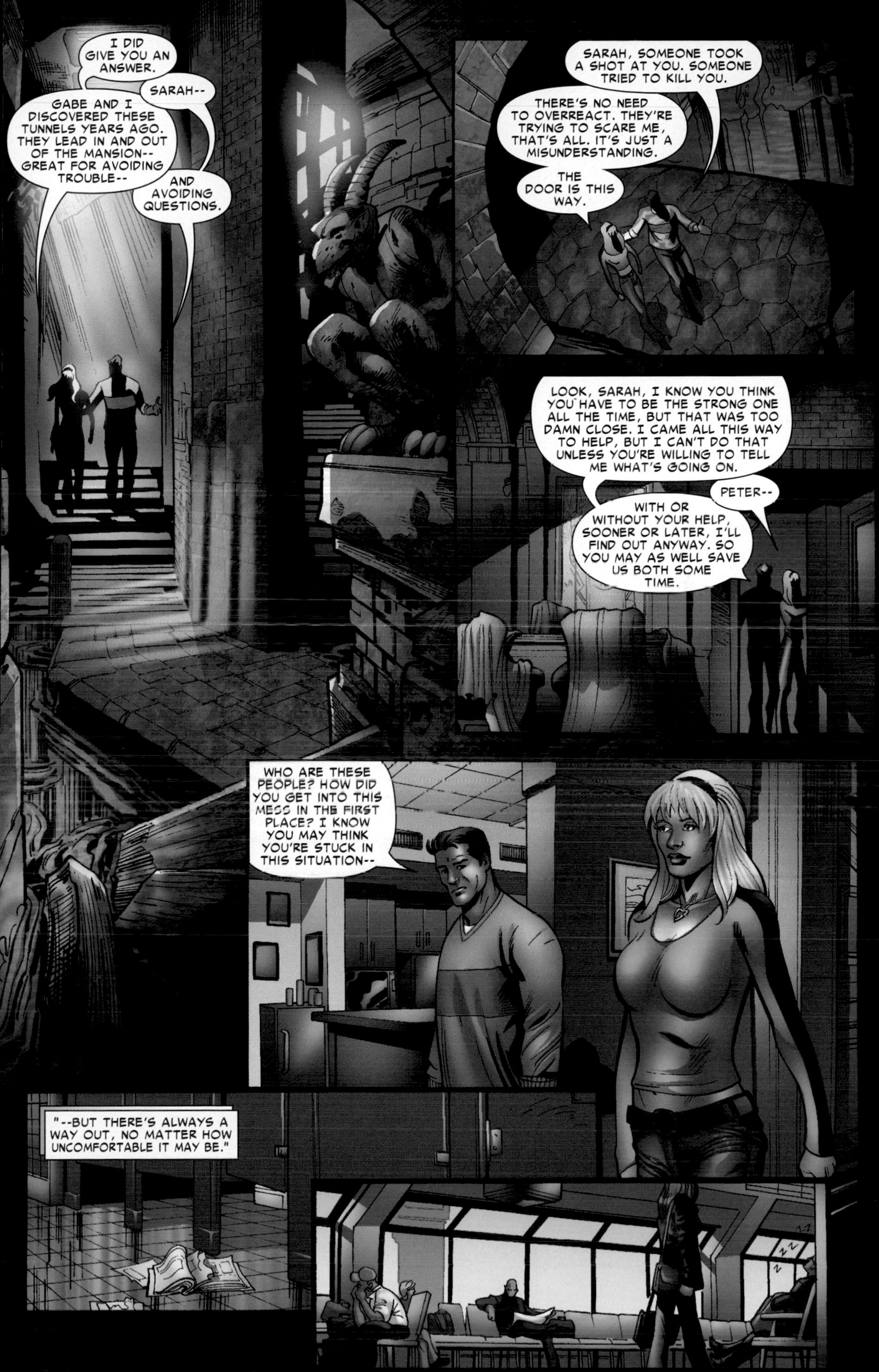
I DID GIVE YOU AN ANSWER.
SARAH--
GABE AND I DISCOVERED THESE TUNNELS YEARS AGO. THEY LEAD IN AND OUT OF THE MANSION-- GREAT FOR AVOIDING TROUBLE--
AND AVOIDING QUESTIONS.
SARAH, SOMEONE TOOK A SHOT AT YOU. SOMEONE TRIED TO KILL YOU.
THERE'S NO NEED TO OVERREACT. THEY'RE TRYING TO SCARE ME, THAT'S ALL. IT'S JUST A MISUNDERSTANDING.
THE DOOR IS THIS WAY.
LOOK, SARAH, I KNOW YOU THINK YOU HAVE TO BE THE STRONG ONE ALL THE TIME, BUT THAT WAS TOO DAMN CLOSE. I CAME ALL THIS WAY TO HELP, BUT I CAN'T DO THAT UNLESS YOU'RE WILLING TO TELL ME WHAT'S GOING ON.
PETER--
WITH OR WITHOUT YOUR HELP, SOONER OR LATER, I'LL FIND OUT ANYWAY. SO YOU MAY AS WELL SAVE US BOTH SOME TIME.
WHO ARE THESE PEOPLE? HOW DID YOU GET INTO THIS MESS IN THE FIRST PLACE? I KNOW YOU MAY THINK YOU'RE STUCK IN THIS SITUATION--
"--BUT THERE'S ALWAYS A WAY OUT, NO MATTER HOW UNCOMFORTABLE IT MAY BE."

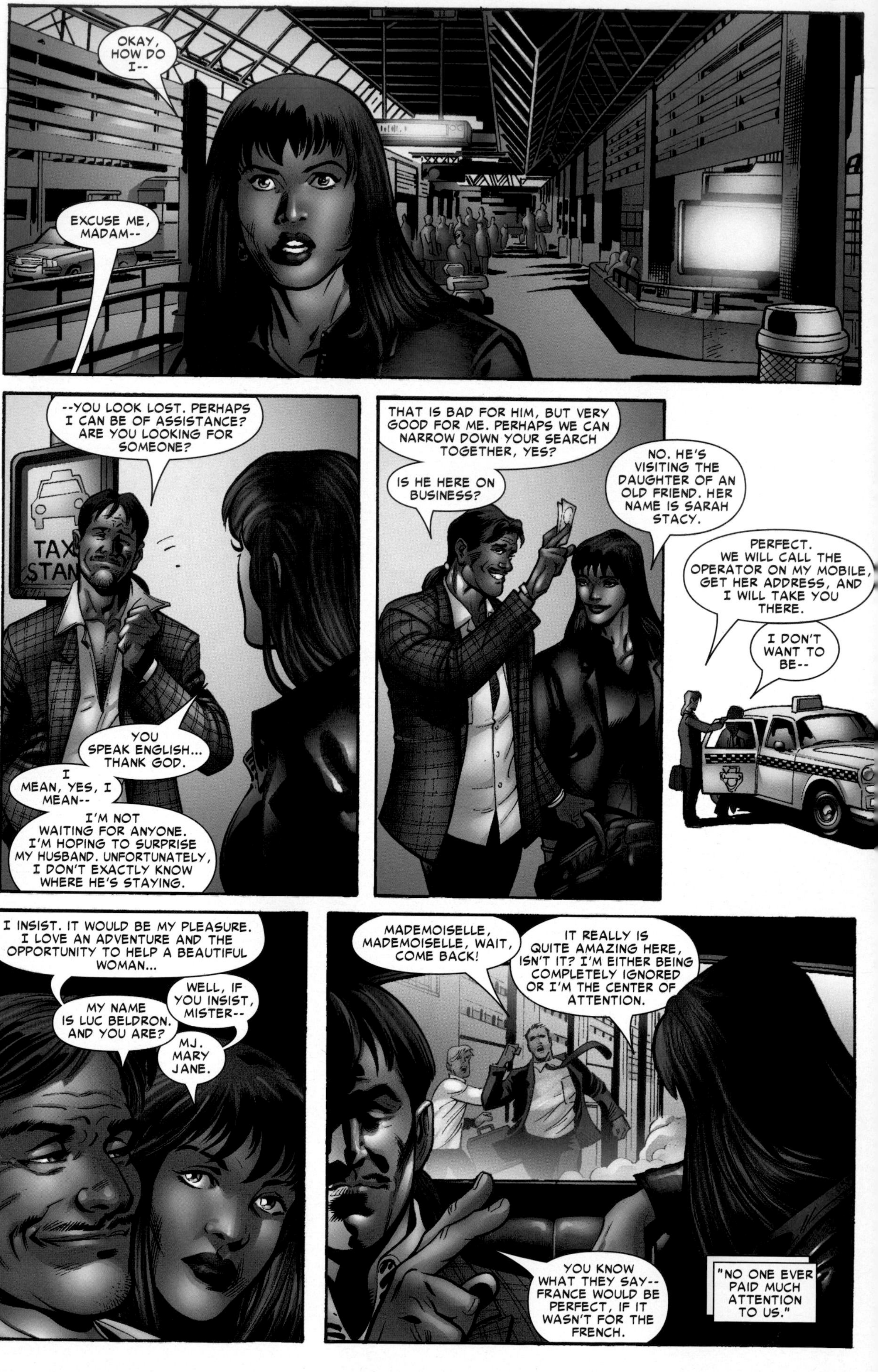
OKAY, HOW DO I--
EXCUSE ME, MADAM--
--YOU LOOK LOST. PERHAPS I CAN BE OF ASSISTANCE? ARE YOU LOOKING FOR SOMEONE?
TAXI STAND
YOU SPEAK ENGLISH... THANK GOD.
I MEAN, YES, I MEAN--
I'M NOT WAITING FOR ANYONE. I'M HOPING TO SURPRISE MY HUSBAND. UNFORTUNATELY, I DON'T EXACTLY KNOW WHERE HE'S STAYING.
THAT IS BAD FOR HIM, BUT VERY GOOD FOR ME. PERHAPS WE CAN NARROW DOWN YOUR SEARCH TOGETHER, YES?
IS HE HERE ON BUSINESS?
NO. HE'S VISITING THE DAUGHTER OF AN OLD FRIEND. HER NAME IS SARAH STACY.
PERFECT. WE WILL CALL THE OPERATOR ON MY MOBILE, GET HER ADDRESS, AND I WILL TAKE YOU THERE.
I DON'T WANT TO BE--
I INSIST. IT WOULD BE MY PLEASURE. I LOVE AN ADVENTURE AND THE OPPORTUNITY TO HELP A BEAUTIFUL WOMAN...
MY NAME IS LUC BELDRON. AND YOU ARE?
WELL, IF YOU INSIST, MISTER--
MJ. MARY JANE.
MADEMOISELLE, MADEMOISELLE, WAIT, COME BACK!
IT REALLY IS QUITE AMAZING HERE, ISN'T IT? I'M EITHER BEING COMPLETELY IGNORED OR I'M THE CENTER OF ATTENTION.
YOU KNOW WHAT THEY SAY-- FRANCE WOULD BE PERFECT, IF IT WASN'T FOR THE FRENCH.
"NO ONE EVER PAID MUCH ATTENTION TO US."

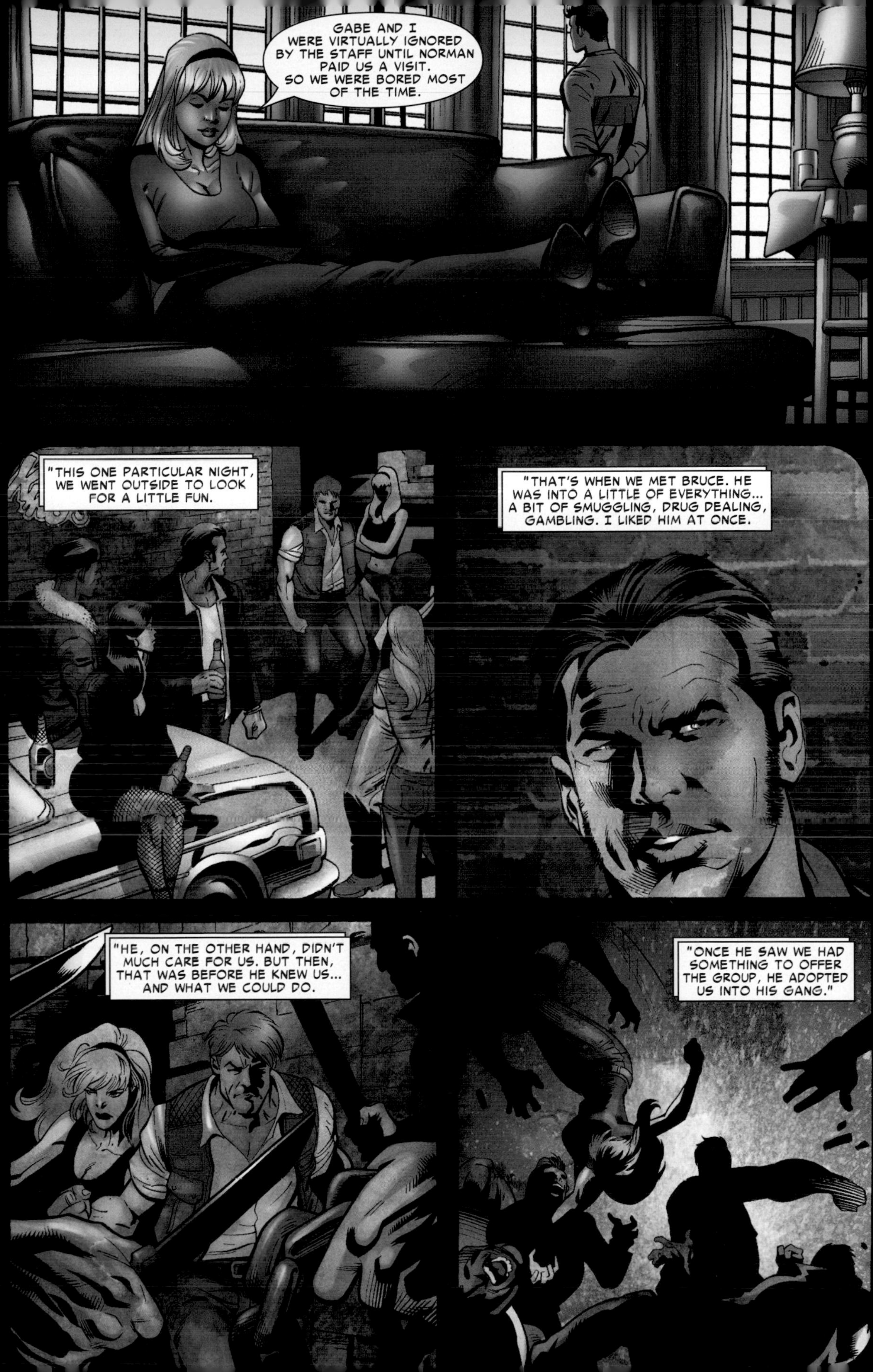
GABE AND I WERE VIRTUALLY IGNORED BY THE STAFF UNTIL NORMAN PAID US A VISIT. SO WE WERE BORED MOST OF THE TIME.
"THIS ONE PARTICULAR NIGHT, WE WENT OUTSIDE TO LOOK FOR A LITTLE FUN.
"THAT'S WHEN WE MET BRUCE. HE WAS INTO A LITTLE OF EVERYTHING... A BIT OF SMUGGLING, DRUG DEALING, GAMBLING. I LIKED HIM AT ONCE.
"HE, ON THE OTHER HAND, DIDN'T MUCH CARE FOR US. BUT THEN, THAT WAS BEFORE HE KNEW US... AND WHAT WE COULD DO.
"ONCE HE SAW WE HAD SOMETHING TO OFFER THE GROUP, HE ADOPTED US INTO HIS GANG."

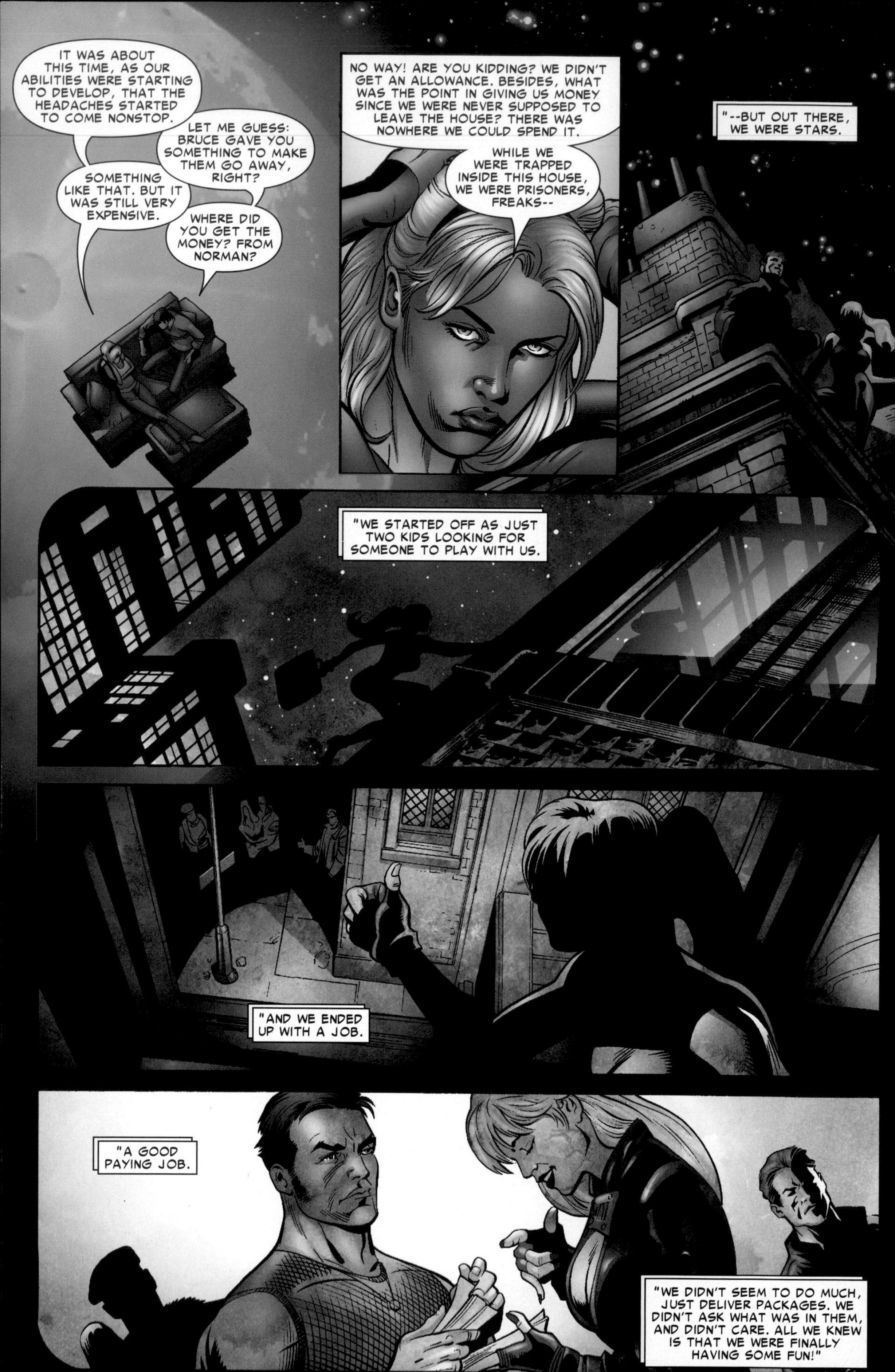
IT WAS ABOUT THIS TIME, AS OUR ABILITIES WERE STARTING TO DEVELOP, THAT THE HEADACHES STARTED TO COME NONSTOP.
LET ME GUESS: BRUCE GAVE YOU SOMETHING TO MAKE THEM GO AWAY, RIGHT?
SOMETHING LIKE THAT. BUT IT WAS STILL VERY EXPENSIVE.
WHERE DID YOU GET THE MONEY? FROM NORMAN?
NO WAY! ARE YOU KIDDING? WE DIDN'T GET AN ALLOWANCE. BESIDES, WHAT WAS THE POINT IN GIVING US MONEY SINCE WE WERE NEVER SUPPOSED TO LEAVE THE HOUSE? THERE WAS NOWHERE WE COULD SPEND IT.
WHILE WE WERE TRAPPED INSIDE THIS HOUSE, WE WERE PRISONERS, FREAKS--
"--BUT OUT THERE, WE WERE STARS.
"WE STARTED OFF AS JUST TWO KIDS LOOKING FOR SOMEONE TO PLAY WITH US.
"AND WE ENDED UP WITH A JOB.
"A GOOD PAYING JOB.
"WE DIDN'T SEEM TO DO MUCH, JUST DELIVER PACKAGES. WE DIDN'T ASK WHAT WAS IN THEM, AND DIDN'T CARE. ALL WE KNEW IS THAT WE WERE FINALLY HAVING SOME FUN!"

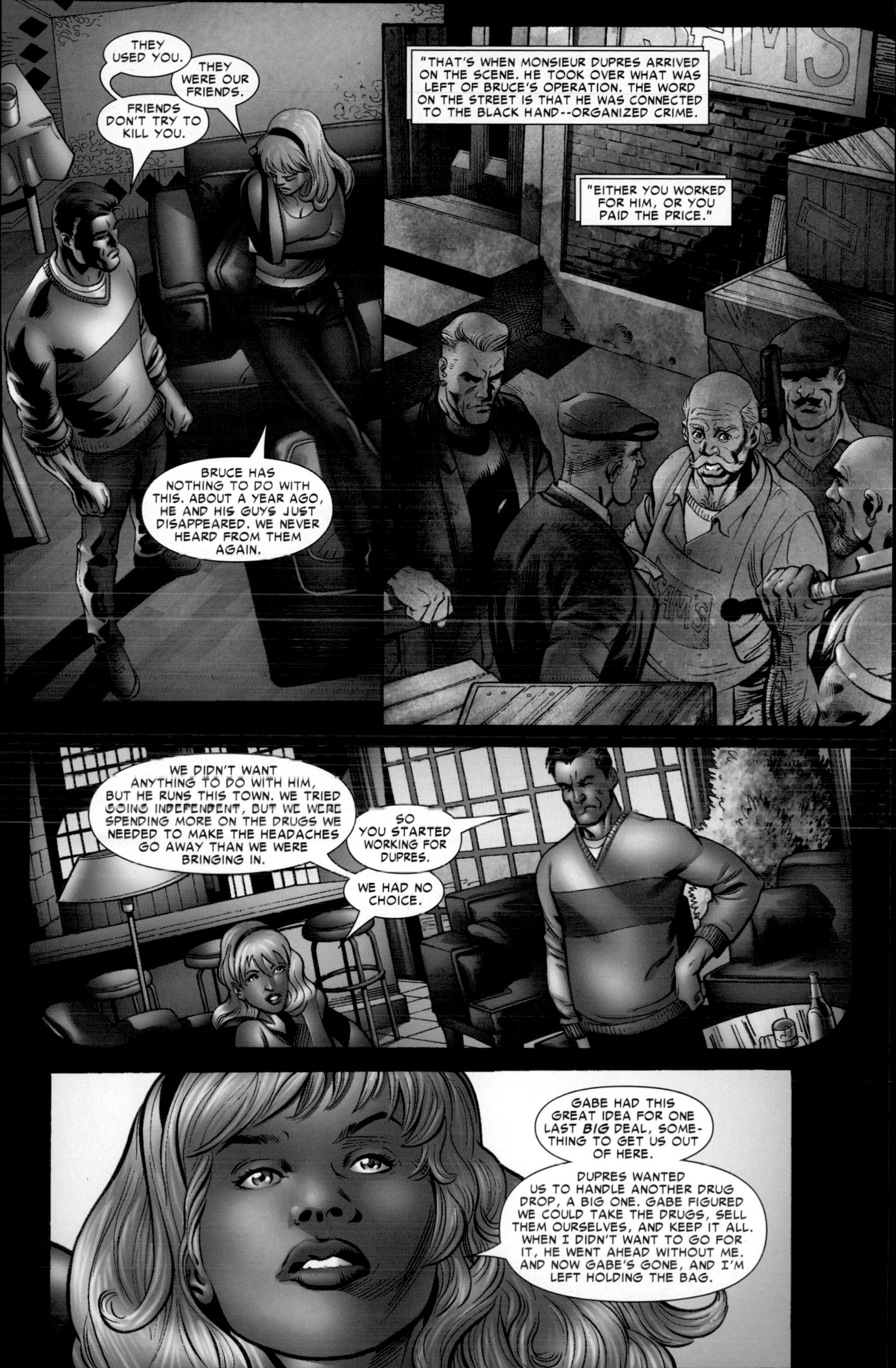
THEY USED YOU.
THEY WERE OUR FRIENDS.
FRIENDS DON'T TRY TO KILL YOU.
"THAT'S WHEN MONSIEUR DUPRES ARRIVED ON THE SCENE. HE TOOK OVER WHAT WAS LEFT OF BRUCE'S OPERATION. THE WORD ON THE STREET IS THAT HE WAS CONNECTED TO THE BLACK HAND--ORGANIZED CRIME.
"EITHER YOU WORKED FOR HIM, OR YOU PAID THE PRICE."
BRUCE HAS NOTHING TO DO WITH THIS. ABOUT A YEAR AGO, HE AND HIS GUYS JUST DISAPPEARED. WE NEVER HEARD FROM THEM AGAIN.
WE DIDN'T WANT ANYTHING TO DO WITH HIM, BUT HE RUNS THIS TOWN. WE TRIED GOING INDEPENDENT, BUT WE WERE SPENDING MORE ON THE DRUGS WE NEEDED TO MAKE THE HEADACHES GO AWAY THAN WE WERE BRINGING IN.
SO YOU STARTED WORKING FOR DUPRES.
WE HAD NO CHOICE.
GABE HAD THIS GREAT IDEA FOR ONE LAST *BIG* DEAL, SOMETHING TO GET US OUT OF HERE.
DUPRES WANTED US TO HANDLE ANOTHER DRUG DROP, A BIG ONE. GABE FIGURED WE COULD TAKE THE DRUGS, SELL THEM OURSELVES, AND KEEP IT ALL. WHEN I DIDN'T WANT TO GO FOR IT, HE WENT AHEAD WITHOUT ME. AND NOW GABE'S GONE, AND I'M LEFT HOLDING THE BAG.

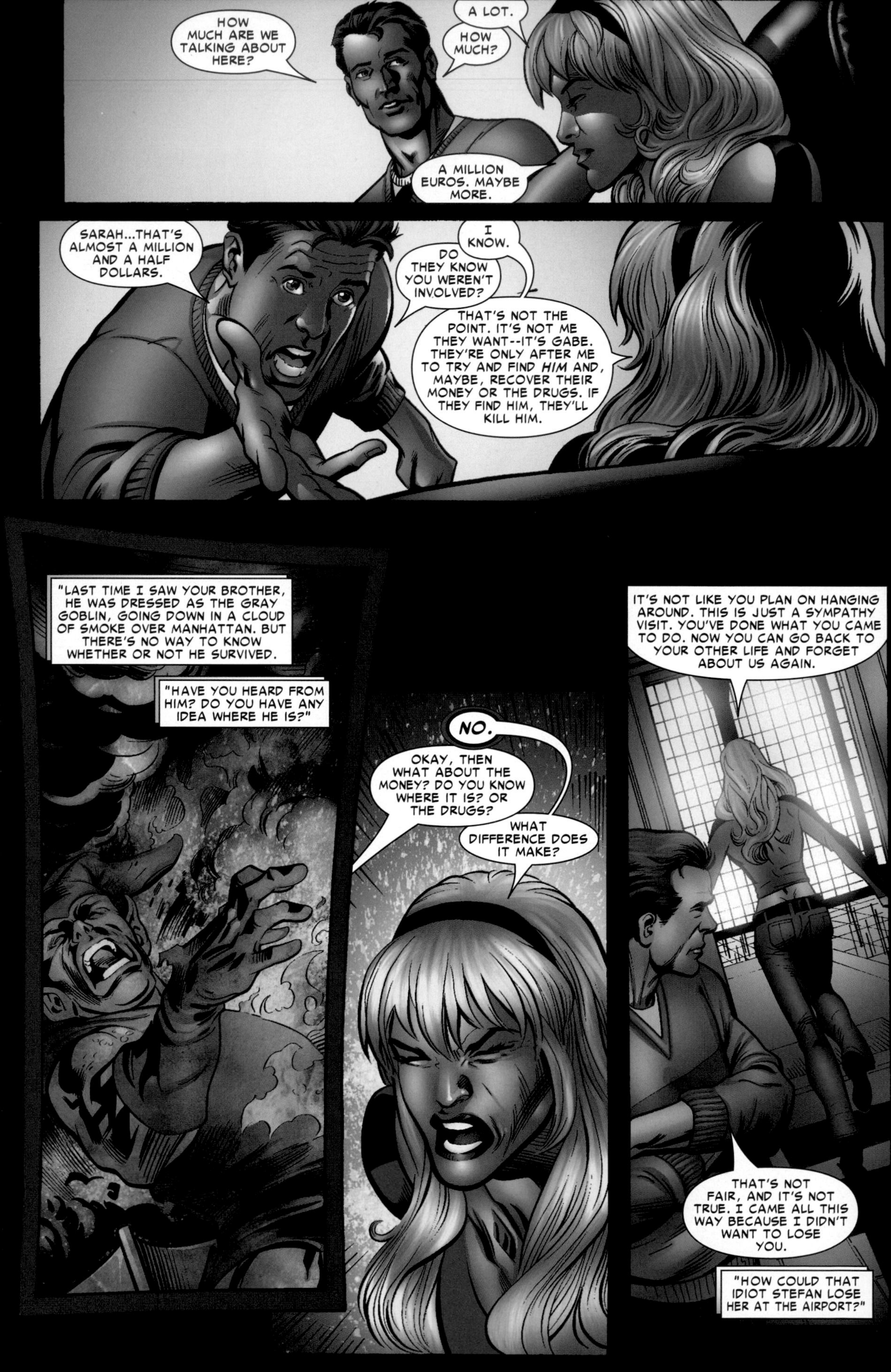
HOW MUCH ARE WE TALKING ABOUT HERE?
A LOT.
HOW MUCH?
A MILLION EUROS. MAYBE MORE.
SARAH...THAT'S ALMOST A MILLION AND A HALF DOLLARS.
I KNOW.
DO THEY KNOW YOU WEREN'T INVOLVED?
THAT'S NOT THE POINT. IT'S NOT ME THEY WANT--IT'S GABE. THEY'RE ONLY AFTER ME TO TRY AND FIND *HIM* AND, MAYBE, RECOVER THEIR MONEY OR THE DRUGS. IF THEY FIND HIM, THEY'LL KILL HIM.
"LAST TIME I SAW YOUR BROTHER, HE WAS DRESSED AS THE GRAY GOBLIN, GOING DOWN IN A CLOUD OF SMOKE OVER MANHATTAN. BUT THERE'S NO WAY TO KNOW WHETHER OR NOT HE SURVIVED.
"HAVE YOU HEARD FROM HIM? DO YOU HAVE ANY IDEA WHERE HE IS?"
NO.
OKAY, THEN WHAT ABOUT THE MONEY? DO YOU KNOW WHERE IT IS? OR THE DRUGS?
WHAT DIFFERENCE DOES IT MAKE?
IT'S NOT LIKE YOU PLAN ON HANGING AROUND. THIS IS JUST A SYMPATHY VISIT. YOU'VE DONE WHAT YOU CAME TO DO. NOW YOU CAN GO BACK TO YOUR OTHER LIFE AND FORGET ABOUT US AGAIN.
THAT'S NOT FAIR, AND IT'S NOT TRUE. I CAME ALL THIS WAY BECAUSE I DIDN'T WANT TO LOSE YOU.
"HOW COULD THAT IDIOT STEFAN LOSE HER AT THE AIRPORT?"

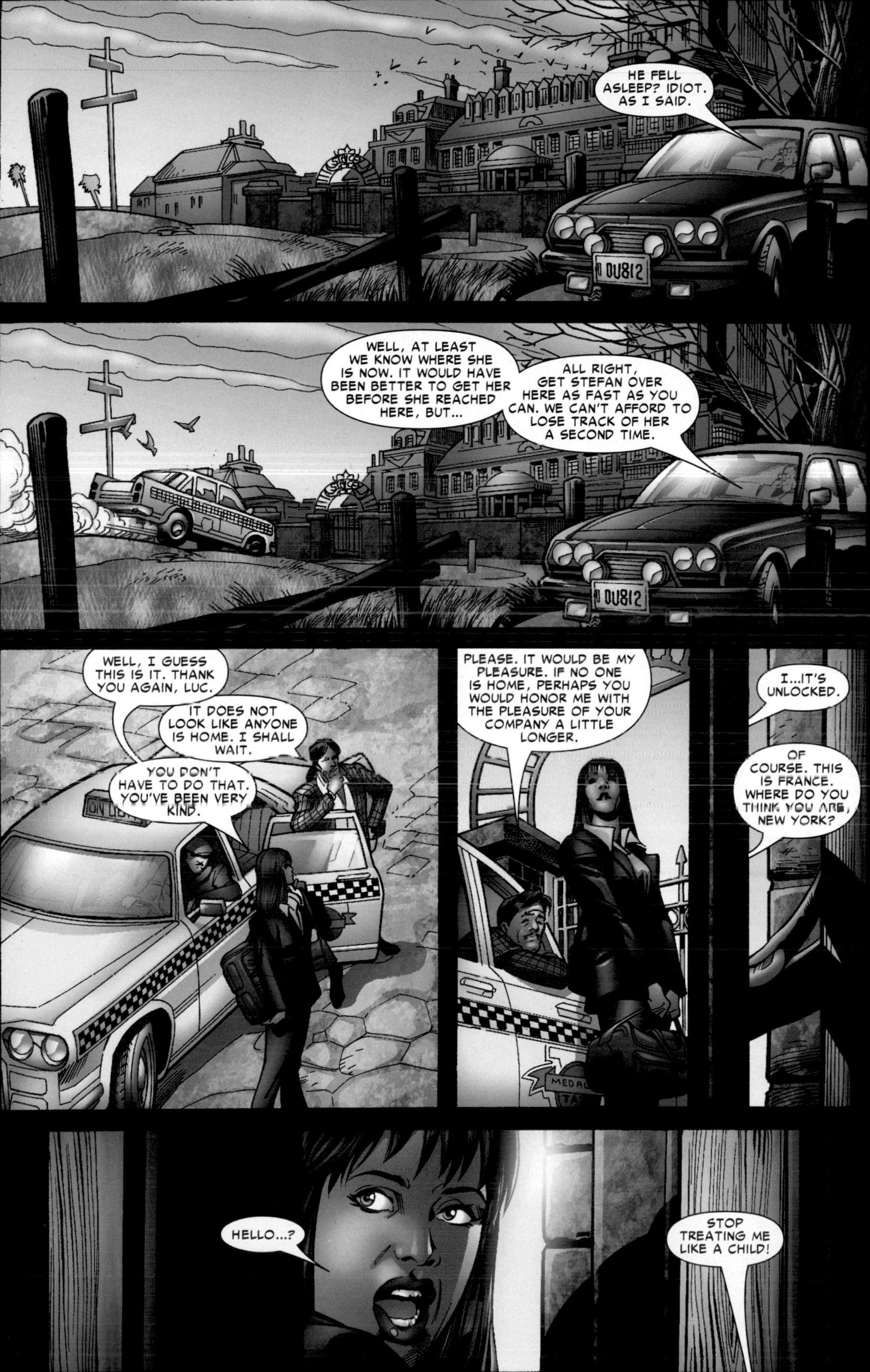
HE FELL ASLEEP? IDIOT. AS I SAID.
DU812
WELL, AT LEAST WE KNOW WHERE SHE IS NOW. IT WOULD HAVE BEEN BETTER TO GET HER BEFORE SHE REACHED HERE, BUT...
ALL RIGHT, GET STEFAN OVER HERE AS FAST AS YOU CAN. WE CAN'T AFFORD TO LOSE TRACK OF HER A SECOND TIME.
DU812
WELL, I GUESS THIS IS IT. THANK YOU AGAIN, LUC.
IT DOES NOT LOOK LIKE ANYONE IS HOME. I SHALL WAIT.
YOU DON'T HAVE TO DO THAT. YOU'VE BEEN VERY KIND.
PLEASE. IT WOULD BE MY PLEASURE. IF NO ONE IS HOME, PERHAPS YOU WOULD HONOR ME WITH THE PLEASURE OF YOUR COMPANY A LITTLE LONGER.
I...IT'S UNLOCKED.
OF COURSE. THIS IS FRANCE. WHERE DO YOU THINK YOU ARE, NEW YORK?
HELLO...?
STOP TREATING ME LIKE A CHILD!

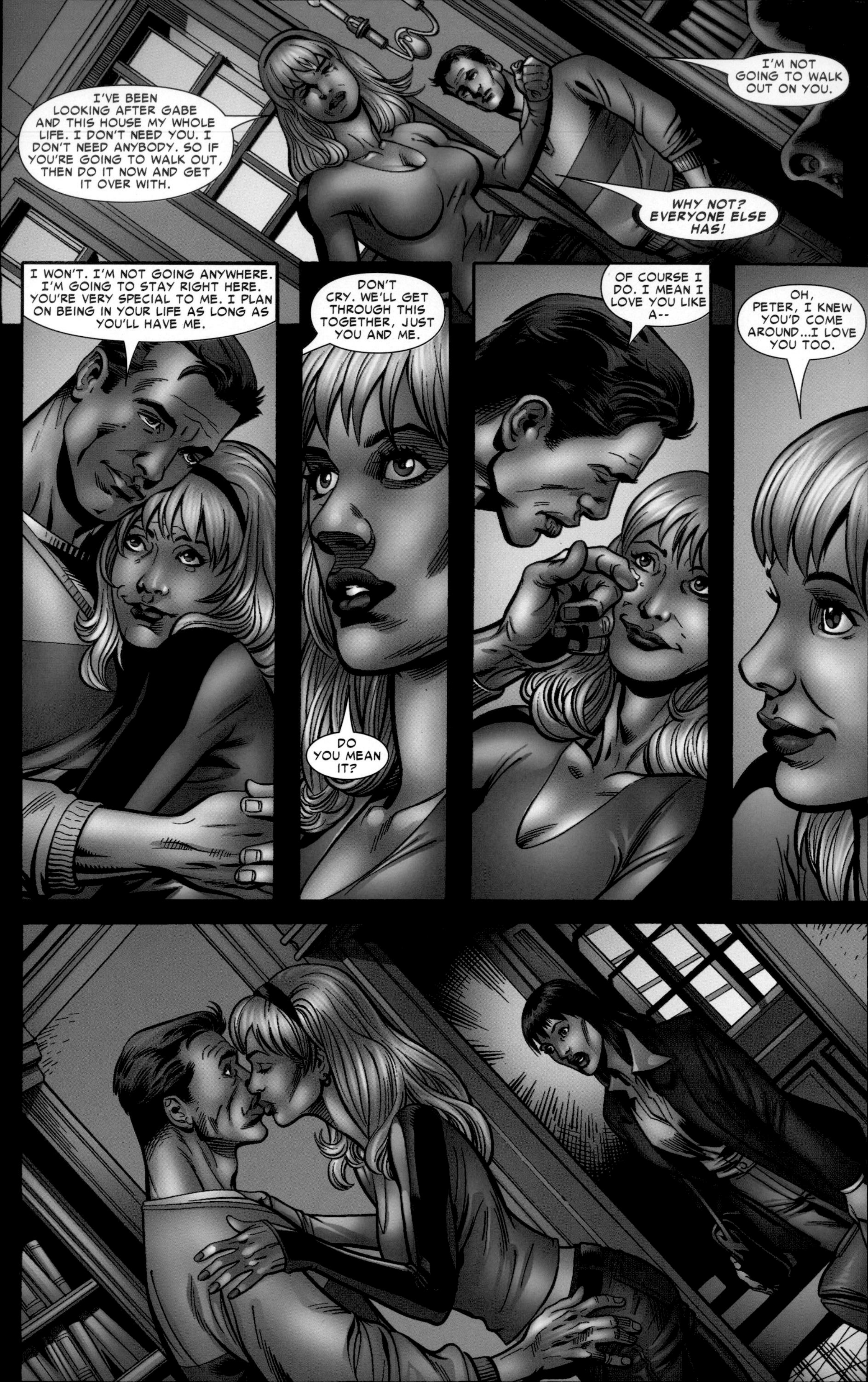
I'VE BEEN LOOKING AFTER GABE AND THIS HOUSE MY WHOLE LIFE. I DON'T NEED YOU. I DON'T NEED ANYBODY. SO IF YOU'RE GOING TO WALK OUT, THEN DO IT NOW AND GET IT OVER WITH.
I'M NOT GOING TO WALK OUT ON YOU.
WHY NOT? EVERYONE ELSE HAS!
I WON'T. I'M NOT GOING ANYWHERE. I'M GOING TO STAY RIGHT HERE. YOU'RE VERY SPECIAL TO ME. I PLAN ON BEING IN YOUR LIFE AS LONG AS YOU'LL HAVE ME.
DON'T CRY. WE'LL GET THROUGH THIS TOGETHER, JUST YOU AND ME.
DO YOU MEAN IT?
OF COURSE I DO. I MEAN I LOVE YOU LIKE A--
OH, PETER, I KNEW YOU'D COME AROUND...I LOVE YOU TOO.

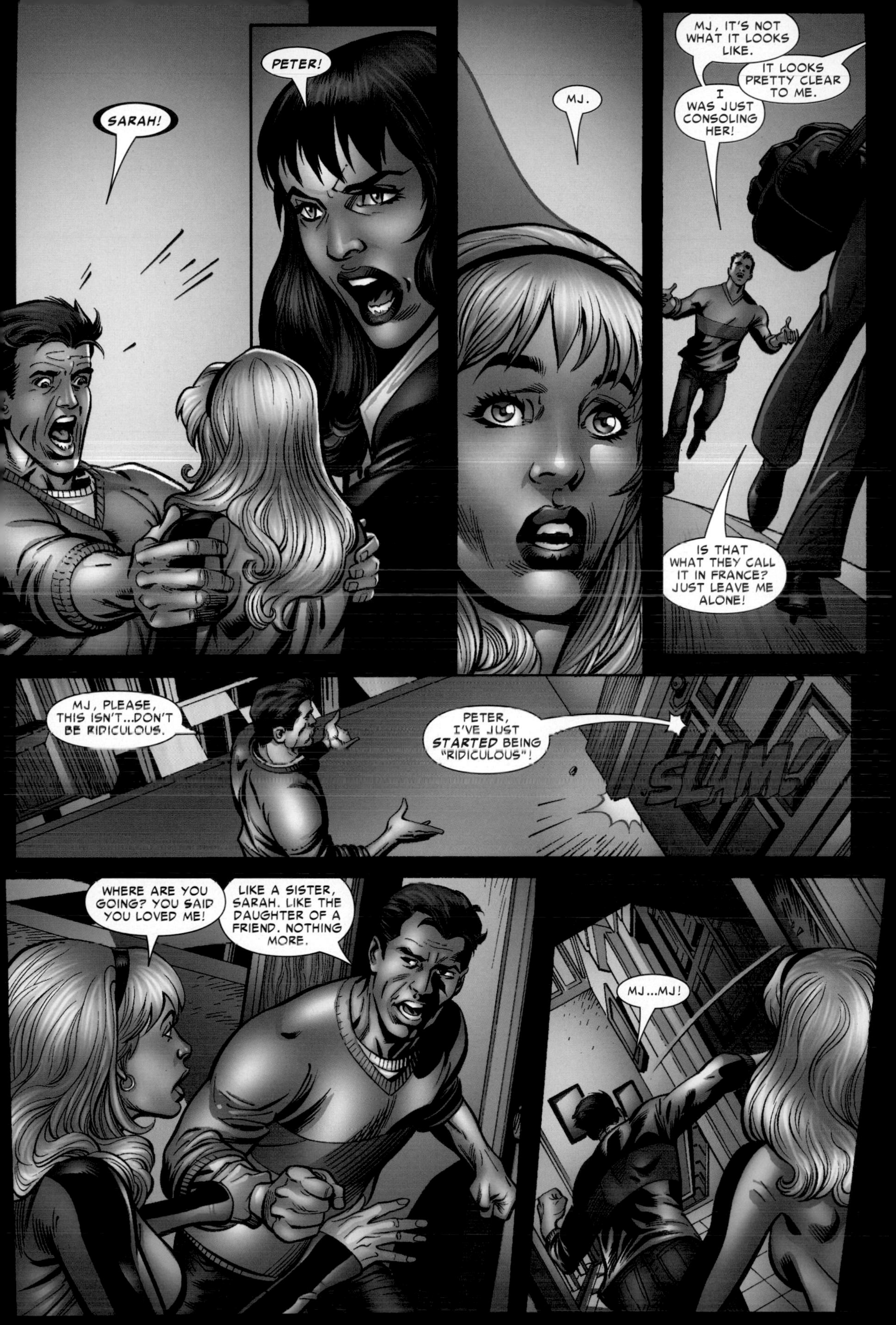
SARAH!
PETER!
MJ.
MJ, IT'S NOT WHAT IT LOOKS LIKE.
IT LOOKS PRETTY CLEAR TO ME.
I WAS JUST CONSOLING HER!
IS THAT WHAT THEY CALL IT IN FRANCE? JUST LEAVE ME ALONE!
MJ, PLEASE, THIS ISN'T...DON'T BE RIDICULOUS.
PETER, I'VE JUST STARTED BEING "RIDICULOUS"!
SLAM!
WHERE ARE YOU GOING? YOU SAID YOU LOVED ME!
LIKE A SISTER, SARAH. LIKE THE DAUGHTER OF A FRIEND. NOTHING MORE.
MJ...MJ!

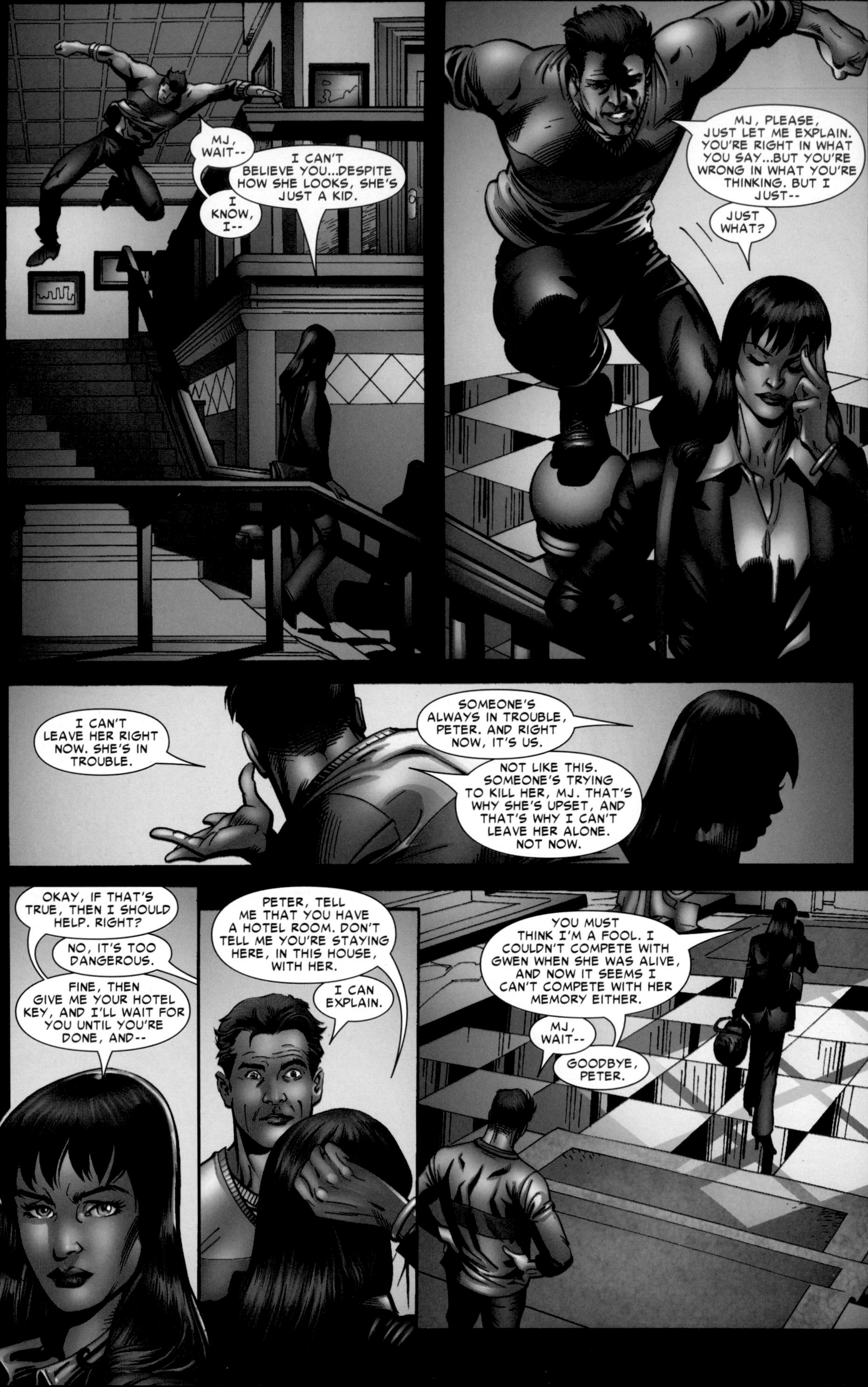
MJ, WAIT--
I CAN'T BELIEVE YOU...DESPITE HOW SHE LOOKS, SHE'S JUST A KID.
I KNOW, I--
MJ, PLEASE, JUST LET ME EXPLAIN. YOU'RE RIGHT IN WHAT YOU SAY...BUT YOU'RE WRONG IN WHAT YOU'RE THINKING. BUT I JUST--
JUST WHAT?
I CAN'T LEAVE HER RIGHT NOW. SHE'S IN TROUBLE.
SOMEONE'S ALWAYS IN TROUBLE, PETER. AND RIGHT NOW, IT'S US.
NOT LIKE THIS. SOMEONE'S TRYING TO KILL HER, MJ. THAT'S WHY SHE'S UPSET, AND THAT'S WHY I CAN'T LEAVE HER ALONE. NOT NOW.
OKAY, IF THAT'S TRUE, THEN I SHOULD HELP. RIGHT?
NO, IT'S TOO DANGEROUS.
FINE, THEN GIVE ME YOUR HOTEL KEY, AND I'LL WAIT FOR YOU UNTIL YOU'RE DONE, AND--
PETER, TELL ME THAT YOU HAVE A HOTEL ROOM. DON'T TELL ME YOU'RE STAYING HERE, IN THIS HOUSE, WITH HER.
I CAN EXPLAIN.
YOU MUST THINK I'M A FOOL. I COULDN'T COMPETE WITH GWEN WHEN SHE WAS ALIVE, AND NOW IT SEEMS I CAN'T COMPETE WITH HER MEMORY EITHER.
MJ, WAIT--
GOODBYE, PETER.

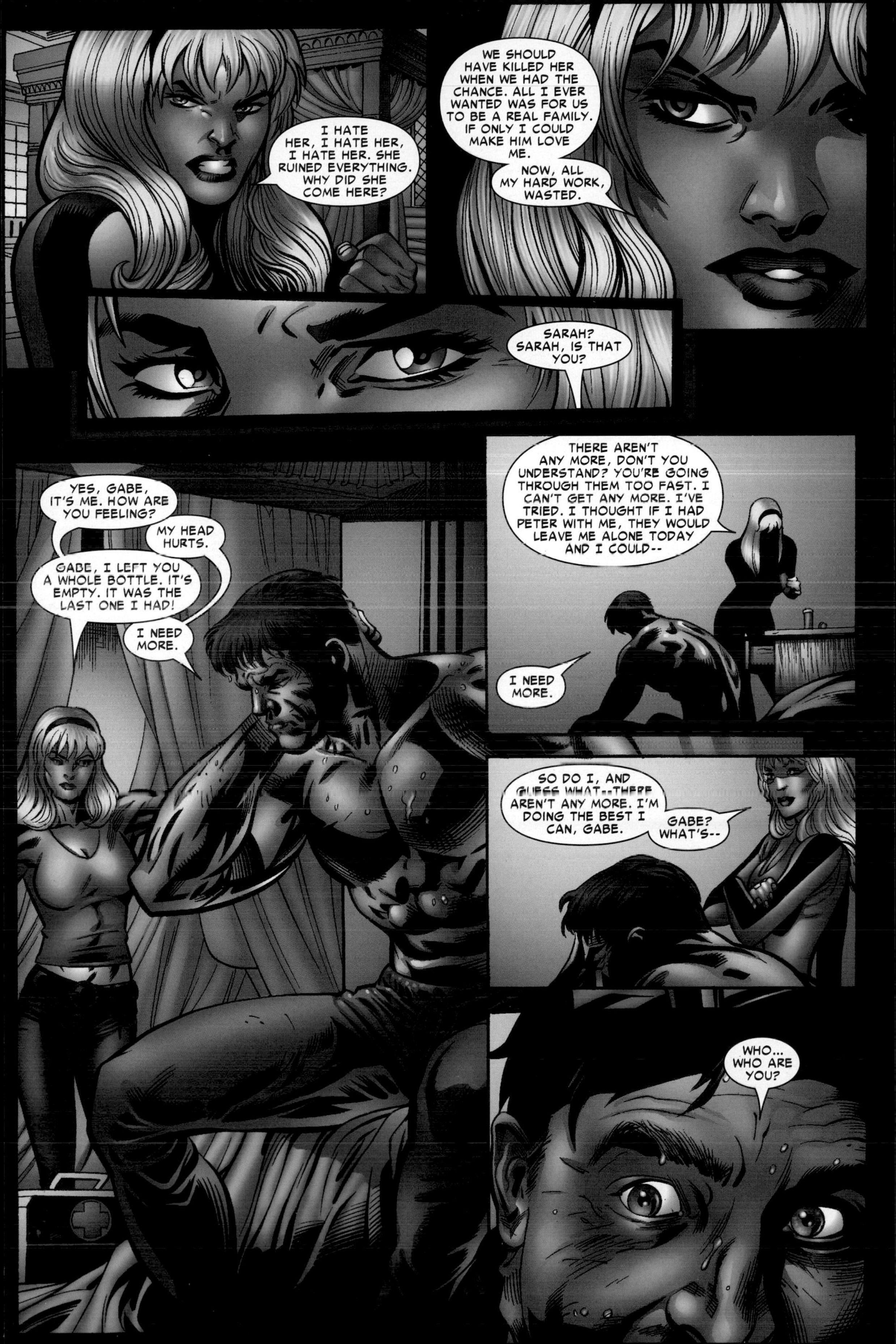

I HATE HER, I HATE HER, I HATE HER. SHE RUINED EVERYTHING. WHY DID SHE COME HERE?
WE SHOULD HAVE KILLED HER WHEN WE HAD THE CHANCE. ALL I EVER WANTED WAS FOR US TO BE A REAL FAMILY. IF ONLY I COULD MAKE HIM LOVE ME.
NOW, ALL MY HARD WORK, WASTED.
SARAH? SARAH, IS THAT YOU?
YES, GABE, IT'S ME. HOW ARE YOU FEELING?
MY HEAD HURTS.
GABE, I LEFT YOU A WHOLE BOTTLE. IT'S EMPTY. IT WAS THE LAST ONE I HAD!
I NEED MORE.
THERE AREN'T ANY MORE, DON'T YOU UNDERSTAND? YOU'RE GOING THROUGH THEM TOO FAST. I CAN'T GET ANY MORE. I'VE TRIED. I THOUGHT IF I HAD PETER WITH ME, THEY WOULD LEAVE ME ALONE TODAY AND I COULD--
I NEED MORE.
SO DO I, AND GUESS WHAT--THERE AREN'T ANY MORE. I'M DOING THE BEST I CAN, GABE.
GABE? WHAT'S--
WHO... WHO ARE YOU?

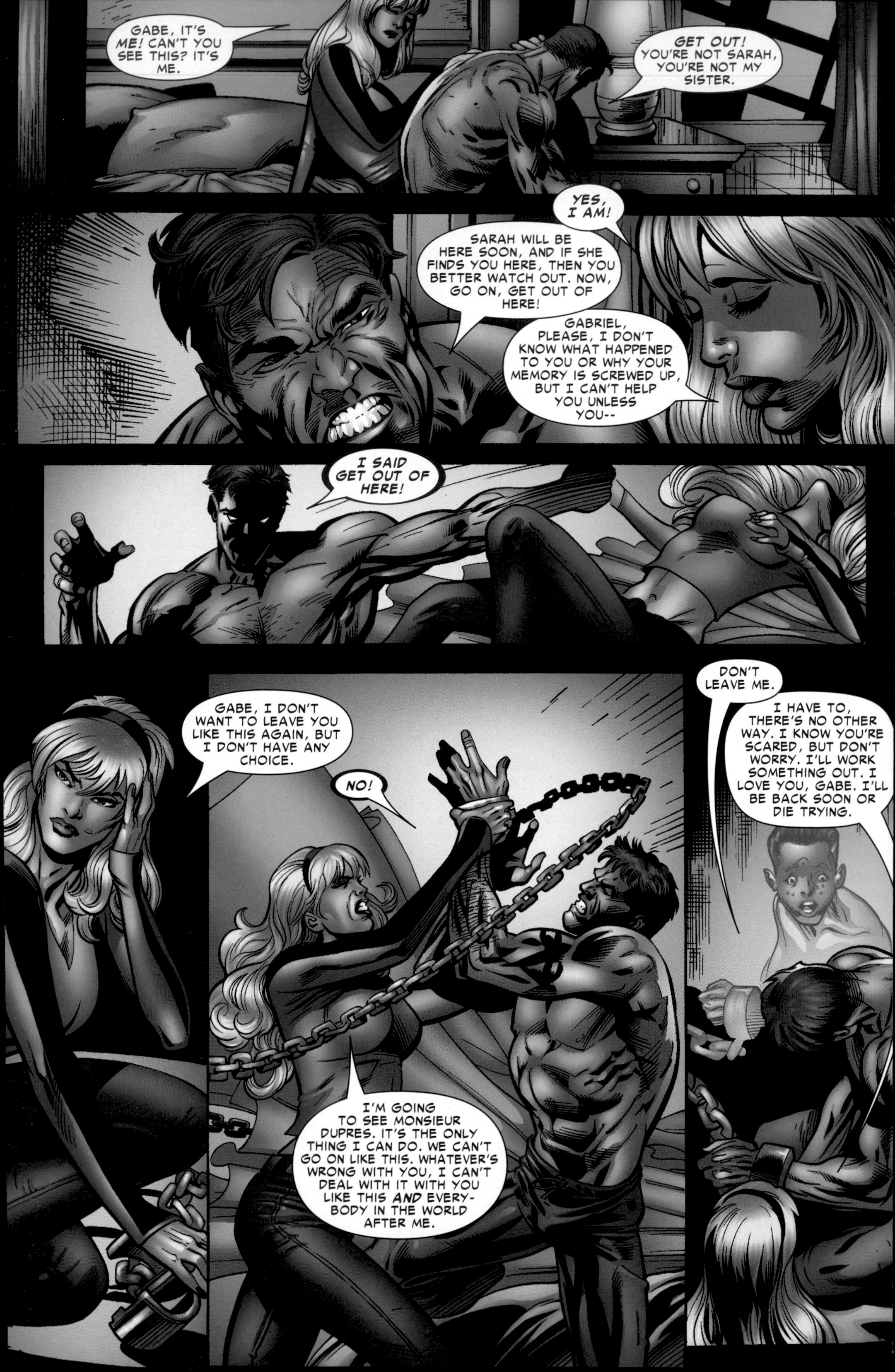
GABE, IT'S ME! CAN'T YOU SEE THIS? IT'S ME.
GET OUT! YOU'RE NOT SARAH, YOU'RE NOT MY SISTER.
YES, I AM!
SARAH WILL BE HERE SOON, AND IF SHE FINDS YOU HERE, THEN YOU BETTER WATCH OUT. NOW, GO ON, GET OUT OF HERE!
GABRIEL, PLEASE, I DON'T KNOW WHAT HAPPENED TO YOU OR WHY YOUR MEMORY IS SCREWED UP, BUT I CAN'T HELP YOU UNLESS YOU--
I SAID GET OUT OF HERE!
GABE, I DON'T WANT TO LEAVE YOU LIKE THIS AGAIN, BUT I DON'T HAVE ANY CHOICE.
NO!
I'M GOING TO SEE MONSIEUR DUPRES. IT'S THE ONLY THING I CAN DO. WE CAN'T GO ON LIKE THIS. WHATEVER'S WRONG WITH YOU, I CAN'T DEAL WITH IT WITH YOU LIKE THIS AND EVERY-BODY IN THE WORLD AFTER ME.
DON'T LEAVE ME.
I HAVE TO, THERE'S NO OTHER WAY. I KNOW YOU'RE SCARED, BUT DON'T WORRY. I'LL WORK SOMETHING OUT. I LOVE YOU, GABE. I'LL BE BACK SOON OR DIE TRYING.

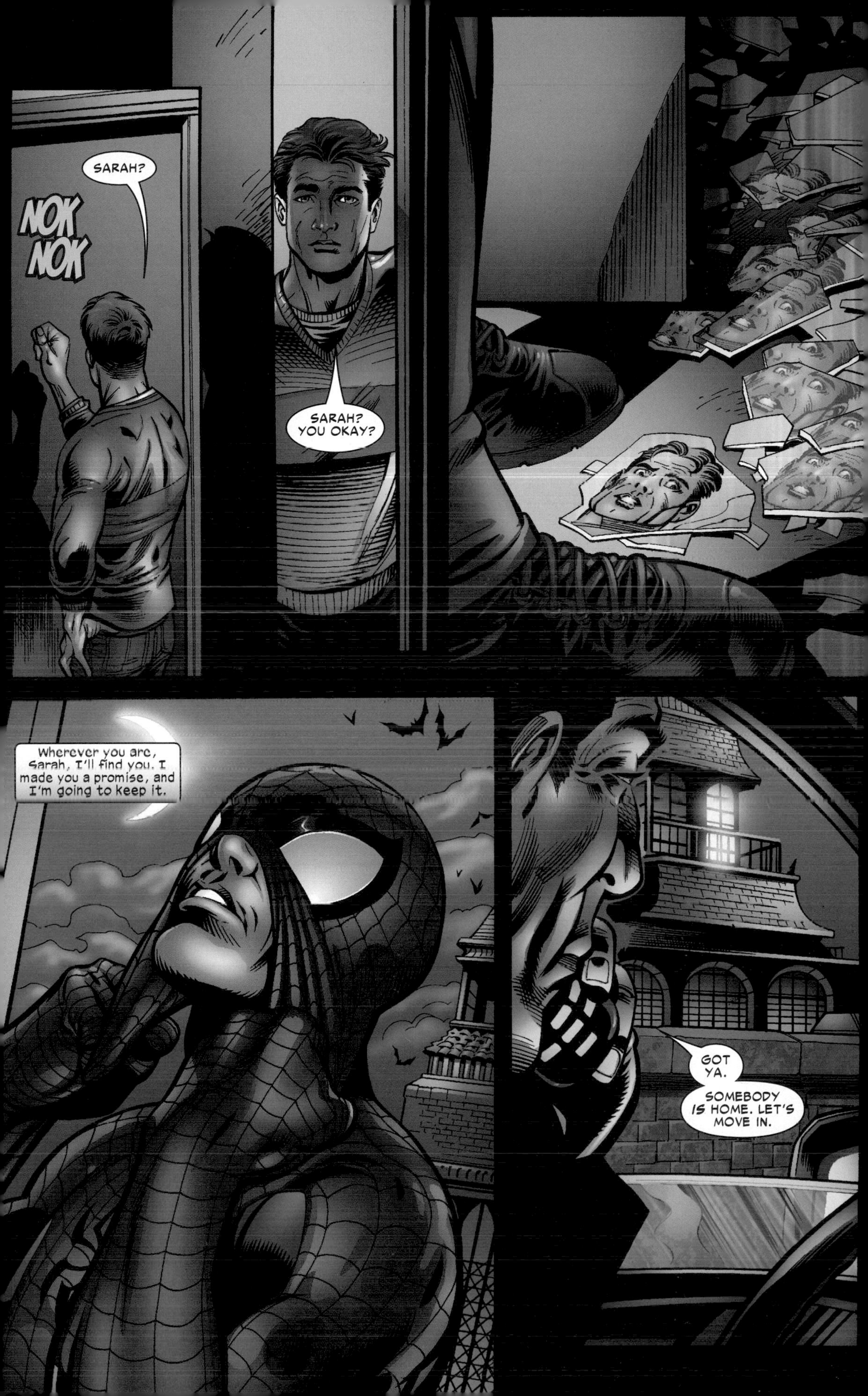

NOK NOK
SARAH?
SARAH? YOU OKAY?
Wherever you are, Sarah, I'll find you. I made you a promise, and I'm going to keep it.
GOT YA.
SOMEBODY IS HOME. LET'S MOVE IN.

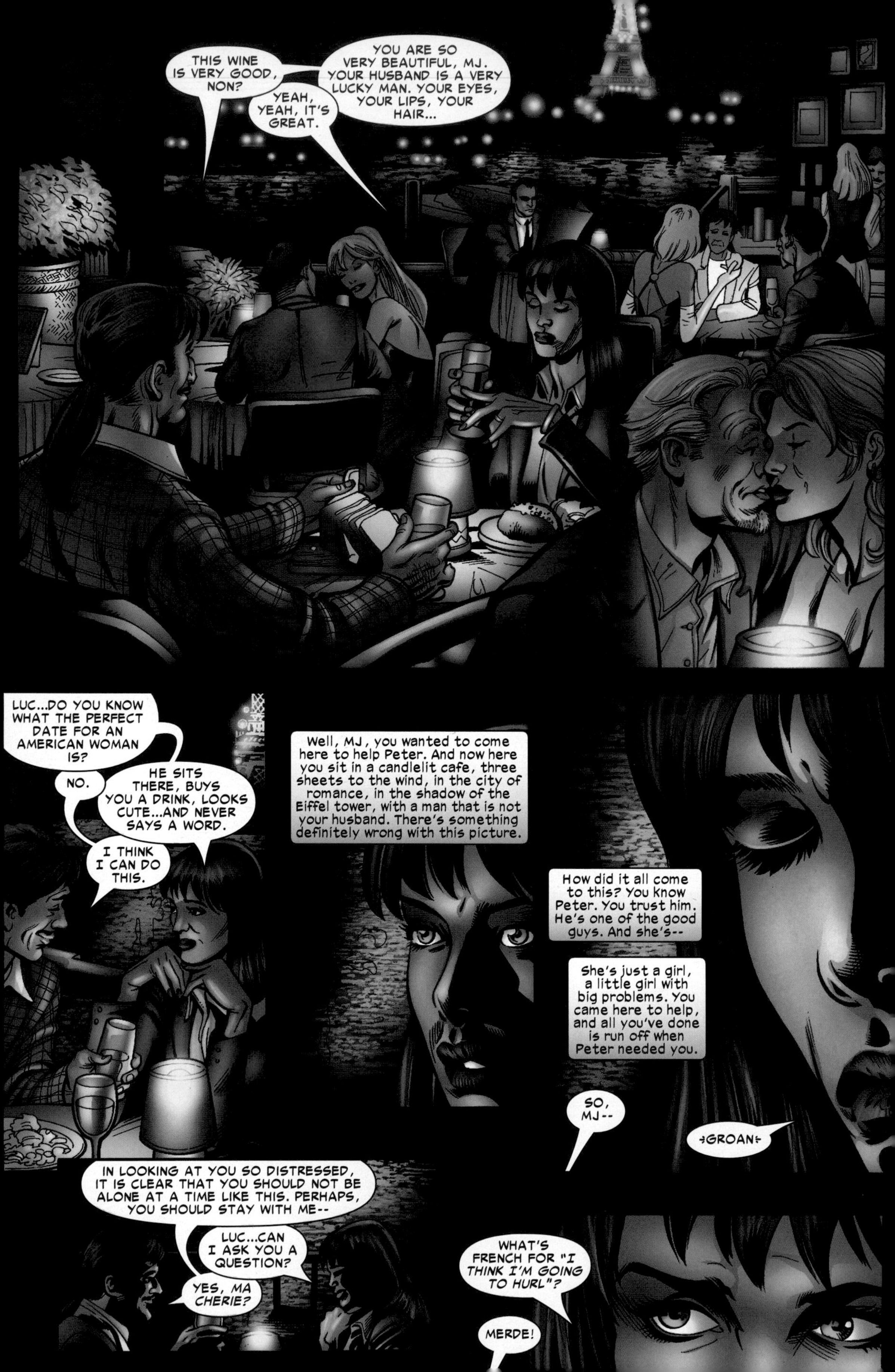

THIS WINE IS VERY GOOD, NON?
YOU ARE SO VERY BEAUTIFUL, MJ. YOUR HUSBAND IS A VERY LUCKY MAN. YOUR EYES, YOUR LIPS, YOUR HAIR...
YEAH, YEAH, IT'S GREAT.
LUC...DO YOU KNOW WHAT THE PERFECT DATE FOR AN AMERICAN WOMAN IS?
NO.
HE SITS THERE, BUYS YOU A DRINK, LOOKS CUTE...AND NEVER SAYS A WORD.
I THINK I CAN DO THIS.
Well, MJ, you wanted to come here to help Peter. And now here you sit in a candlelit cafe, three sheets to the wind, in the city of romance, in the shadow of the Eiffel tower, with a man that is not your husband. There's something definitely wrong with this picture.
How did it all come to this? You know Peter. You trust him. He's one of the good guys. And she's--
She's just a girl, a little girl with big problems. You came here to help, and all you've done is run off when Peter needed you.
SO, MJ--
GROAN
IN LOOKING AT YOU SO DISTRESSED, IT IS CLEAR THAT YOU SHOULD NOT BE ALONE AT A TIME LIKE THIS. PERHAPS, YOU SHOULD STAY WITH ME--
LUC...CAN I ASK YOU A QUESTION?
YES, MA CHERIE?
WHAT'S FRENCH FOR "I THINK I'M GOING TO HURL"?
MERDE!

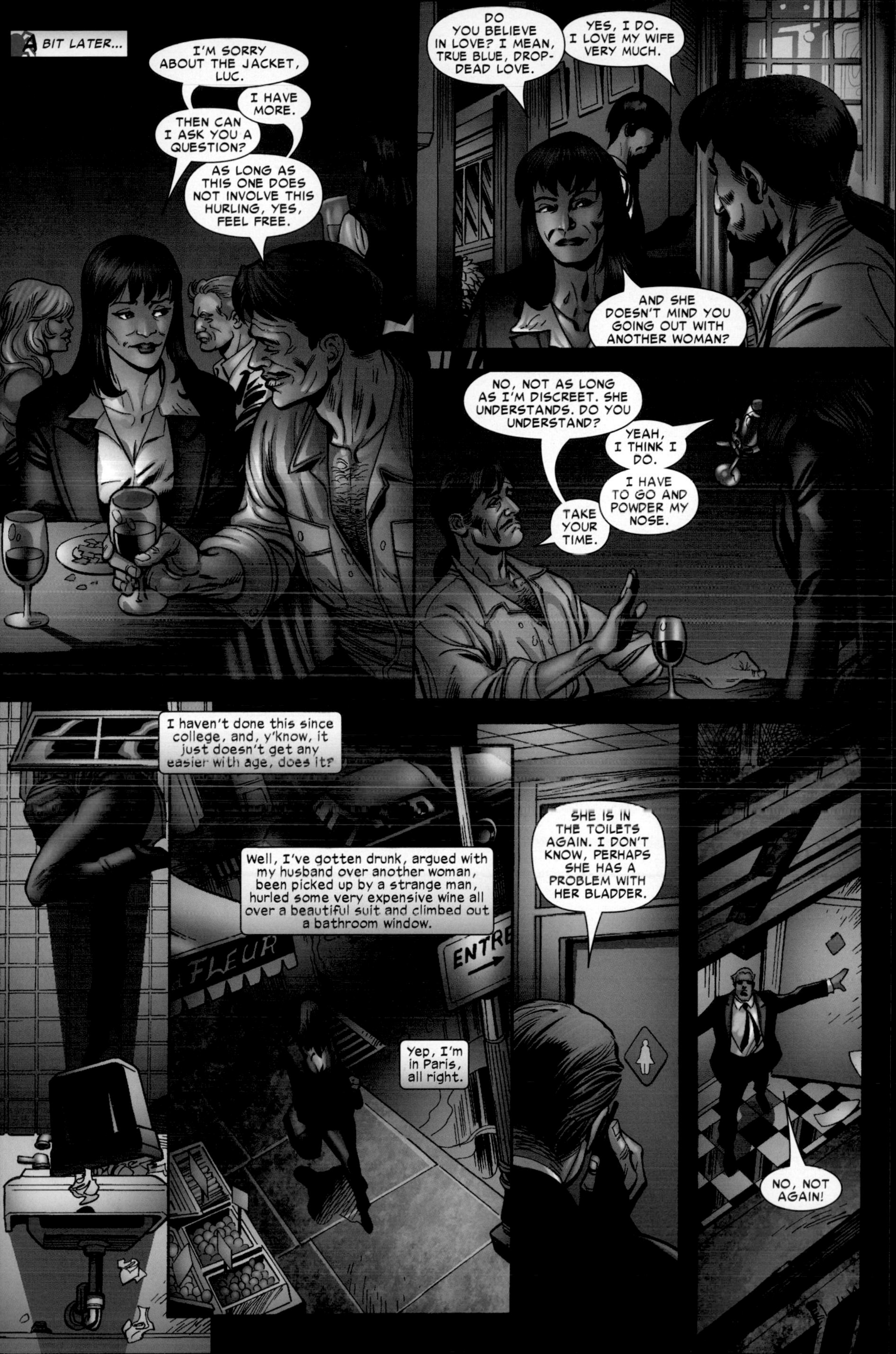
A BIT LATER...
I'M SORRY ABOUT THE JACKET, LUC.
I HAVE MORE.
THEN CAN I ASK YOU A QUESTION?
AS LONG AS THIS ONE DOES NOT INVOLVE THIS HURLING, YES, FEEL FREE.
DO YOU BELIEVE IN LOVE? I MEAN, TRUE BLUE, DROP-DEAD LOVE.
YES, I DO. I LOVE MY WIFE VERY MUCH.
AND SHE DOESN'T MIND YOU GOING OUT WITH ANOTHER WOMAN?
NO, NOT AS LONG AS I'M DISCREET. SHE UNDERSTANDS. DO YOU UNDERSTAND?
YEAH, I THINK I DO.
I HAVE TO GO AND POWDER MY NOSE.
TAKE YOUR TIME.
I haven't done this since college, and, y'know, it just doesn't get any easier with age, does it?
Well, I've gotten drunk, argued with my husband over another woman, been picked up by a strange man, hurled some very expensive wine all over a beautiful suit and climbed out a bathroom window.
FLEUR
ENTRE
Yep, I'm in Paris, all right.
SHE IS IN THE TOILETS AGAIN. I DON'T KNOW, PERHAPS SHE HAS A PROBLEM WITH HER BLADDER.
NO, NOT AGAIN!

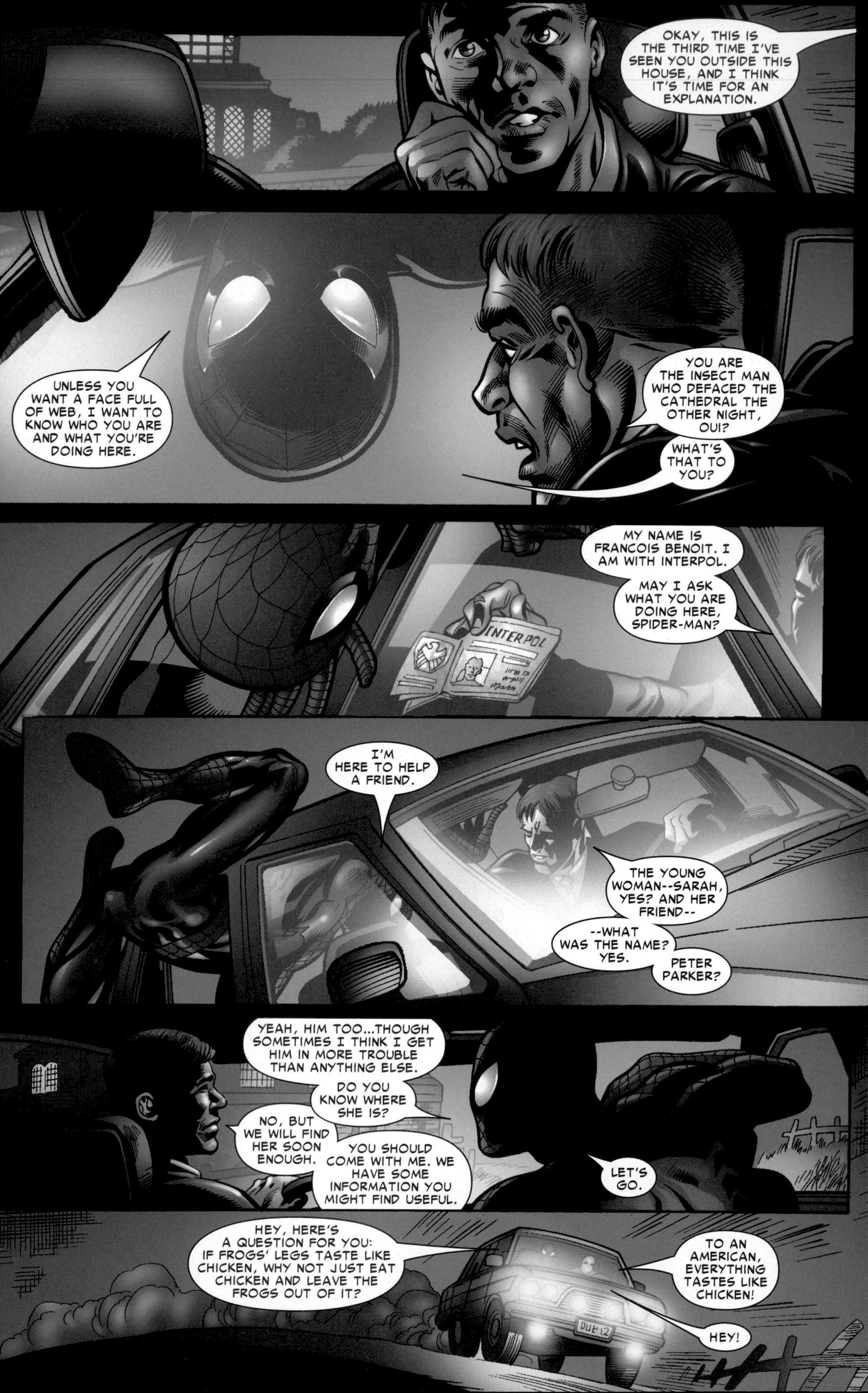
OKAY, THIS IS THE THIRD TIME I'VE SEEN YOU OUTSIDE THIS HOUSE, AND I THINK IT'S TIME FOR AN EXPLANATION.
UNLESS YOU WANT A FACE FULL OF WEB, I WANT TO KNOW WHO YOU ARE AND WHAT YOU'RE DOING HERE.
YOU ARE THE INSECT MAN WHO DEFACED THE CATHEDRAL THE OTHER NIGHT, OUI?
WHAT'S THAT TO YOU?
MY NAME IS FRANCOIS BENOIT. I AM WITH INTERPOL.
MAY I ASK WHAT YOU ARE DOING HERE, SPIDER-MAN?
INTERPOL
I'M HERE TO HELP A FRIEND.
THE YOUNG WOMAN--SARAH, YES? AND HER FRIEND--
--WHAT WAS THE NAME? YES.
PETER PARKER?
YEAH, HIM TOO...THOUGH SOMETIMES I THINK I GET HIM IN MORE TROUBLE THAN ANYTHING ELSE.
DO YOU KNOW WHERE SHE IS?
NO, BUT WE WILL FIND HER SOON ENOUGH.
YOU SHOULD COME WITH ME. WE HAVE SOME INFORMATION YOU MIGHT FIND USEFUL.
LET'S GO.
HEY, HERE'S A QUESTION FOR YOU: IF FROGS' LEGS TASTE LIKE CHICKEN, WHY NOT JUST EAT CHICKEN AND LEAVE THE FROGS OUT OF IT?
TO AN AMERICAN, EVERYTHING TASTES LIKE CHICKEN!
HEY!

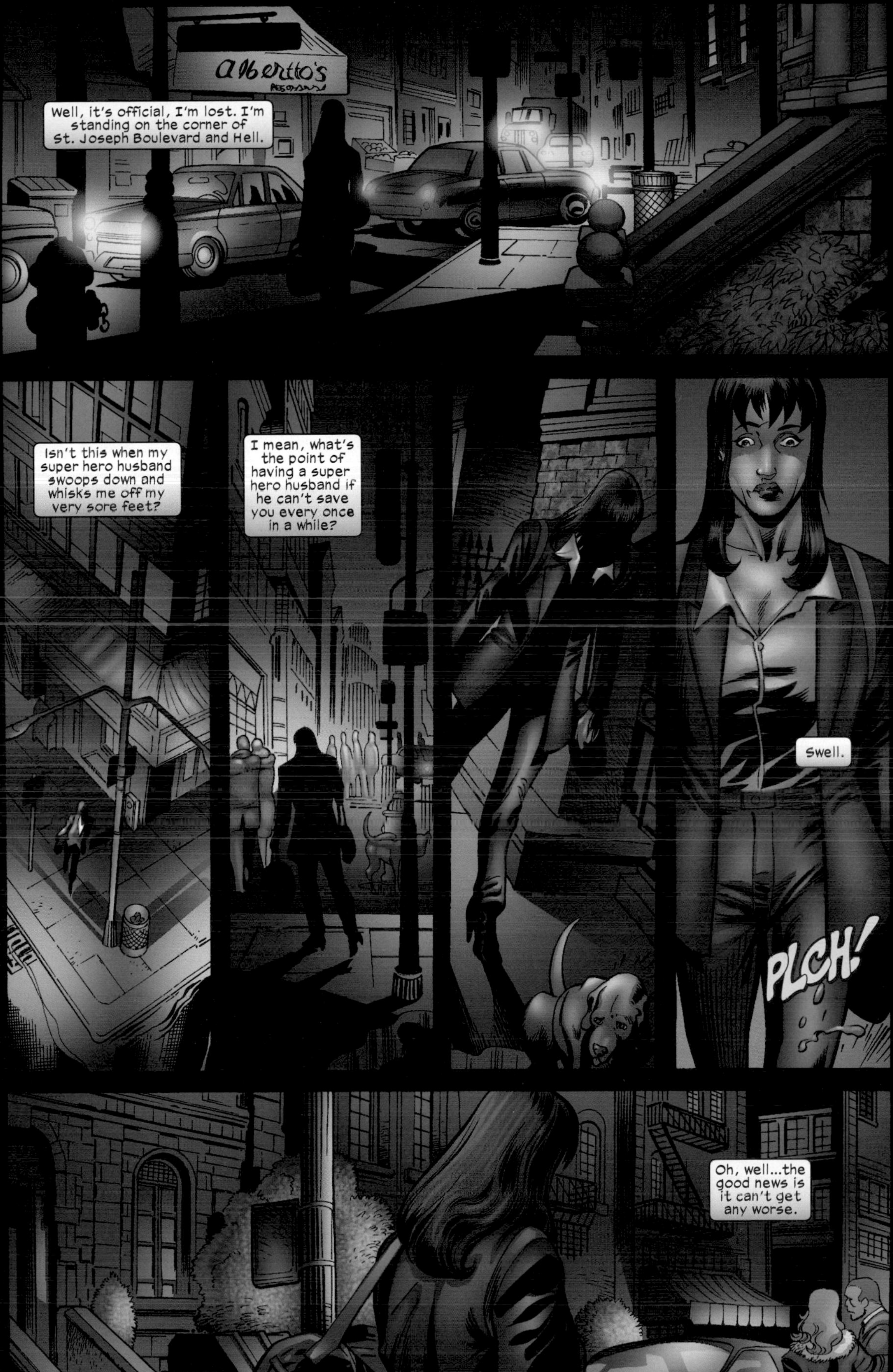
Albertto's
Well, it's official, I'm lost. I'm standing on the corner of St. Joseph Boulevard and Hell.
Isn't this when my super hero husband swoops down and whisks me off my very sore feet?
I mean, what's the point of having a super hero husband if he can't save you every once in a while?
Swell.
PLCH!
Oh, well...the good news is it can't get any worse.

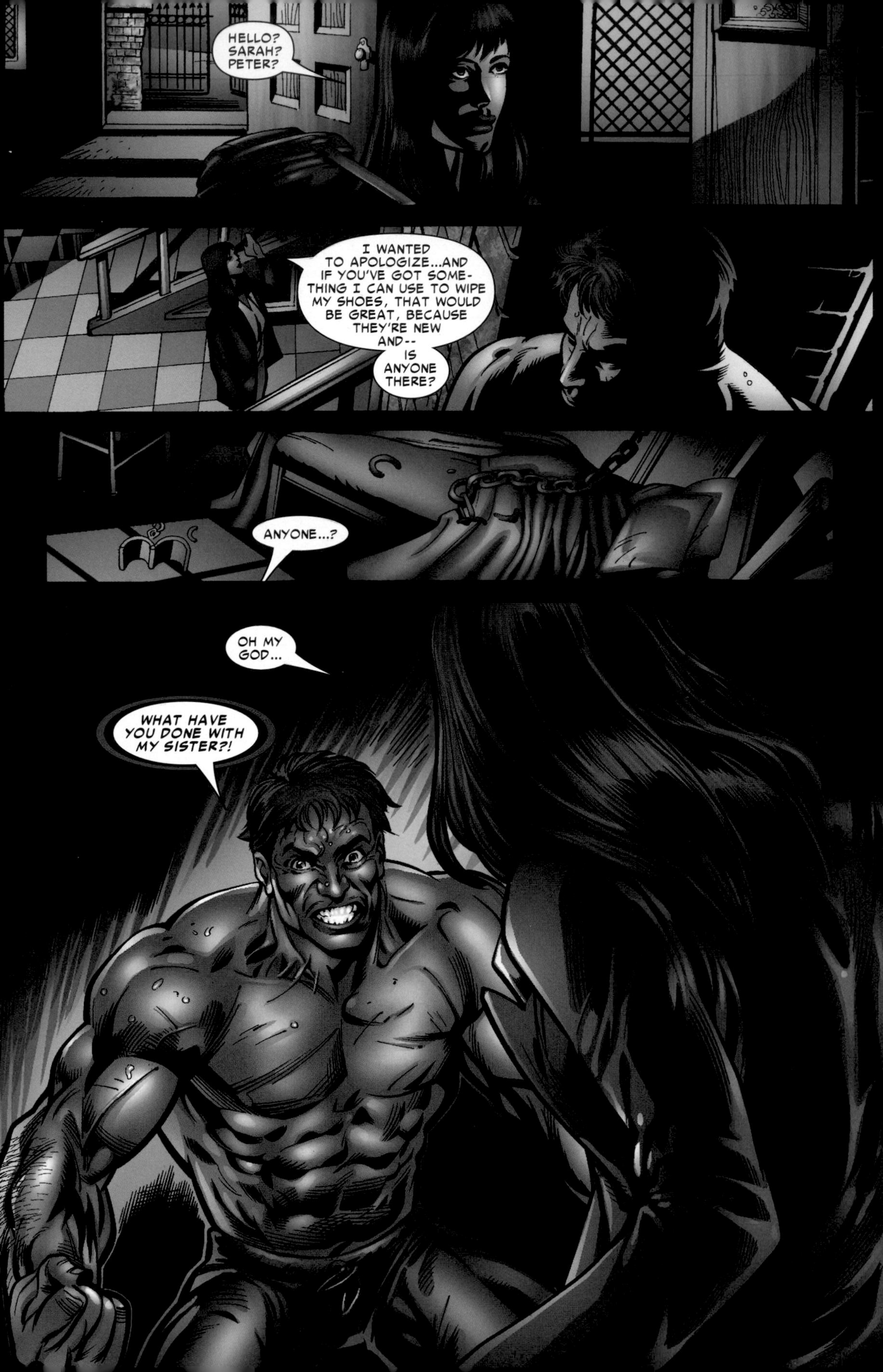
HELLO? SARAH? PETER?
I WANTED TO APOLOGIZE...AND IF YOU'VE GOT SOME-THING I CAN USE TO WIPE MY SHOES, THAT WOULD BE GREAT, BECAUSE THEY'RE NEW AND--
IS ANYONE THERE?
ANYONE...?
OH MY GOD...
WHAT HAVE YOU DONE WITH MY SISTER?!

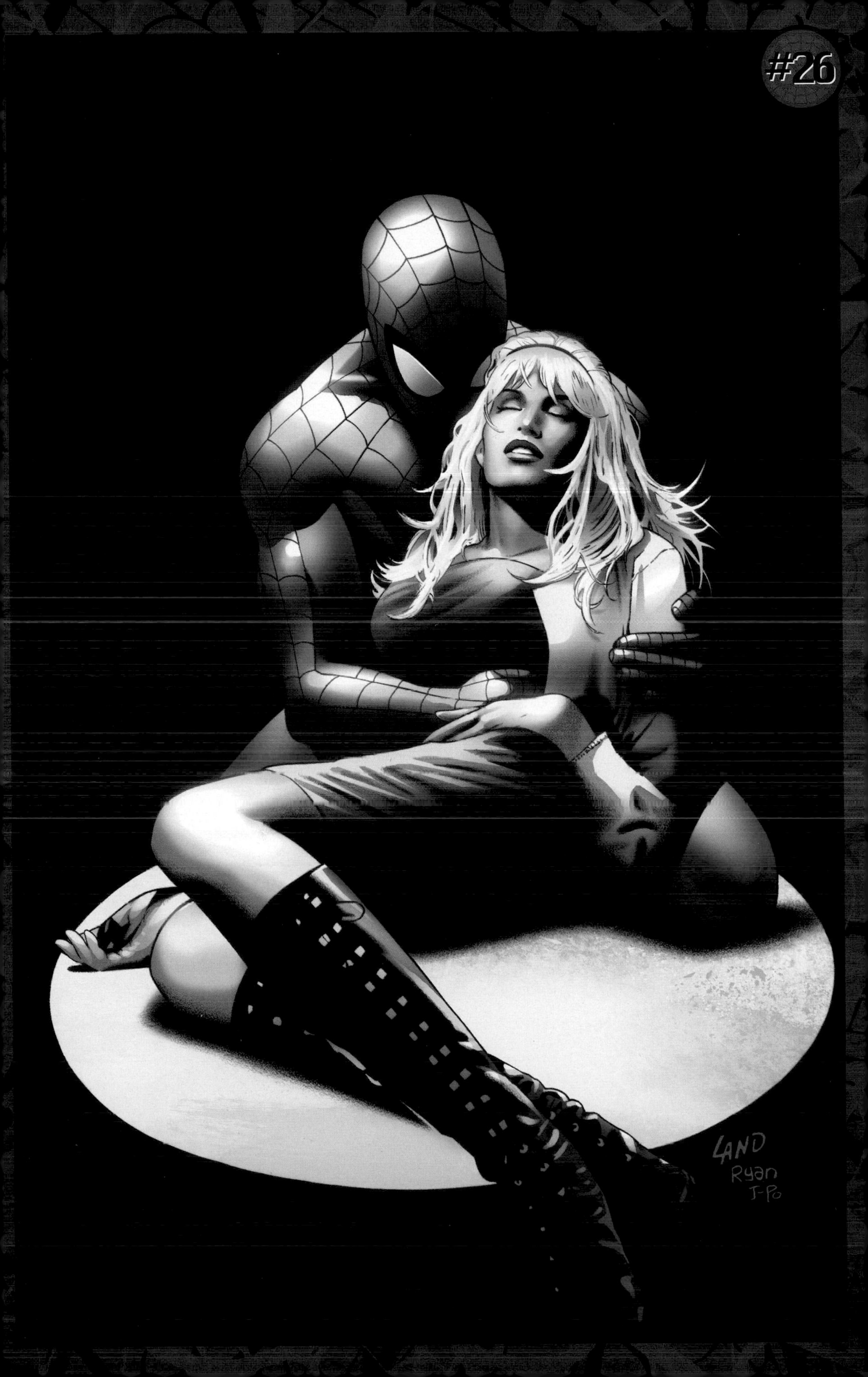
#26
LAND
Ryan
J-Po

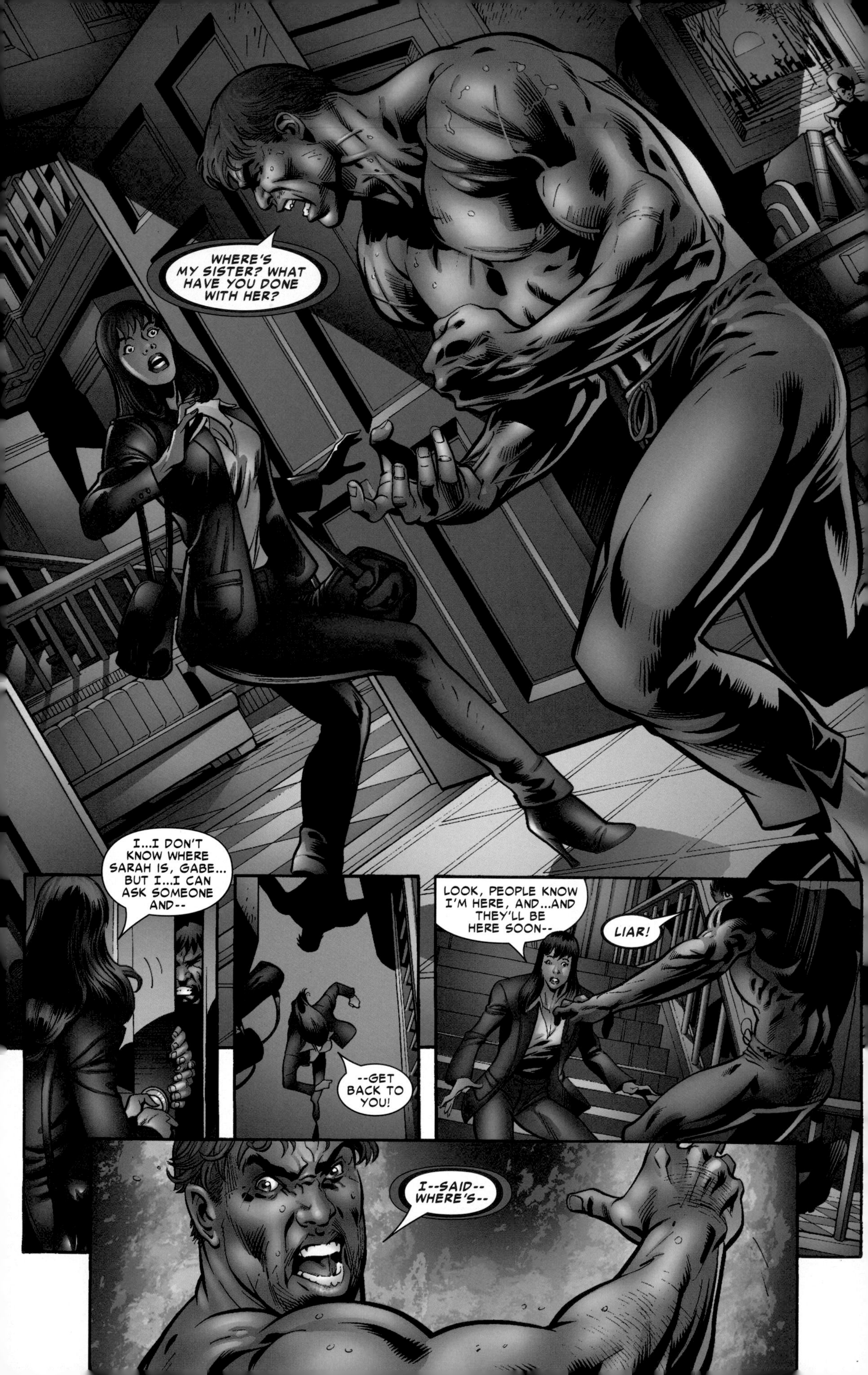
WHERE'S MY SISTER? WHAT HAVE YOU DONE WITH HER?
I...I DON'T KNOW WHERE SARAH IS, GABE... BUT I...I CAN ASK SOMEONE AND--
--GET BACK TO YOU!
LOOK, PEOPLE KNOW I'M HERE, AND...AND THEY'LL BE HERE SOON--
LIAR!
I--SAID-- WHERE'S--

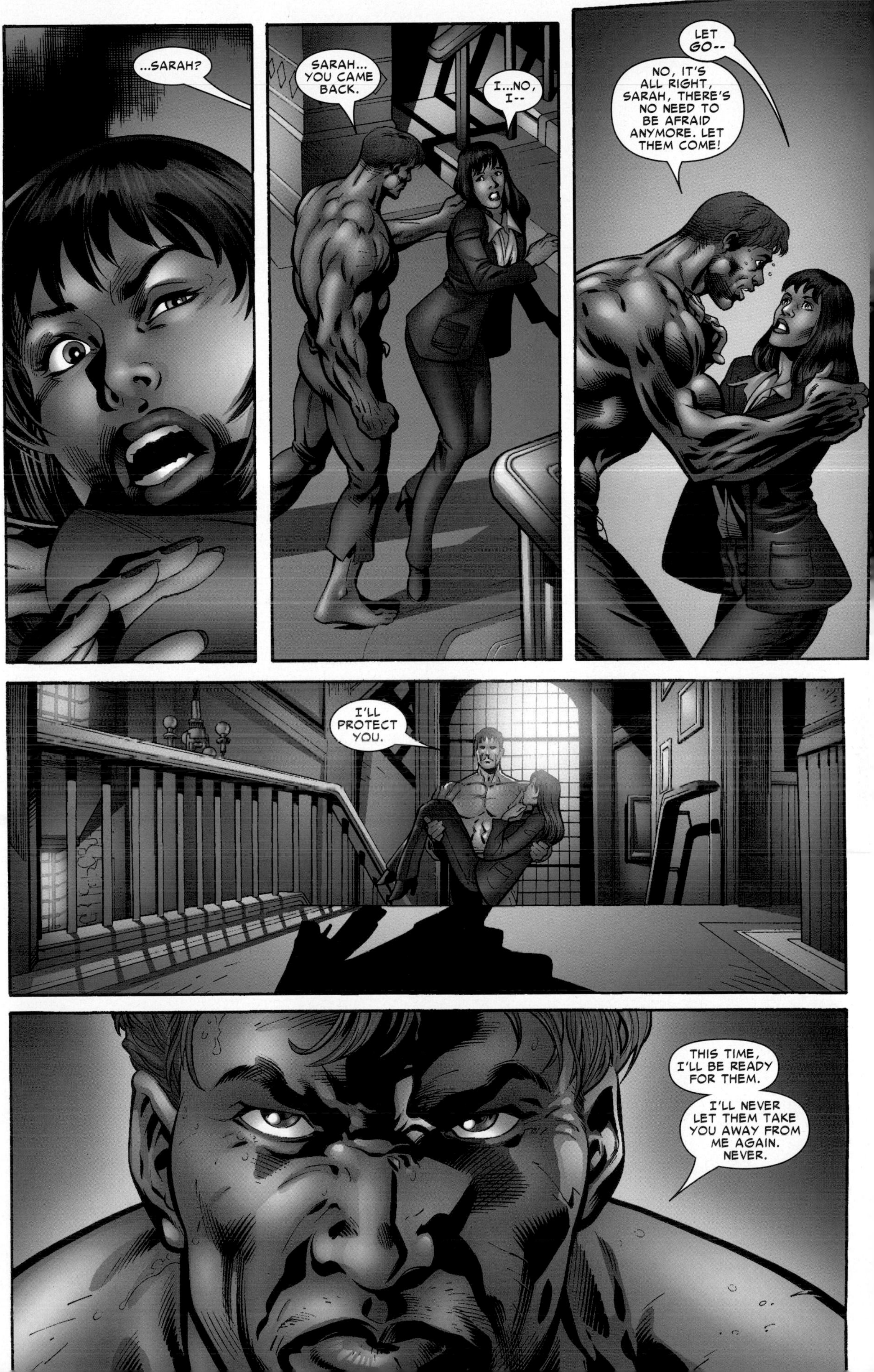
...SARAH?
SARAH... YOU CAME BACK.
I...NO, I--
LET GO--
NO, IT'S ALL RIGHT, SARAH, THERE'S NO NEED TO BE AFRAID ANYMORE. LET THEM COME!
I'LL PROTECT YOU.
THIS TIME, I'LL BE READY FOR THEM.
I'LL NEVER LET THEM TAKE YOU AWAY FROM ME AGAIN. NEVER.

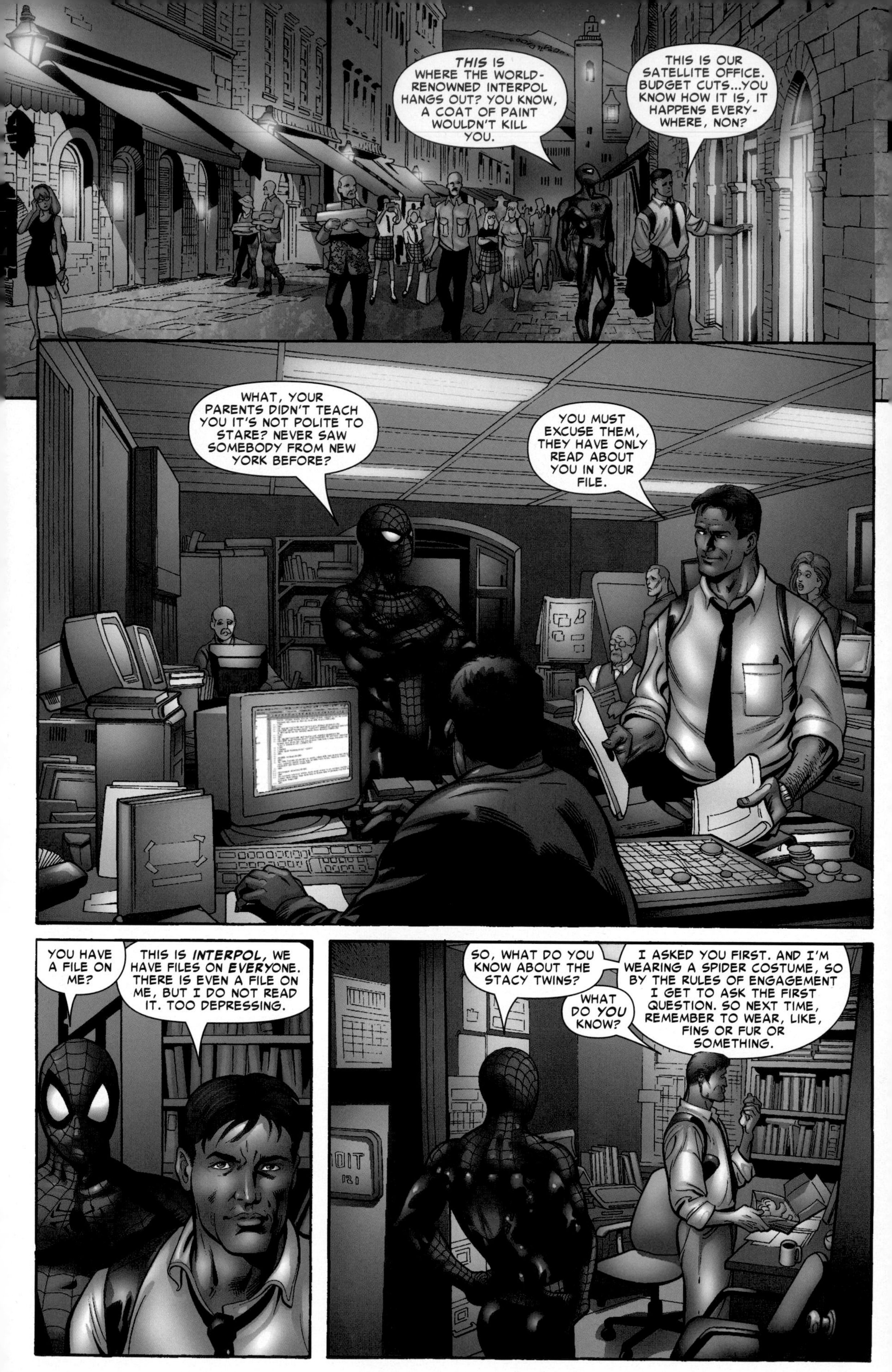
THIS IS WHERE THE WORLD-RENOWNED INTERPOL HANGS OUT? YOU KNOW, A COAT OF PAINT WOULDN'T KILL YOU.
THIS IS OUR SATELLITE OFFICE. BUDGET CUTS...YOU KNOW HOW IT IS, IT HAPPENS EVERY-WHERE, NON?
WHAT, YOUR PARENTS DIDN'T TEACH YOU IT'S NOT POLITE TO STARE? NEVER SAW SOMEBODY FROM NEW YORK BEFORE?
YOU MUST EXCUSE THEM, THEY HAVE ONLY READ ABOUT YOU IN YOUR FILE.
YOU HAVE A FILE ON ME?
THIS IS INTERPOL, WE HAVE FILES ON EVERYONE. THERE IS EVEN A FILE ON ME, BUT I DO NOT READ IT. TOO DEPRESSING.
SO, WHAT DO YOU KNOW ABOUT THE STACY TWINS?
WHAT DO YOU KNOW?
I ASKED YOU FIRST. AND I'M WEARING A SPIDER COSTUME, SO BY THE RULES OF ENGAGEMENT I GET TO ASK THE FIRST QUESTION. SO NEXT TIME, REMEMBER TO WEAR, LIKE, FINS OR FUR OR SOMETHING.

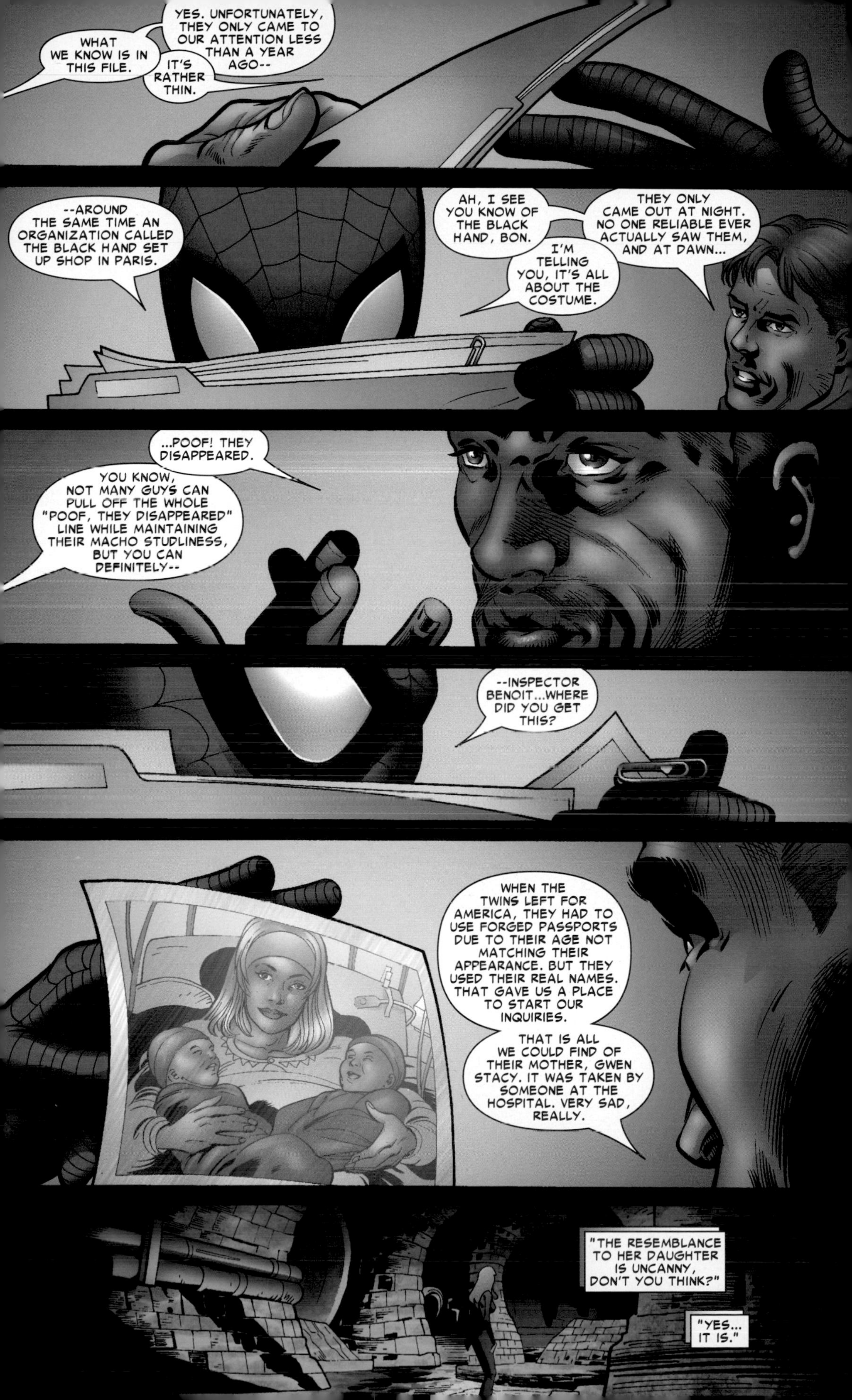
WHAT WE KNOW IS IN THIS FILE.
YES. UNFORTUNATELY, THEY ONLY CAME TO OUR ATTENTION LESS THAN A YEAR AGO--
IT'S RATHER THIN.
--AROUND THE SAME TIME AN ORGANIZATION CALLED THE BLACK HAND SET UP SHOP IN PARIS.
AH, I SEE YOU KNOW OF THE BLACK HAND, BON.
THEY ONLY CAME OUT AT NIGHT. NO ONE RELIABLE EVER ACTUALLY SAW THEM, AND AT DAWN...
I'M TELLING YOU, IT'S ALL ABOUT THE COSTUME.
...POOF! THEY DISAPPEARED.
YOU KNOW, NOT MANY GUYS CAN PULL OFF THE WHOLE "POOF, THEY DISAPPEARED" LINE WHILE MAINTAINING THEIR MACHO STUDLINESS, BUT YOU CAN DEFINITELY--
--INSPECTOR BENOIT...WHERE DID YOU GET THIS?
WHEN THE TWINS LEFT FOR AMERICA, THEY HAD TO USE FORGED PASSPORTS DUE TO THEIR AGE NOT MATCHING THEIR APPEARANCE. BUT THEY USED THEIR REAL NAMES. THAT GAVE US A PLACE TO START OUR INQUIRIES.
THAT IS ALL WE COULD FIND OF THEIR MOTHER, GWEN STACY. IT WAS TAKEN BY SOMEONE AT THE HOSPITAL. VERY SAD, REALLY.
"THE RESEMBLANCE TO HER DAUGHTER IS UNCANNY, DON'T YOU THINK?"
"YES... IT IS."

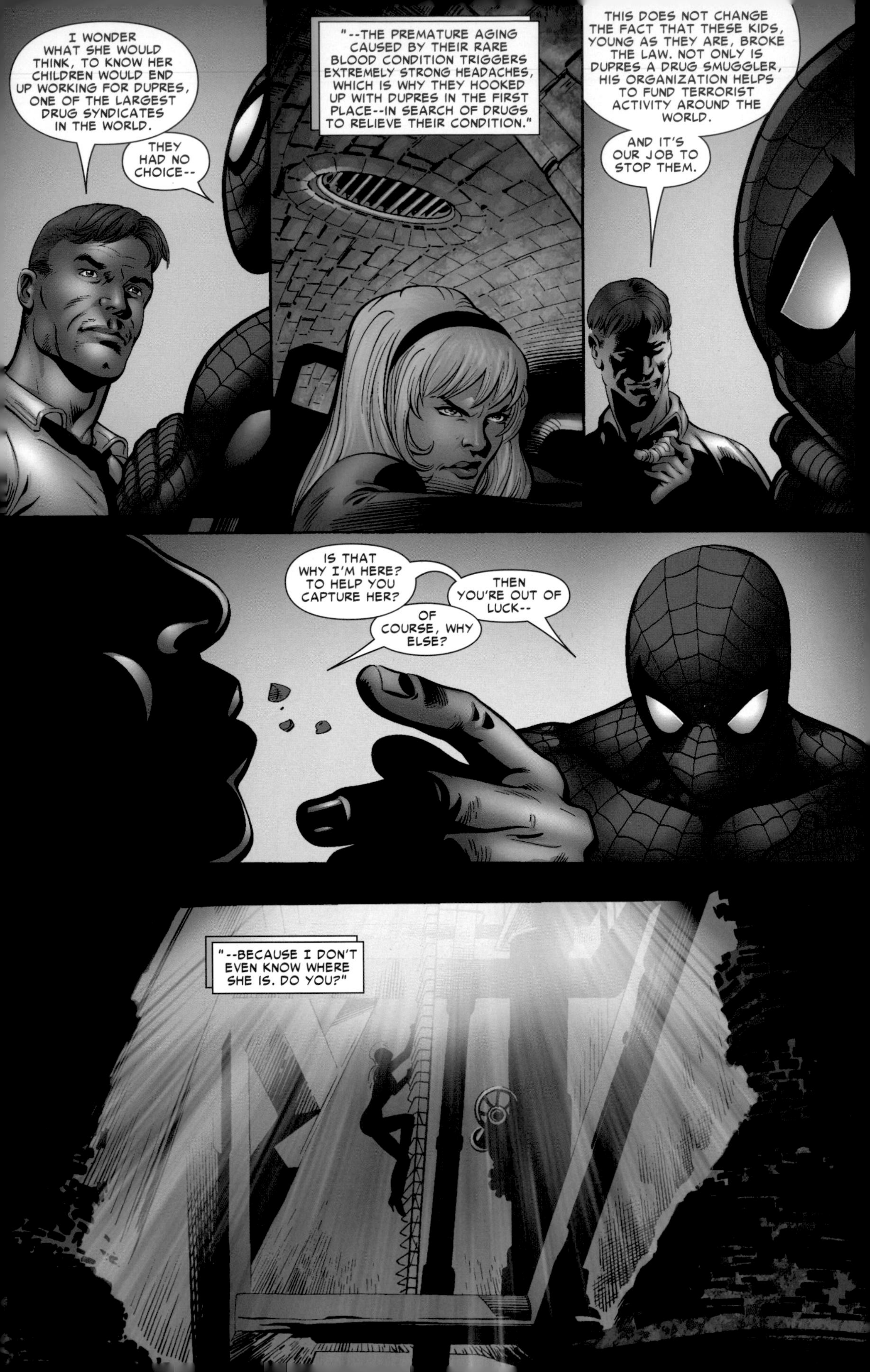
I WONDER WHAT SHE WOULD THINK, TO KNOW HER CHILDREN WOULD END UP WORKING FOR DUPRES, ONE OF THE LARGEST DRUG SYNDICATES IN THE WORLD.
THEY HAD NO CHOICE--
"--THE PREMATURE AGING CAUSED BY THEIR RARE BLOOD CONDITION TRIGGERS EXTREMELY STRONG HEADACHES, WHICH IS WHY THEY HOOKED UP WITH DUPRES IN THE FIRST PLACE--IN SEARCH OF DRUGS TO RELIEVE THEIR CONDITION."
THIS DOES NOT CHANGE THE FACT THAT THESE KIDS, YOUNG AS THEY ARE, BROKE THE LAW. NOT ONLY IS DUPRES A DRUG SMUGGLER, HIS ORGANIZATION HELPS TO FUND TERRORIST ACTIVITY AROUND THE WORLD.
AND IT'S OUR JOB TO STOP THEM.
IS THAT WHY I'M HERE? TO HELP YOU CAPTURE HER?
OF COURSE, WHY ELSE?
THEN YOU'RE OUT OF LUCK--
"--BECAUSE I DON'T EVEN KNOW WHERE SHE IS. DO YOU?"

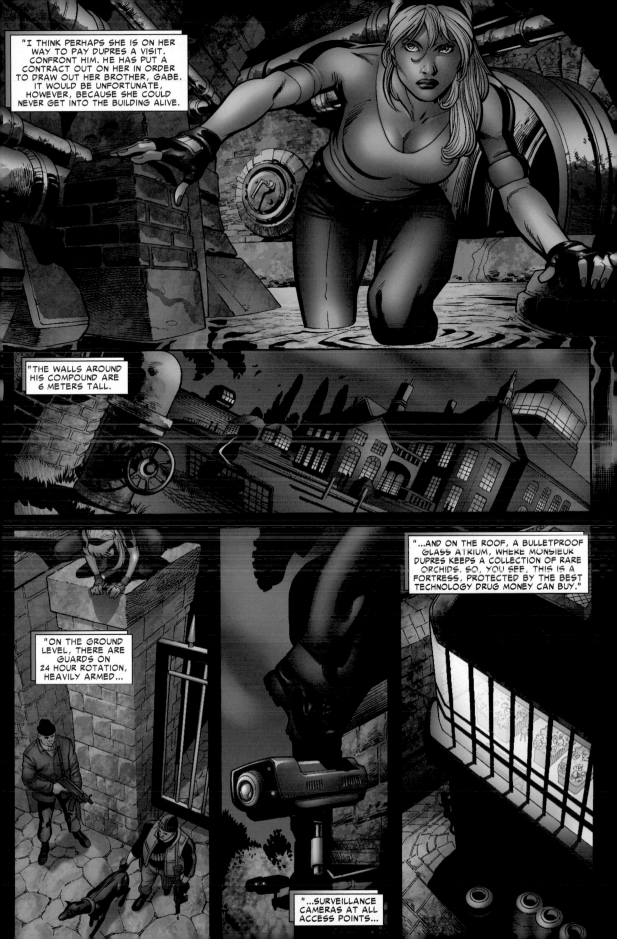

"I THINK PERHAPS SHE IS ON HER WAY TO PAY DUPRES A VISIT. CONFRONT HIM. HE HAS PUT A CONTRACT OUT ON HER IN ORDER TO DRAW OUT HER BROTHER, GABE. IT WOULD BE UNFORTUNATE, HOWEVER, BECAUSE SHE COULD NEVER GET INTO THE BUILDING ALIVE.

"THE WALLS AROUND HIS COMPOUND ARE 6 METERS TALL.

"...AND ON THE ROOF, A BULLETPROOF GLASS ATRIUM, WHERE MONSIEUR DUPRES KEEPS A COLLECTION OF RARE ORCHIDS. SO, YOU SEE, THIS IS A FORTRESS, PROTECTED BY THE BEST TECHNOLOGY DRUG MONEY CAN BUY."

"ON THE GROUND LEVEL, THERE ARE GUARDS ON 24 HOUR ROTATION, HEAVILY ARMED...

"...SURVEILLANCE CAMERAS AT ALL ACCESS POINTS...

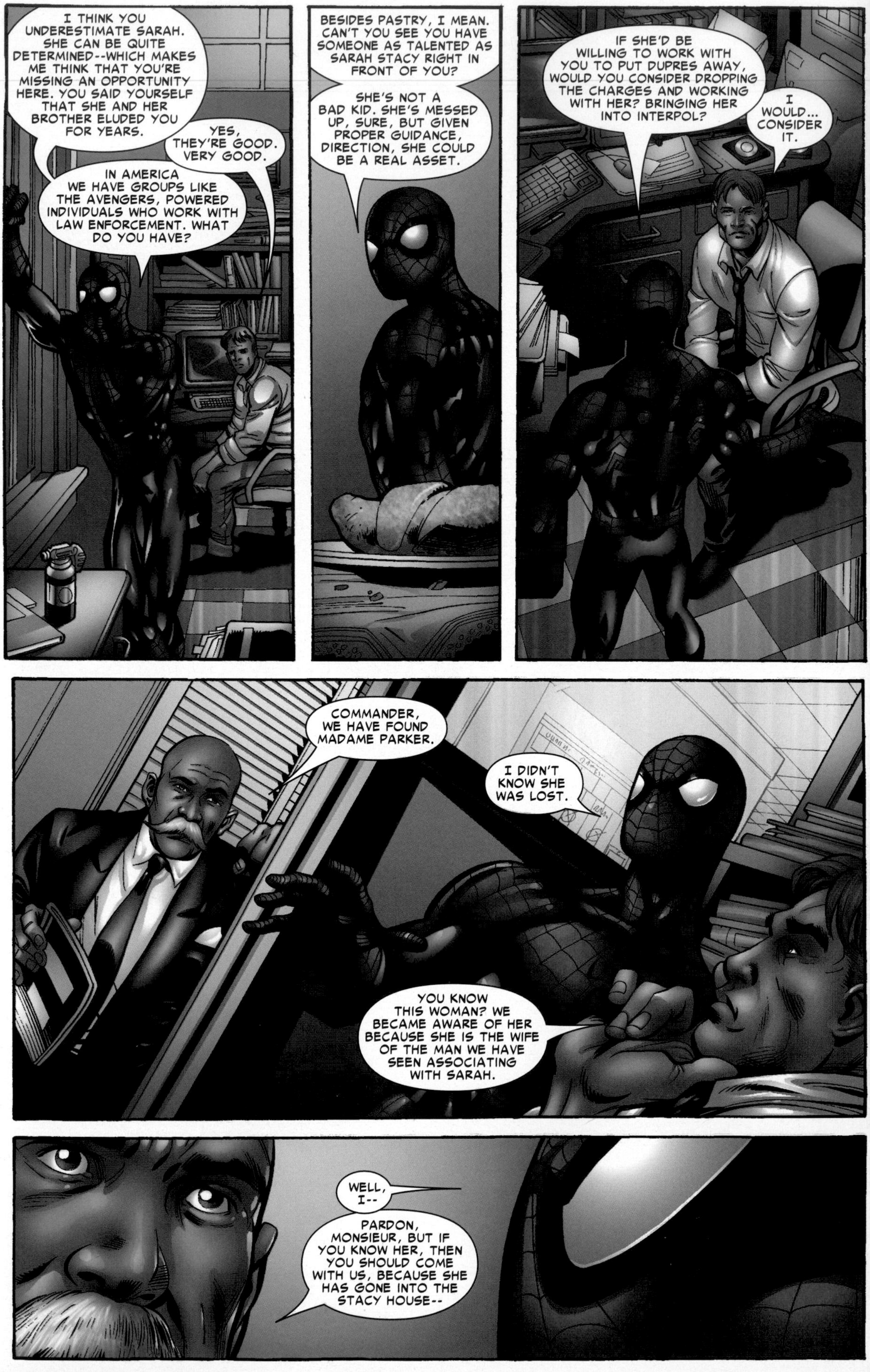
I THINK YOU UNDERESTIMATE SARAH. SHE CAN BE QUITE DETERMINED--WHICH MAKES ME THINK THAT YOU'RE MISSING AN OPPORTUNITY HERE. YOU SAID YOURSELF THAT SHE AND HER BROTHER ELUDED YOU FOR YEARS.
YES, THEY'RE GOOD. VERY GOOD.
IN AMERICA WE HAVE GROUPS LIKE THE AVENGERS, POWERED INDIVIDUALS WHO WORK WITH LAW ENFORCEMENT. WHAT DO YOU HAVE?
BESIDES PASTRY, I MEAN. CAN'T YOU SEE YOU HAVE SOMEONE AS TALENTED AS SARAH STACY RIGHT IN FRONT OF YOU?
SHE'S NOT A BAD KID. SHE'S MESSED UP, SURE, BUT GIVEN PROPER GUIDANCE, DIRECTION, SHE COULD BE A REAL ASSET.
IF SHE'D BE WILLING TO WORK WITH YOU TO PUT DUPRES AWAY, WOULD YOU CONSIDER DROPPING THE CHARGES AND WORKING WITH HER? BRINGING HER INTO INTERPOL?
I WOULD... CONSIDER IT.
COMMANDER, WE HAVE FOUND MADAME PARKER.
I DIDN'T KNOW SHE WAS LOST.
YOU KNOW THIS WOMAN? WE BECAME AWARE OF HER BECAUSE SHE IS THE WIFE OF THE MAN WE HAVE SEEN ASSOCIATING WITH SARAH.
WELL, I--
PARDON, MONSIEUR, BUT IF YOU KNOW HER, THEN YOU SHOULD COME WITH US, BECAUSE SHE HAS GONE INTO THE STACY HOUSE--

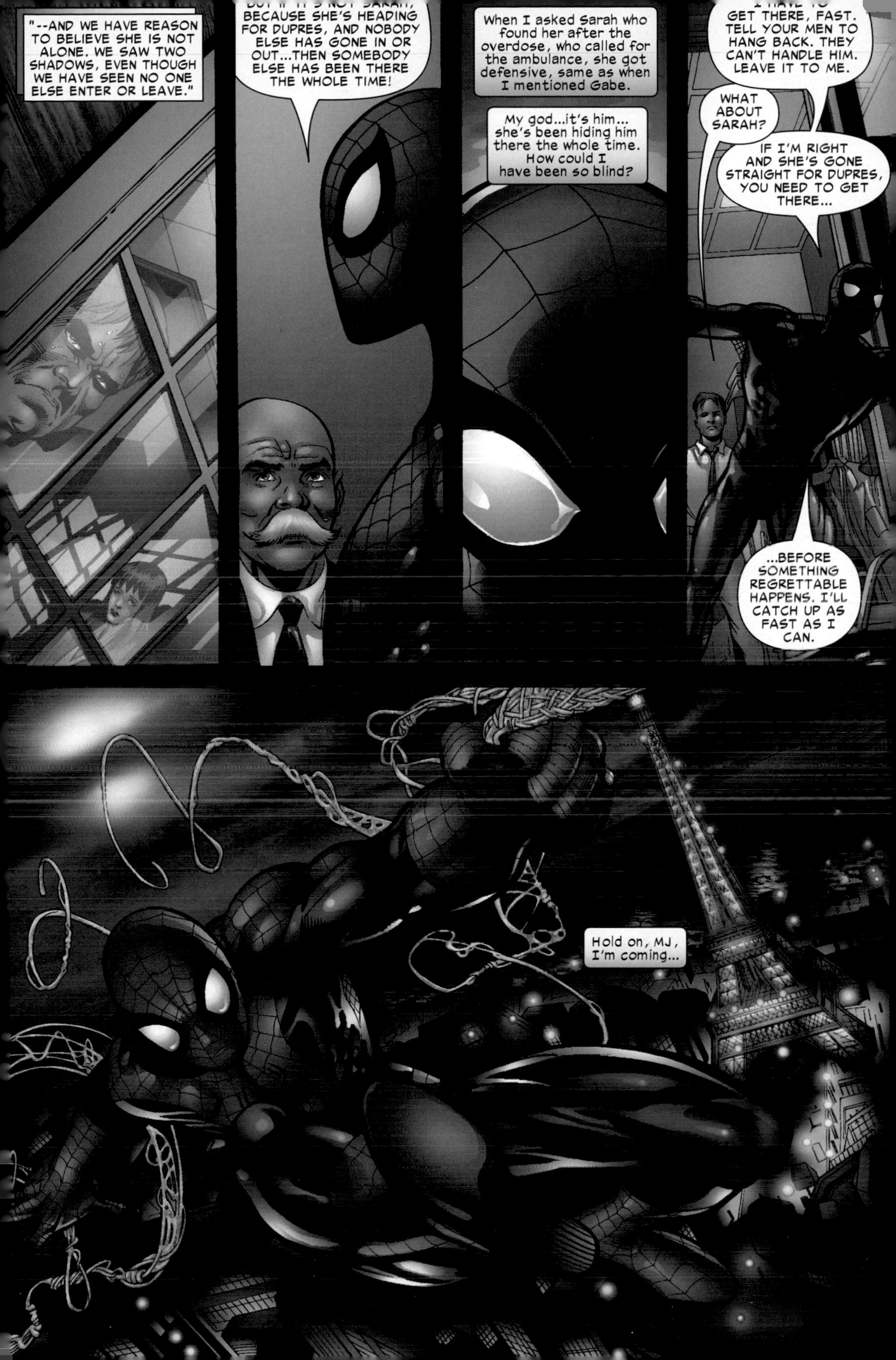
"--AND WE HAVE REASON TO BELIEVE SHE IS NOT ALONE. WE SAW TWO SHADOWS, EVEN THOUGH WE HAVE SEEN NO ONE ELSE ENTER OR LEAVE."
BECAUSE SHE'S HEADING FOR DUPRES, AND NOBODY ELSE HAS GONE IN OR OUT...THEN SOMEBODY ELSE HAS BEEN THERE THE WHOLE TIME!
When I asked Sarah who found her after the overdose, who called for the ambulance, she got defensive, same as when I mentioned Gabe.
My god...it's him... she's been hiding him there the whole time. How could I have been so blind?
GET THERE, FAST. TELL YOUR MEN TO HANG BACK. THEY CAN'T HANDLE HIM. LEAVE IT TO ME.
WHAT ABOUT SARAH?
IF I'M RIGHT AND SHE'S GONE STRAIGHT FOR DUPRES, YOU NEED TO GET THERE...
...BEFORE SOMETHING REGRETTABLE HAPPENS. I'LL CATCH UP AS FAST AS I CAN.
Hold on, MJ, I'm coming...

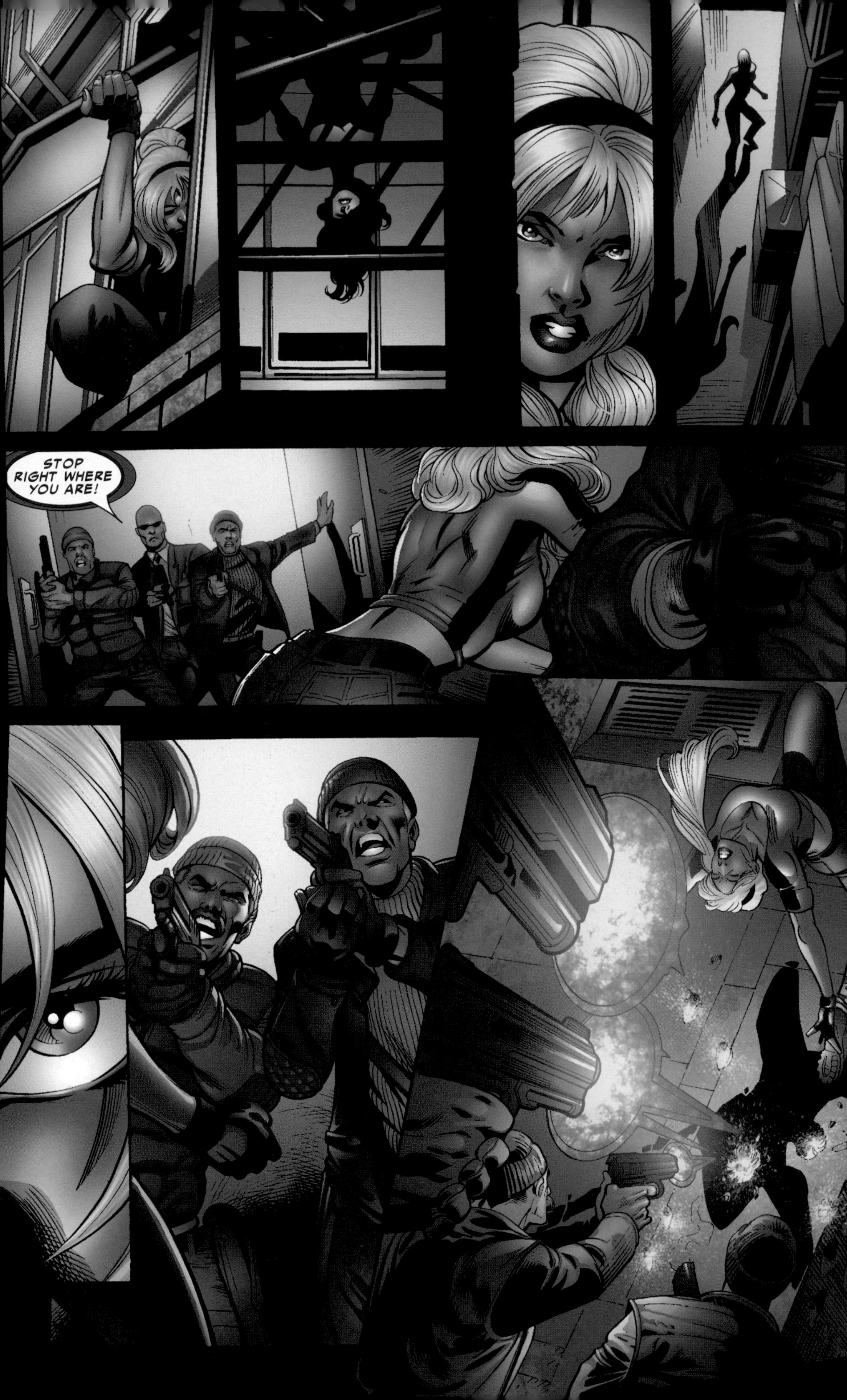
STOP RIGHT WHERE YOU ARE!

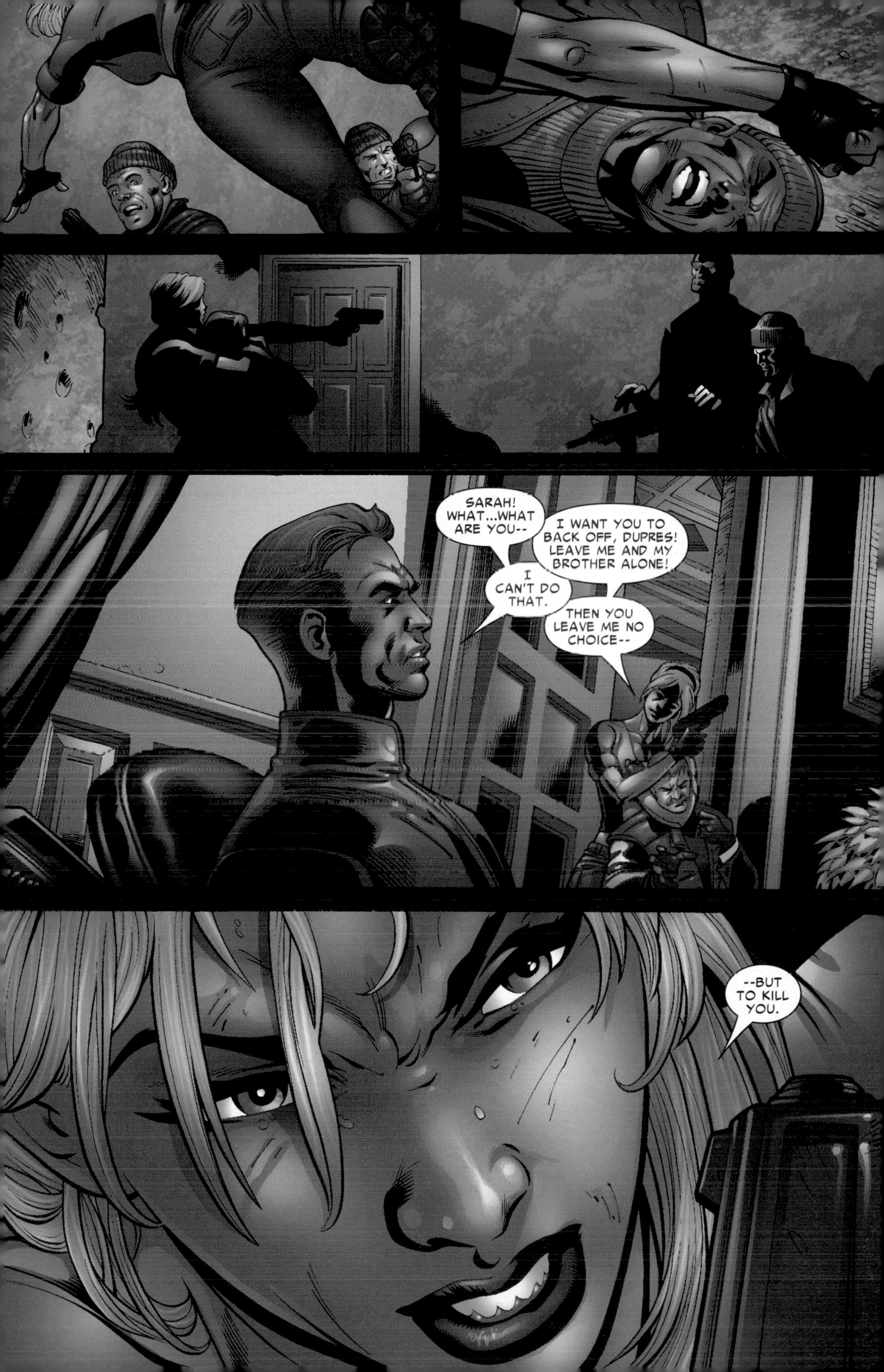
SARAH! WHAT...WHAT ARE YOU--
I WANT YOU TO BACK OFF, DUPRES! LEAVE ME AND MY BROTHER ALONE!
I CAN'T DO THAT.
THEN YOU LEAVE ME NO CHOICE--
--BUT TO KILL YOU.

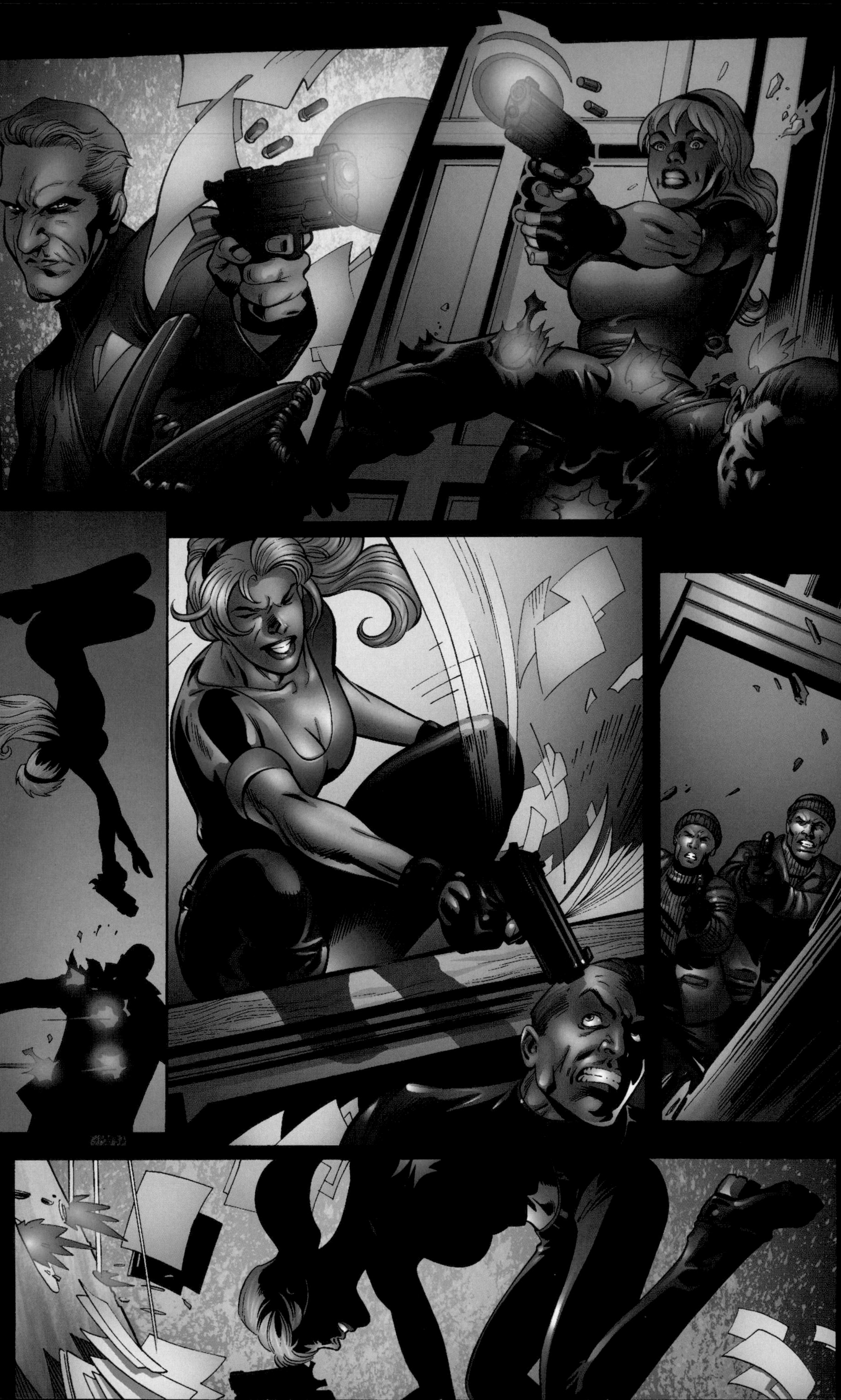

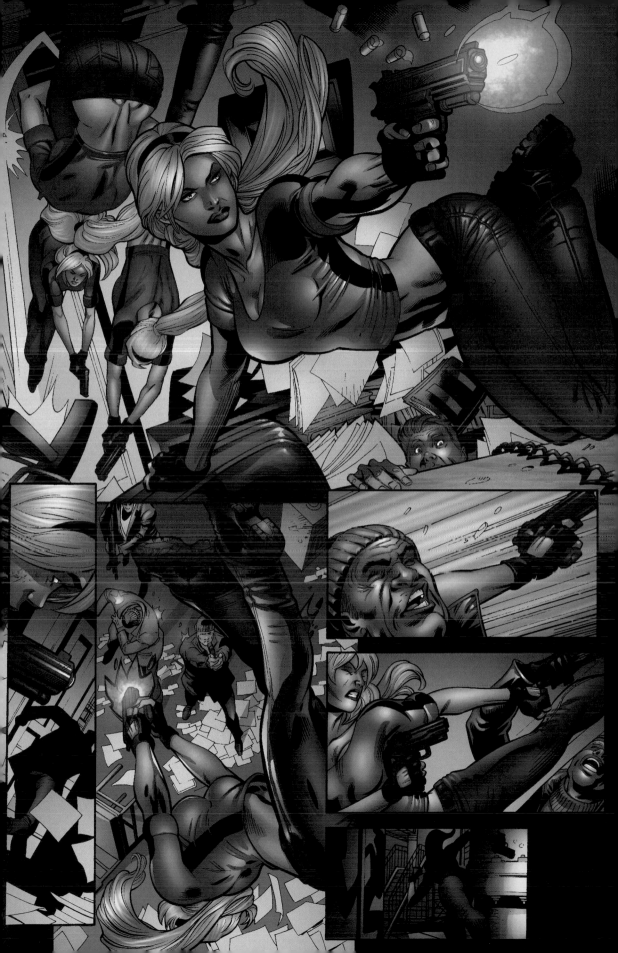

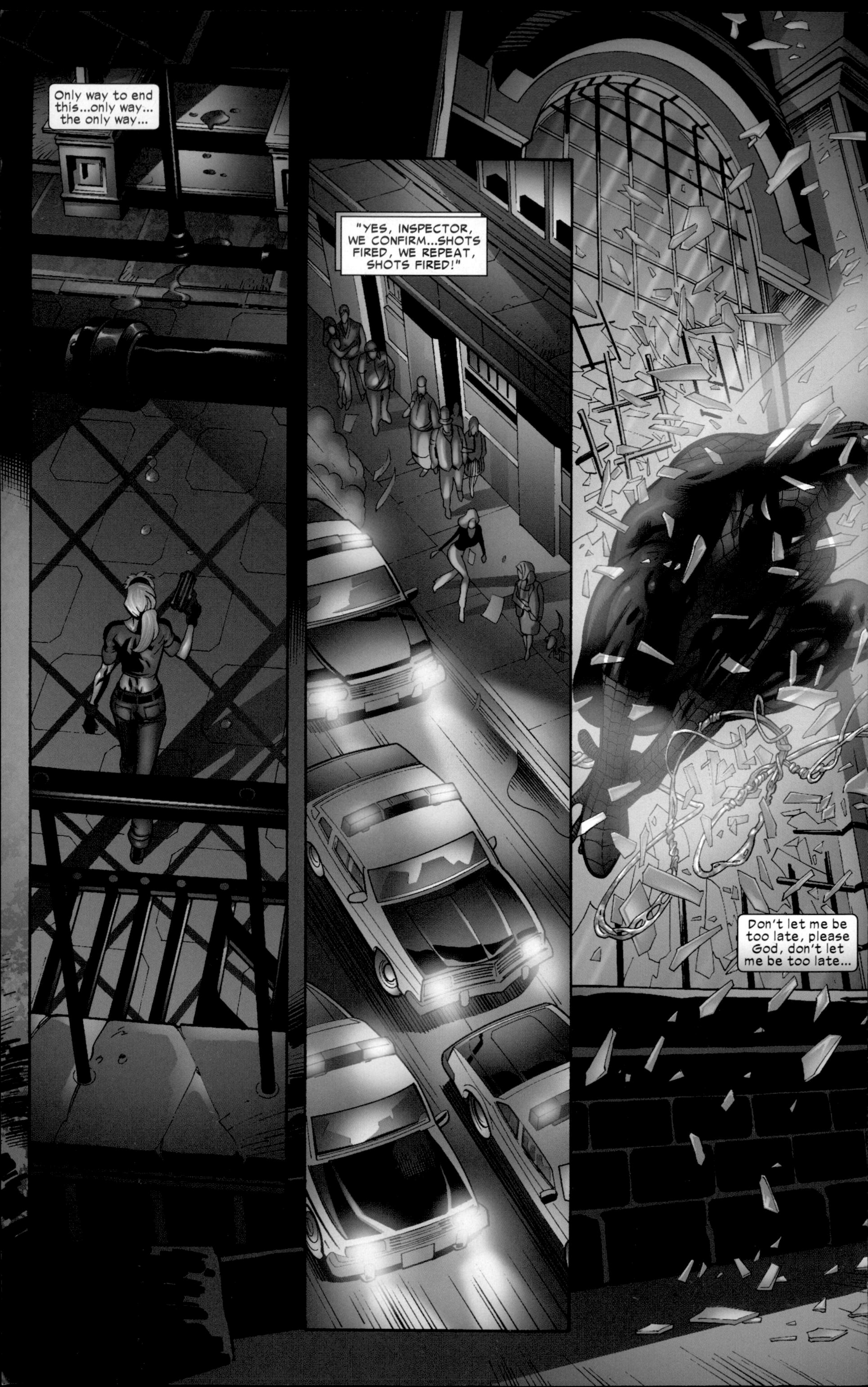
Only way to end this...only way... the only way...
"YES, INSPECTOR, WE CONFIRM...SHOTS FIRED, WE REPEAT, SHOTS FIRED!"
Don't let me be too late, please God, don't let me be too late...

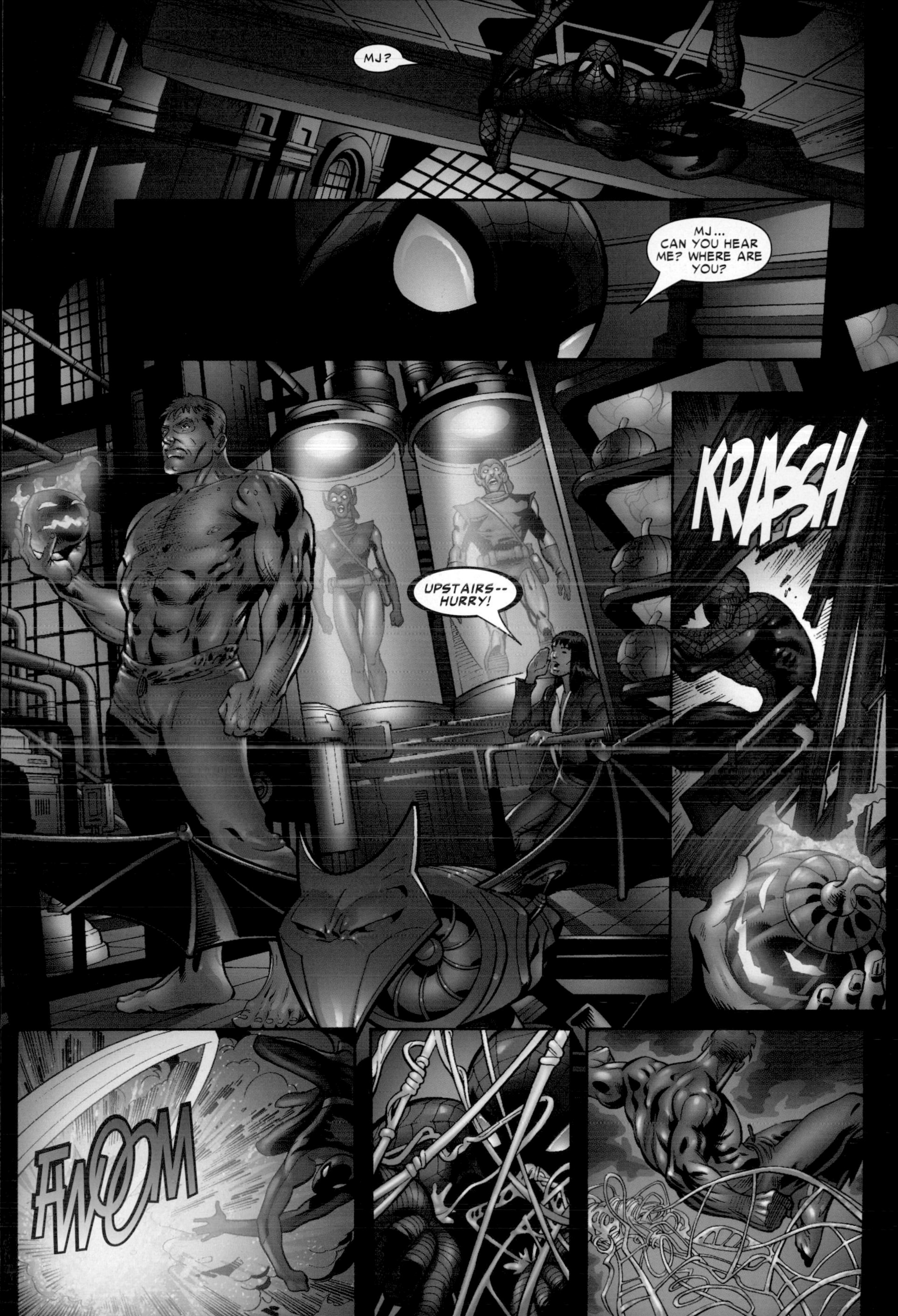
MJ?
MJ... CAN YOU HEAR ME? WHERE ARE YOU?
UPSTAIRS-- HURRY!
KRASCH
FWOOM

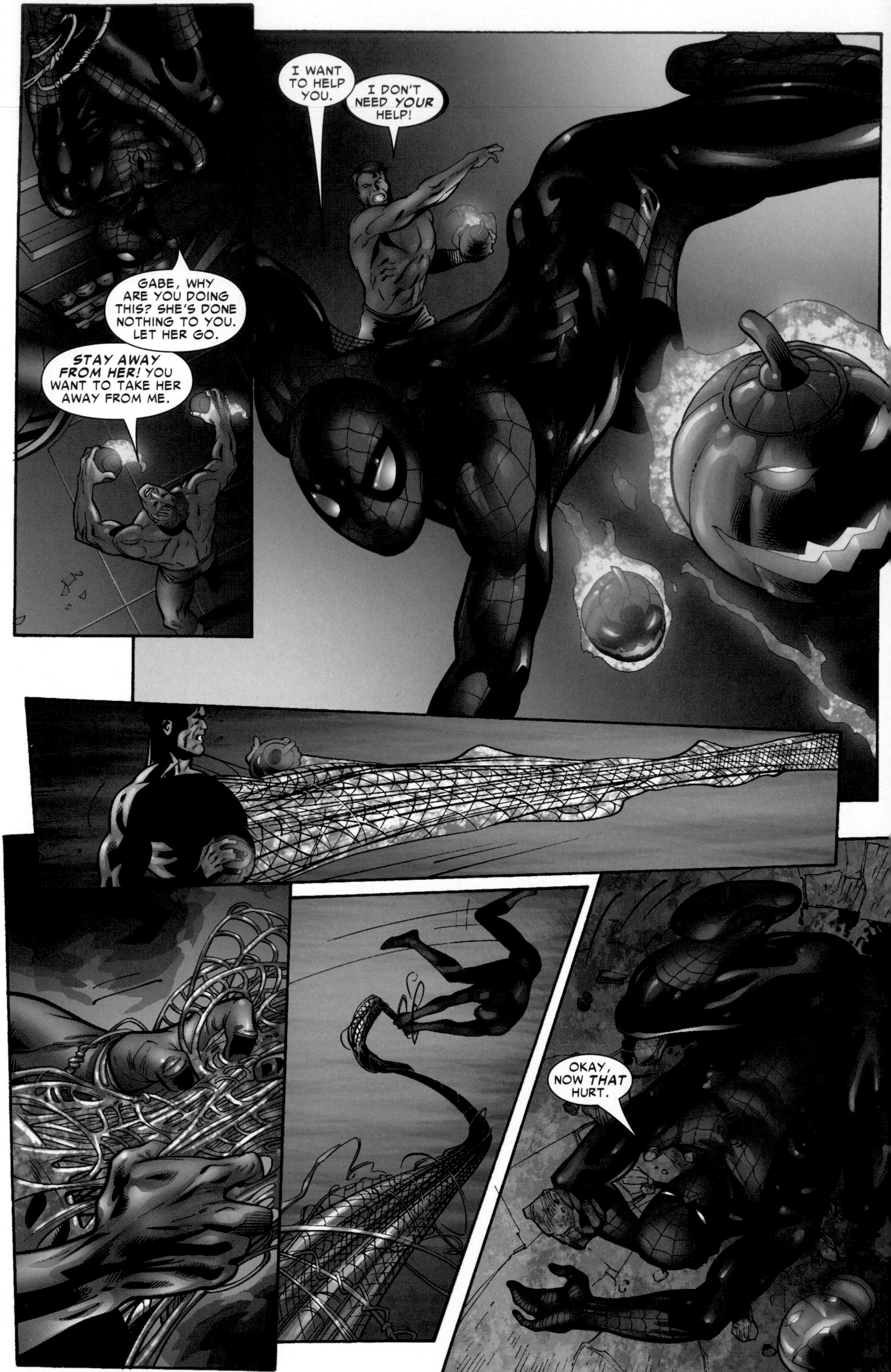
I WANT TO HELP YOU.
I DON'T NEED YOUR HELP!
GABE, WHY ARE YOU DOING THIS? SHE'S DONE NOTHING TO YOU. LET HER GO.
STAY AWAY FROM HER! YOU WANT TO TAKE HER AWAY FROM ME.
OKAY, NOW THAT HURT.

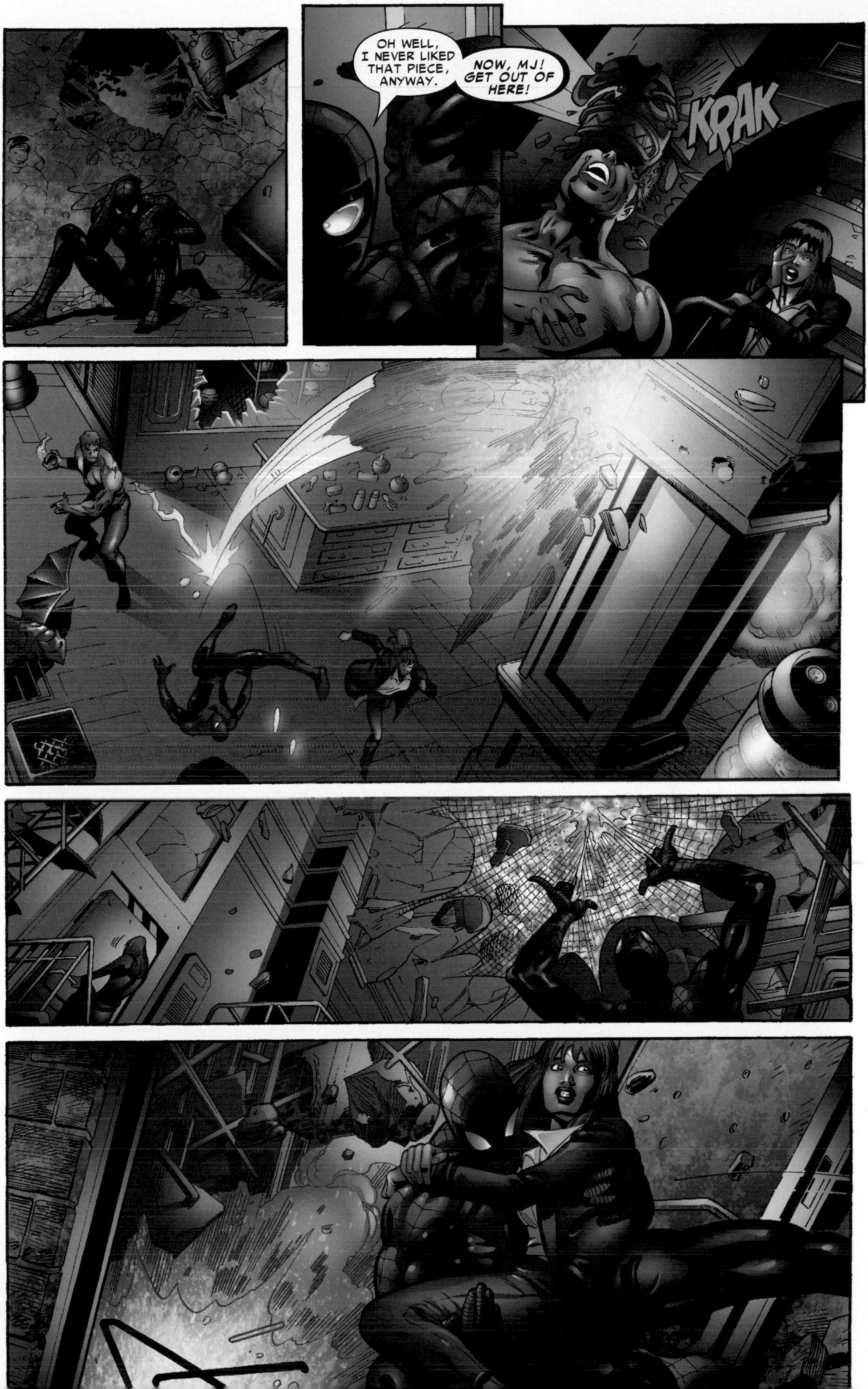
OH WELL, I NEVER LIKED THAT PIECE, ANYWAY.
NOW, MJ! GET OUT OF HERE!
KRAK

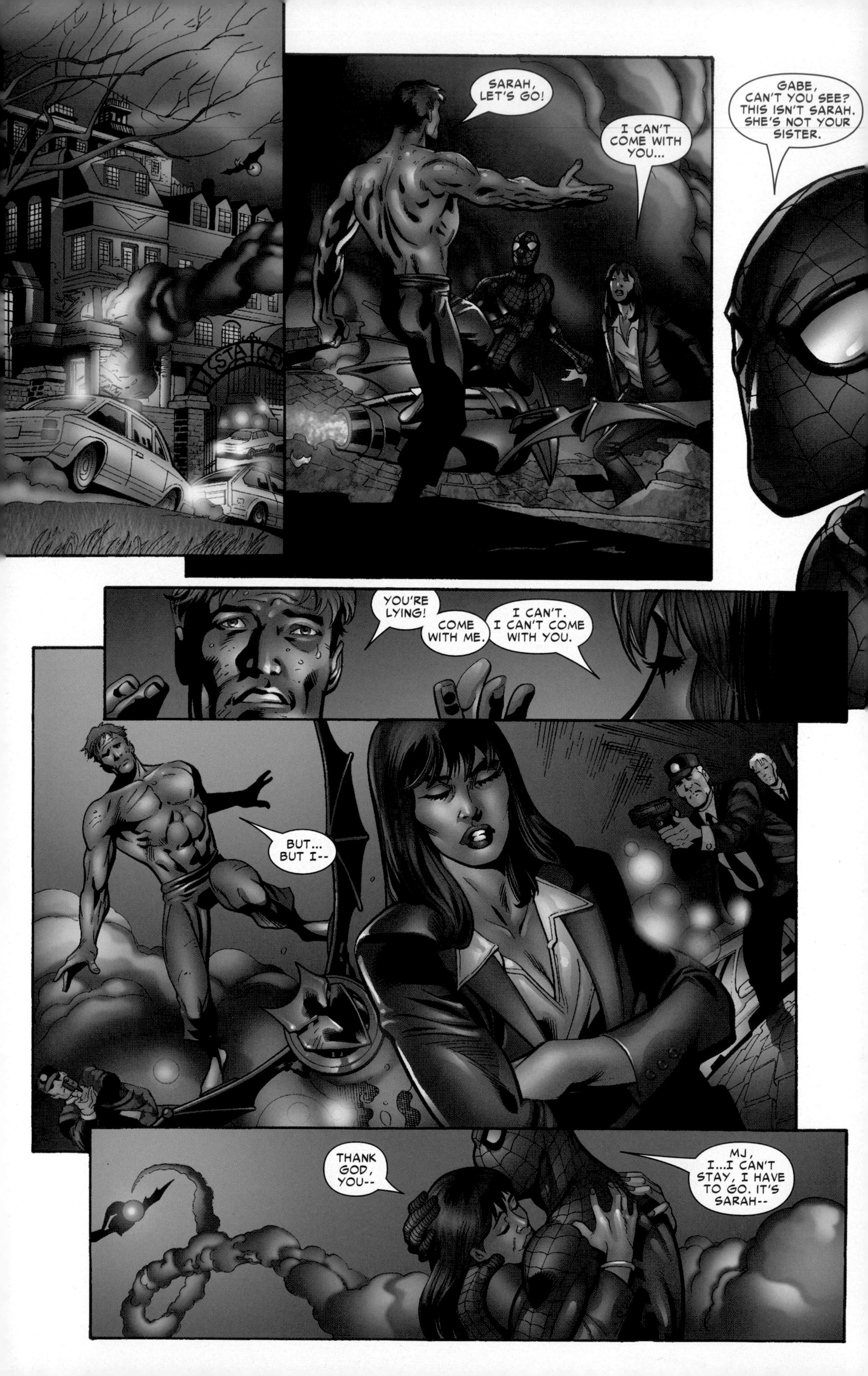
SARAH, LET'S GO!
I CAN'T COME WITH YOU...
GABE, CAN'T YOU SEE? THIS ISN'T SARAH. SHE'S NOT YOUR SISTER.
YOU'RE LYING!
COME WITH ME.
I CAN'T. I CAN'T COME WITH YOU.
BUT... BUT I--
THANK GOD, YOU--
MJ, I...I CAN'T STAY, I HAVE TO GO. IT'S SARAH--

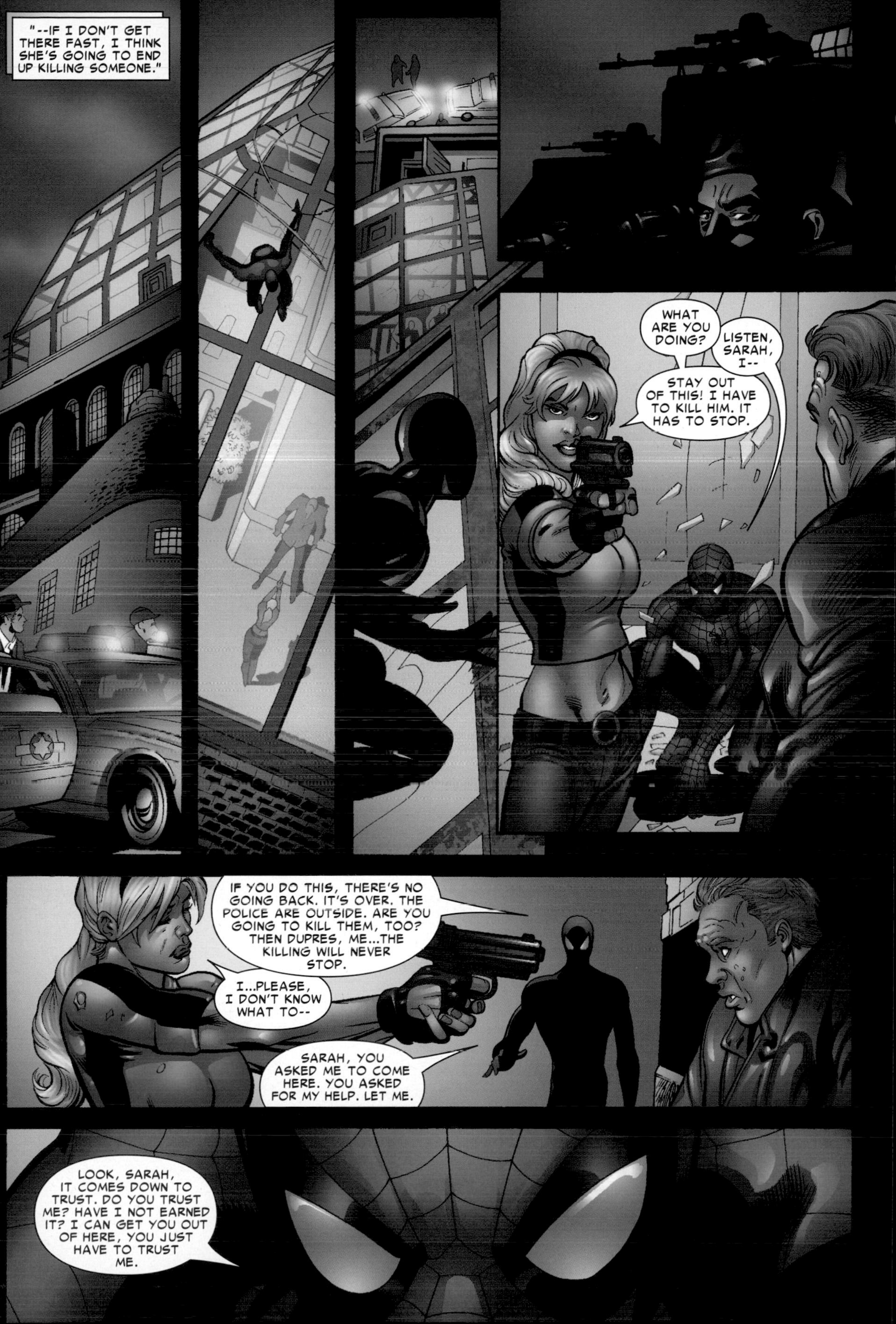
"--IF I DON'T GET THERE FAST, I THINK SHE'S GOING TO END UP KILLING SOMEONE."
WHAT ARE YOU DOING?
LISTEN, SARAH, I--
STAY OUT OF THIS! I HAVE TO KILL HIM. IT HAS TO STOP.
IF YOU DO THIS, THERE'S NO GOING BACK. IT'S OVER. THE POLICE ARE OUTSIDE. ARE YOU GOING TO KILL THEM, TOO? THEN DUPRES, ME...THE KILLING WILL NEVER STOP.
I...PLEASE, I DON'T KNOW WHAT TO--
SARAH, YOU ASKED ME TO COME HERE. YOU ASKED FOR MY HELP. LET ME.
LOOK, SARAH, IT COMES DOWN TO TRUST. DO YOU TRUST ME? HAVE I NOT EARNED IT? I CAN GET YOU OUT OF HERE, YOU JUST HAVE TO TRUST ME.

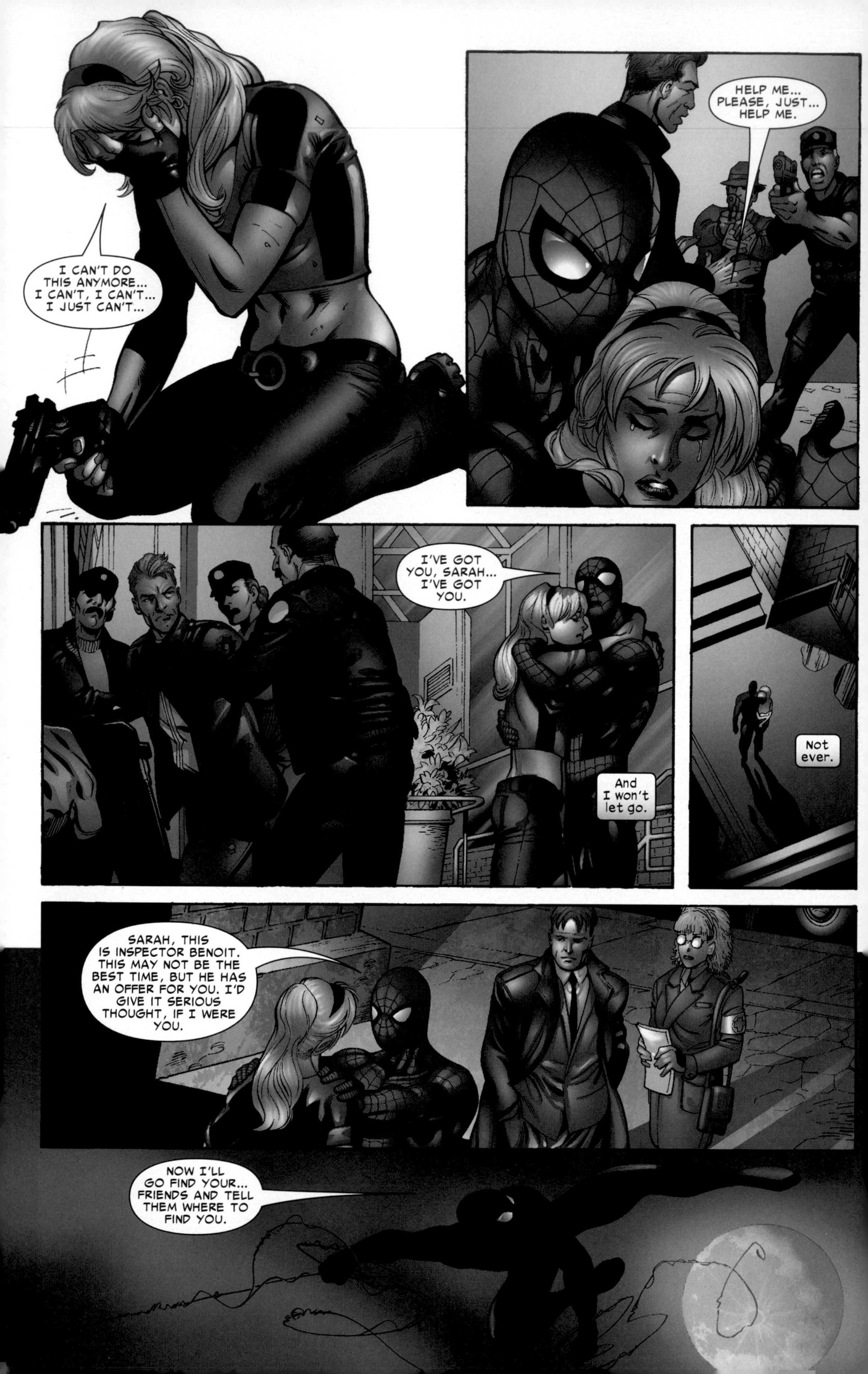
I CAN'T DO THIS ANYMORE... I CAN'T, I CAN'T... I JUST CAN'T...
HELP ME... PLEASE, JUST... HELP ME.
I'VE GOT YOU, SARAH... I'VE GOT YOU.
And I won't let go.
Not ever.
SARAH, THIS IS INSPECTOR BENOIT. THIS MAY NOT BE THE BEST TIME, BUT HE HAS AN OFFER FOR YOU. I'D GIVE IT SERIOUS THOUGHT, IF I WERE YOU.
NOW I'LL GO FIND YOUR... FRIENDS AND TELL THEM WHERE TO FIND YOU.

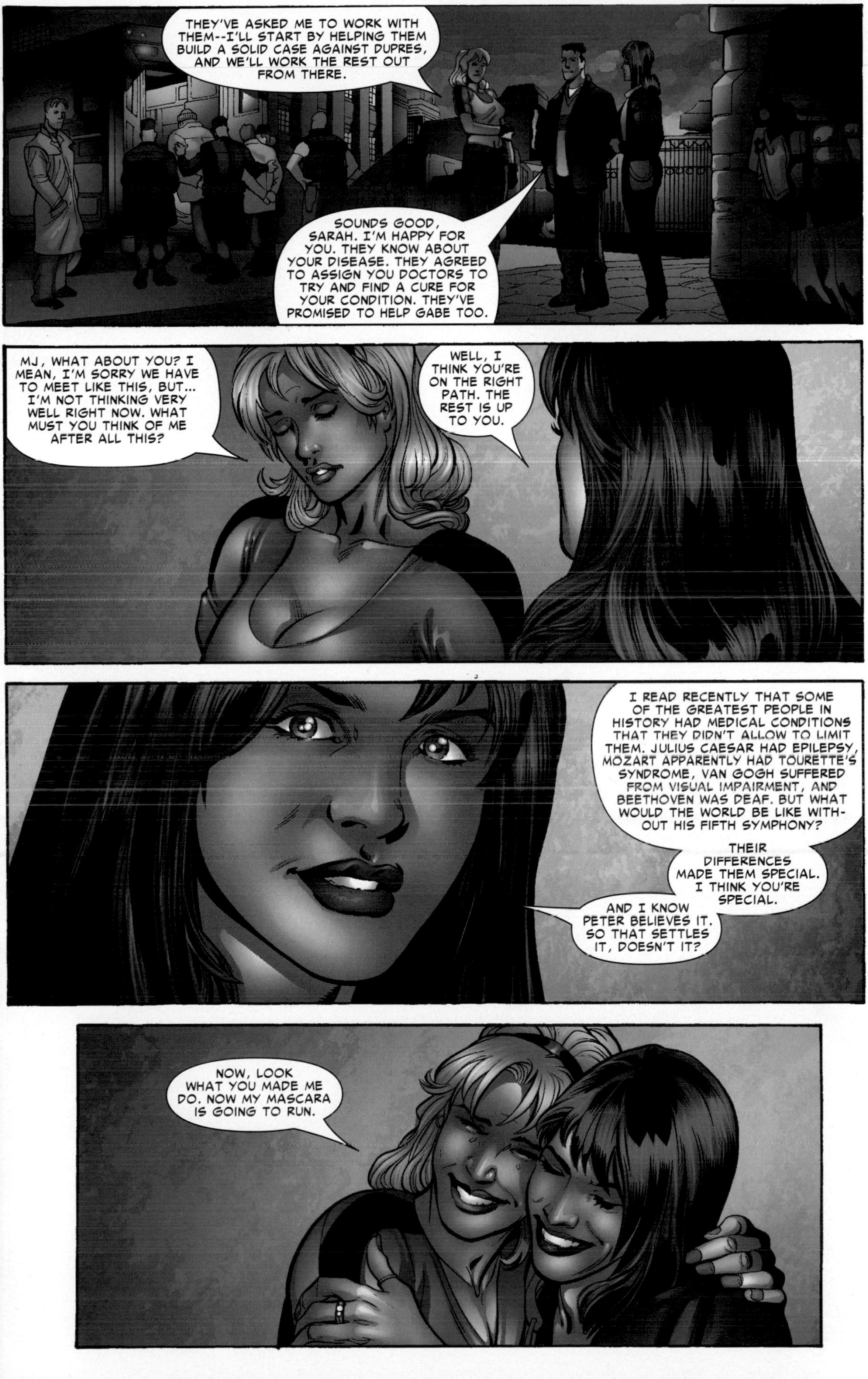

THEY'VE ASKED ME TO WORK WITH THEM--I'LL START BY HELPING THEM BUILD A SOLID CASE AGAINST DUPRES, AND WE'LL WORK THE REST OUT FROM THERE.
SOUNDS GOOD, SARAH. I'M HAPPY FOR YOU. THEY KNOW ABOUT YOUR DISEASE. THEY AGREED TO ASSIGN YOU DOCTORS TO TRY AND FIND A CURE FOR YOUR CONDITION. THEY'VE PROMISED TO HELP GABE TOO.
MJ, WHAT ABOUT YOU? I MEAN, I'M SORRY WE HAVE TO MEET LIKE THIS, BUT... I'M NOT THINKING VERY WELL RIGHT NOW. WHAT MUST YOU THINK OF ME AFTER ALL THIS?
WELL, I THINK YOU'RE ON THE RIGHT PATH. THE REST IS UP TO YOU.
I READ RECENTLY THAT SOME OF THE GREATEST PEOPLE IN HISTORY HAD MEDICAL CONDITIONS THAT THEY DIDN'T ALLOW TO LIMIT THEM. JULIUS CAESAR HAD EPILEPSY, MOZART APPARENTLY HAD TOURETTE'S SYNDROME, VAN GOGH SUFFERED FROM VISUAL IMPAIRMENT, AND BEETHOVEN WAS DEAF. BUT WHAT WOULD THE WORLD BE LIKE WITH-OUT HIS FIFTH SYMPHONY?
THEIR DIFFERENCES MADE THEM SPECIAL. I THINK YOU'RE SPECIAL.
AND I KNOW PETER BELIEVES IT. SO THAT SETTLES IT, DOESN'T IT?
NOW, LOOK WHAT YOU MADE ME DO. NOW MY MASCARA IS GOING TO RUN.

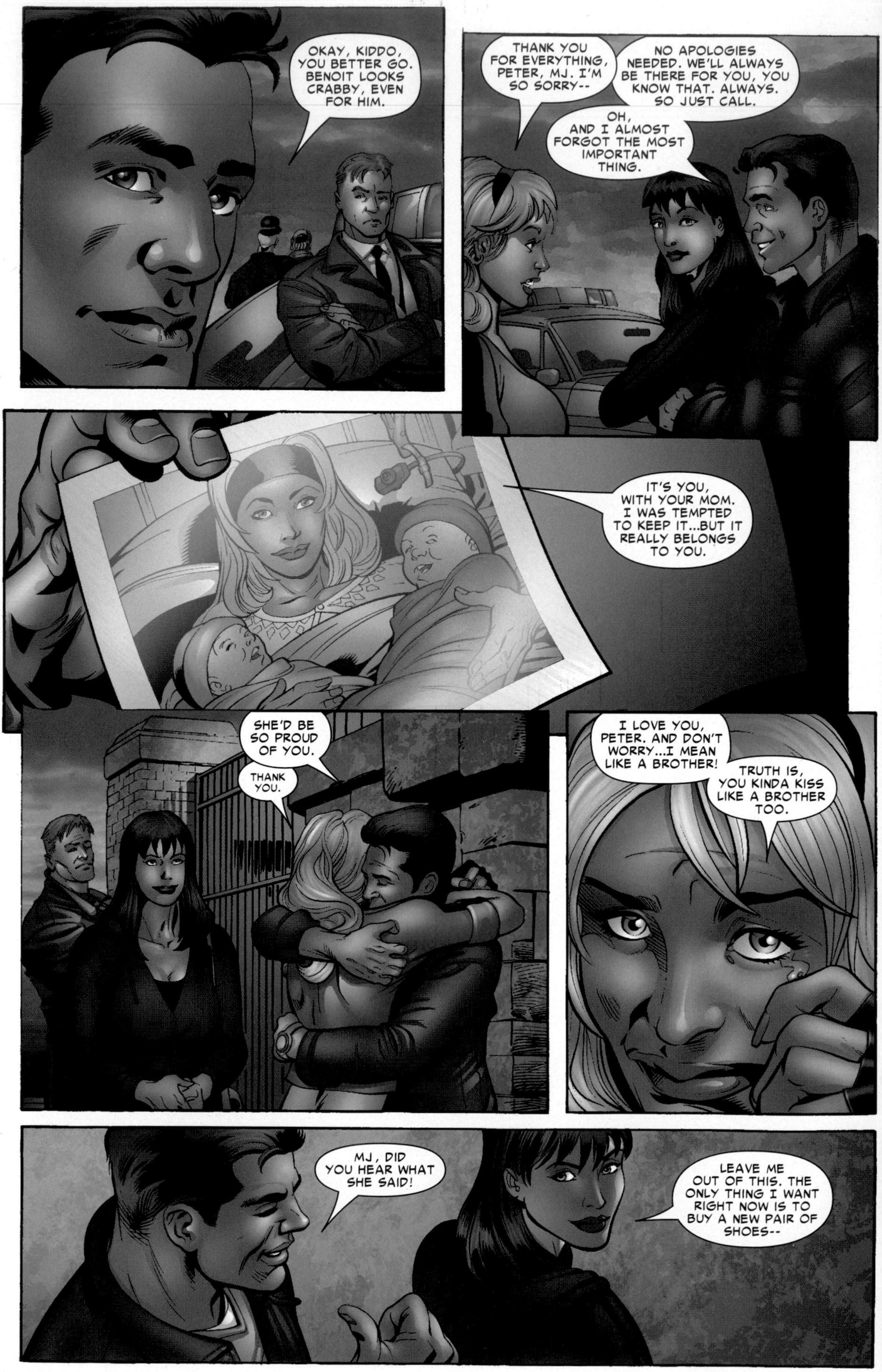
OKAY, KIDDO, YOU BETTER GO. BENOIT LOOKS CRABBY, EVEN FOR HIM.
THANK YOU FOR EVERYTHING, PETER, MJ. I'M SO SORRY--
NO APOLOGIES NEEDED. WE'LL ALWAYS BE THERE FOR YOU, YOU KNOW THAT. ALWAYS. SO JUST CALL.
OH, AND I ALMOST FORGOT THE MOST IMPORTANT THING.
IT'S YOU, WITH YOUR MOM. I WAS TEMPTED TO KEEP IT...BUT IT REALLY BELONGS TO YOU.
SHE'D BE SO PROUD OF YOU.
THANK YOU.
I LOVE YOU, PETER. AND DON'T WORRY...I MEAN LIKE A BROTHER!
TRUTH IS, YOU KINDA KISS LIKE A BROTHER TOO.
MJ, DID YOU HEAR WHAT SHE SAID!
LEAVE ME OUT OF THIS. THE ONLY THING I WANT RIGHT NOW IS TO BUY A NEW PAIR OF SHOES--

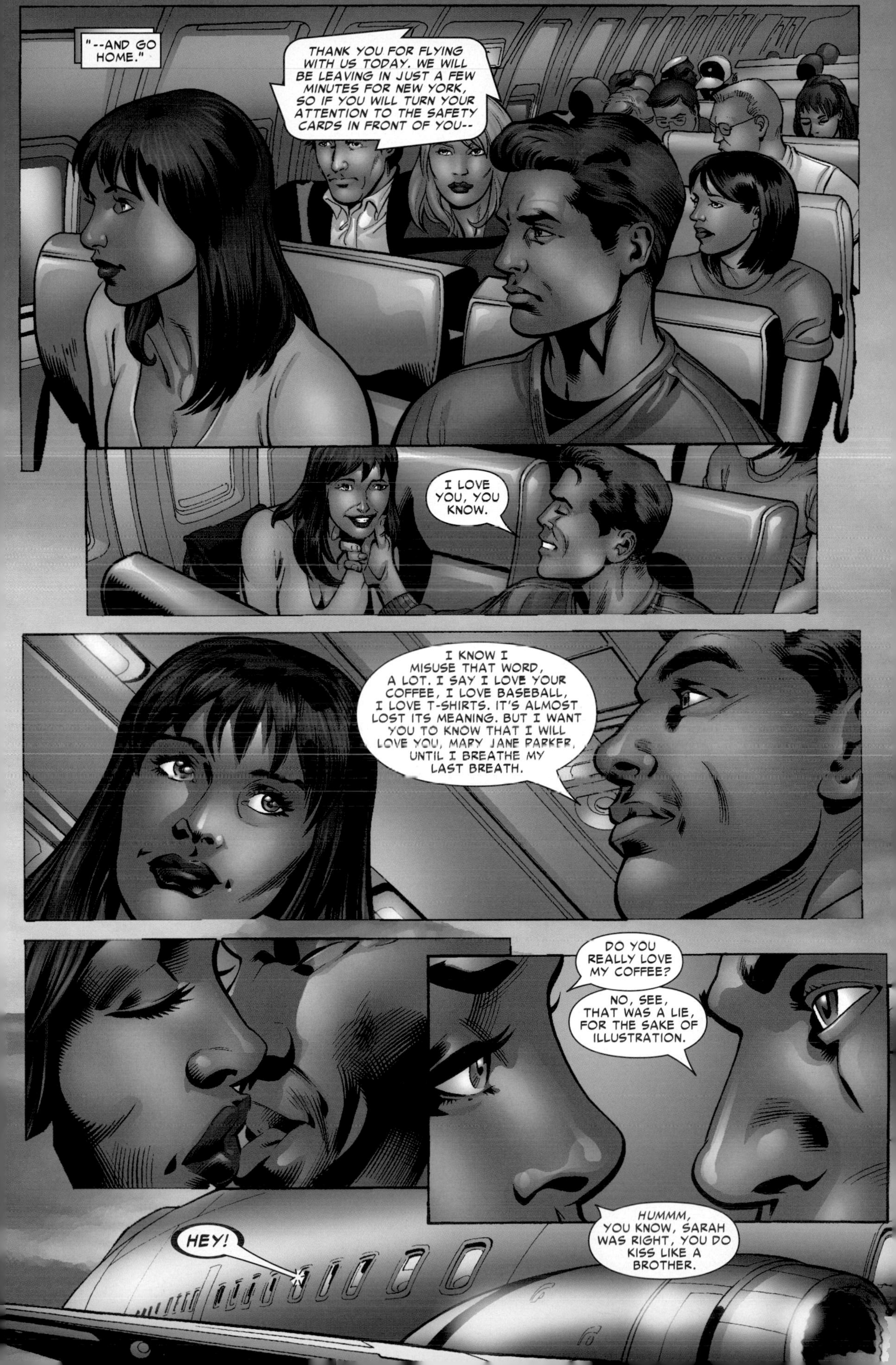
"--AND GO HOME."
THANK YOU FOR FLYING WITH US TODAY. WE WILL BE LEAVING IN JUST A FEW MINUTES FOR NEW YORK, SO IF YOU WILL TURN YOUR ATTENTION TO THE SAFETY CARDS IN FRONT OF YOU--
I LOVE YOU, YOU KNOW.
I KNOW I MISUSE THAT WORD, A LOT. I SAY I LOVE YOUR COFFEE, I LOVE BASEBALL, I LOVE T-SHIRTS. IT'S ALMOST LOST ITS MEANING. BUT I WANT YOU TO KNOW THAT I WILL LOVE YOU, MARY JANE PARKER, UNTIL I BREATHE MY LAST BREATH.
DO YOU REALLY LOVE MY COFFEE?
NO, SEE, THAT WAS A LIE, FOR THE SAKE OF ILLUSTRATION.
HUMMM, YOU KNOW, SARAH WAS RIGHT, YOU DO KISS LIKE A BROTHER.
HEY!

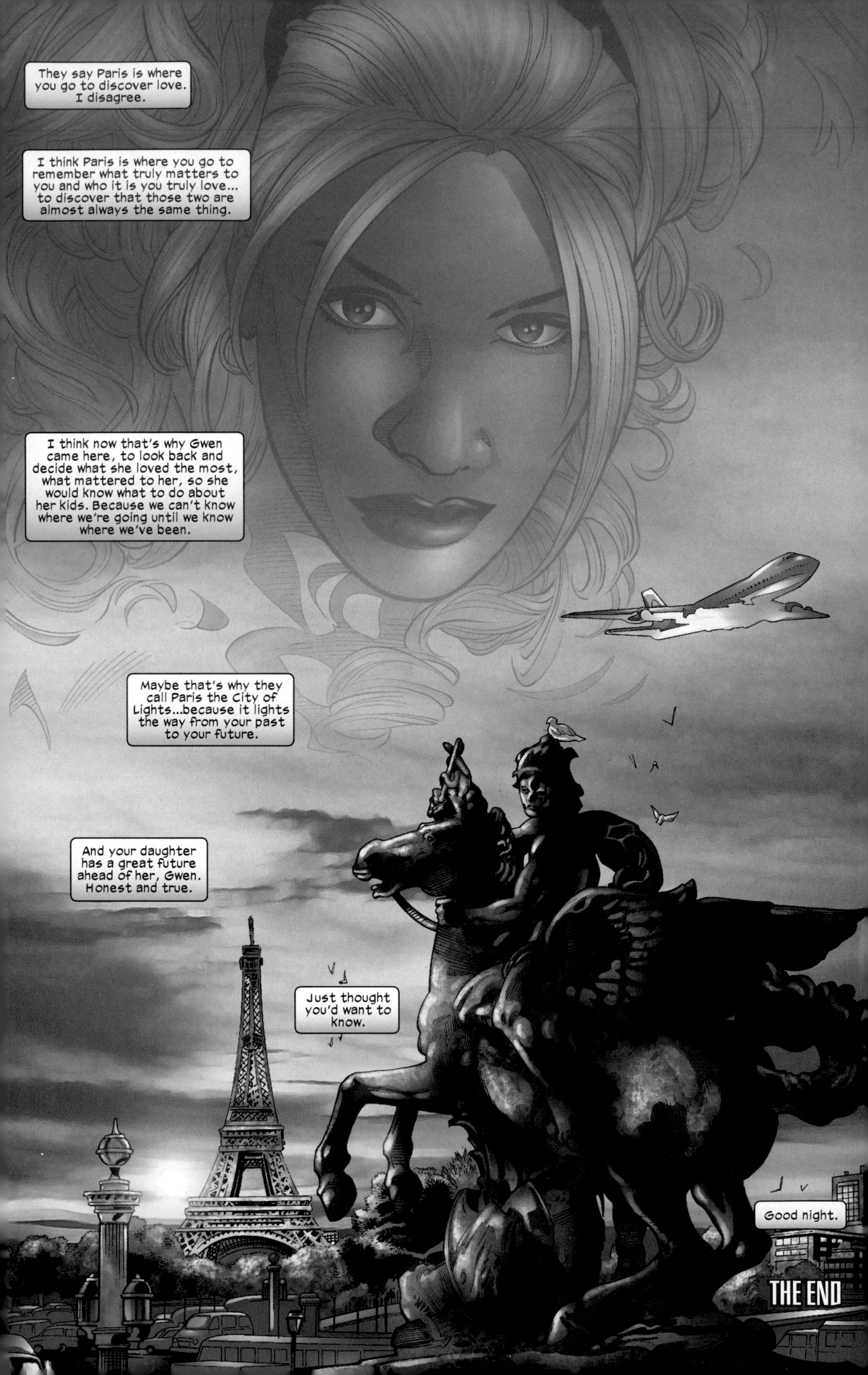
They say Paris is where you go to discover love. I disagree.
I think Paris is where you go to remember what truly matters to you and who it is you truly love... to discover that those two are almost always the same thing.
I think now that's why Gwen came here, to look back and decide what she loved the most, what mattered to her, so she would know what to do about her kids. Because we can't know where we're going until we know where we've been.
Maybe that's why they call Paris the City of Lights...because it lights the way from your past to your future.
And your daughter has a great future ahead of her, Gwen. Honest and true.
Just thought you'd want to know.
Good night.
THE END